Experimental Music and Japanese Aesthetics

Bloomsbury Introductions to World Philosophies

Series Editor:
Monika Kirloskar-Steinbach

Assistant Series Editor:
Leah Kalmanson

Regional Editors:
Nader El-Bizri, James Madaio, Ann A. Pang-White, Takeshi Morisato, Pascah Mungwini, Mickaella Perina, Omar Rivera and Georgina Stewart

Bloomsbury Introductions to World Philosophies delivers primers reflecting exciting new developments in the trajectory of world philosophies. Instead of privileging a single philosophical approach as the basis of comparison, the series provides a platform for diverse philosophical perspectives to accommodate the different dimensions of cross-cultural philosophizing. While introducing thinkers, texts and themes emanating from different world philosophies, each book, in an imaginative and path-breaking way, makes clear how it departs from a conventional treatment of the subject matter.

Titles in the Series:

A Practical Guide to World Philosophies, by Monika Kirloskar-Steinbach and Leah Kalmanson
Daya Krishna and Twentieth-Century Indian Philosophy, by Daniel Raveh
Māori Philosophy, by Georgina Tuari Stewart
Philosophy of Science and The Kyoto School, by Dean Anthony Brink
Tanabe Hajime and the Kyoto School, by Takeshi Morisato
African Philosophy, by Pascah Mungwini
The Zen Buddhist Philosophy of D. T. Suzuki, by Rossa Ó Muireartaigh
Sikh Philosophy, by Arvind-Pal Singh Mandair
The Philosophy of the Brahma-sūtra, by Aleksandar Uskokov
The Philosophy of the Yogasūtra, by Karen O'Brien-Kop
The Life and Thought of H. Odera Oruka, by Gail M. Presbey
Mexican Philosophy for the 21st Century, by Carlos Alberto Sánchez
Buddhist Ethics and the Bodhisattva Path, by Stephen Harris
Contextualizing Angela Davis, by Joy James
Environmental Equity in China and Beyond, by Michael Nylan and Thomas Hahn
Consciousness in Indian Philosophy, by Matthew MacKenzie

Experimental Music and Japanese Aesthetics

Silence, Nature and Hollow Listening

Daryl Jamieson

BLOOMSBURY ACADEMIC
LONDON • NEW YORK • OXFORD • NEW DELHI • SYDNEY

BLOOMSBURY ACADEMIC
Bloomsbury Publishing Plc, 50 Bedford Square, London, WC1B 3DP, UK
Bloomsbury Publishing Inc, 1359 Broadway, New York, NY 10018, USA
Bloomsbury Publishing Ireland, 29 Earlsfort Terrace, Dublin 2, D02 AY28, Ireland

BLOOMSBURY, BLOOMSBURY ACADEMIC and the Diana logo are trademarks of Bloomsbury Publishing Plc

First published in Great Britain 2026

The research was supported by the Japan Society for the Promotion of Science (JSPS) KAKENHI Grant Number 23K00215.

For legal purposes the Acknowledgments on p. ix constitute an extension of this copyright page.

Series design by Louise Dugdale
Cover image © oxygen/Getty Images

A catalogue record for this book is available from the British Library.

A catalog record for this book is available from the Library of Congress.

ISBN: HB: 978-1-3505-4904-3
PB: 978-1-3505-4903-6
ePDF: 978-1-3505-4905-0
eBook: 978-1-3505-4907-4

Series: Bloomsbury Introductions to World Philosophies

Typeset by Deanta Global Publishing Services, Chennai, India
Printed and bound in Great Britain

For product safety related questions contact productsafety@bloomsbury.com.

To find out more about our authors and books visit www.bloomsbury.com and sign up for our newsletters.

Awakening is like the moon reflecting in water.

—Dōgen, '*Genjō Kōan*'

The Sea of Emptiness
Windstill
And yet
of itself
a glimmering golden wave
arises

—Lǐ Tōngxuán

Contents

Illustrations

Preface and Acknowledgements

The research which underpins this book flows from crises both personal and global. From a young age I have been interested in politics almost as much as music. In the late 2000s, as the effects of climate change became ever more palpable and the global capitalist system first wobbled in the wake of the Lehman Brothers collapse and then reoriented towards digital rentierism, I began to question what the point of being a composer is. If the world is in crisis, am I not literally and metaphorically fiddling while it burns? Why would anyone devote their life to experimental, obscure art music or sound art amidst a society which seems to be collapsing under its economic, political and especially environmental contradictions?

There is probably not a single satisfactory answer to this question. Maybe, for some, making music is akin to a religious calling. For others, it is simply, naturally what they have always done, and they can no more stop singing or playing or composing than they could stop speaking – which is to say, they could stop, but only through a force of will (e.g. a vow of silence). A third group simply don't know how to do anything else, having been groomed from childhood into a career that was imposed on them before they were mature enough to know what the other choices might be (a great many professional musicians are members of this category to at least some extent, given how early in life training usually has to begin in order to have a successful career). I suppose I am more of the second and third type of music maker myself: I keep composing because it is natural to compose, and because it gives me pleasure, and – however much I dislike self-promotion and the entrepreneurism that has become compulsory for independent creative artists – it's a bit too late to retrain as a trauma surgeon and join Médecins Sans Frontières in Gaza.

But, over this past decade and a half I was also able to find some meaning in music and art creation by reconnecting with the earth and the roots of the musical traditions of the place I live. I was guided on this path by my study – practical and theoretical – of Japanese traditional music, especially nō theatre. Realizing that nō has its roots in so many diverse spiritual, intellectual and artistic traditions, I have been studying these ever since. In Buddhist philosophy, and especially the Buddhist-influenced artistic and intellectual practice of fifteenth-century nō composer Konparu Zenchiku, I found at least some reasons to keep listening to and making experimental music.

Composer and esoteric Buddhist practitioner Jonathan Harvey said that 'The Buddhist view of reality as lacking in inherent existence from its own side is one of the most important insights into the "reality" of music that I know'.[1] I have two hopes for this book. The first is that musicians and other artists who might be exploring ways of mending the disconnection between the art world and society as a whole can, like Harvey, find something generative in ways of listening and ways of being which are indebted to Buddhist views of reality, ways which I explore in this book. The second hope is that philosophers who are well versed in Japanese or post-modern Western philosophy can find something generative in my outsider's perspective on these disciplines and my practical application of Japanese Buddhist philosophy to listening (in art and in life, which are, despite the best efforts of modernism, always already interdependent and interpenetrating).

* * *

As is emphasized in the main text, every book, every artistic work and every speech act is a jewel through which all of the so-called creator's readings, listenings, discussions with colleagues and everyday experiences are reflected and refracted. There are of course too many people and organizations who have guided me over the years to

1 Jonathan Harvey, 'The Genesis of Quartet No. 4', in *Identity and Difference: Essays on Music, Language and Time*, ed. Peter Dejans (Leuven: Leuven University Press, 2004), 43–4.

acknowledge here, but I want to thank some of the people who had the greatest impact on the conceptualization and realization of this book.

Firstly, my research was supported by the Japan Society for the Promotion of Science (JSPS) KAKENHI Grant Number 23K00215. Any opinions, findings and conclusions or recommendations expressed in this material are those of the author(s) and do not necessarily reflect the views of the author's organization, JSPS nor MEXT.

Intellectual support came from philosophers and scholars Yuko Ishihara, Takeshi Morisato, Fabio Rambelli, Romona Fotiade, Graham Eatough and Yi Chen, among many others, who variously invited me to lecture, give workshops, and simply to discuss at length the ideas that became this book. Several composers, musicians and writers graciously provided me with material to help me understand the works or ideas discussed in this book. Thank you to all of them, including Frank Denyer, Jon Hargreaves, Michael Pisaro-Liu, Heather Roche and Koichiro Osaka, among others.

The *Digital Dictionary of Buddhism* has been a constant source of assistance with understanding Buddhist terminology across several languages. Because I have not directly quoted or cited it anywhere in the main text, I want to acknowledge the existence of such an immensely helpful and free resource here and thank its contributors and editor Charles Muller for all their work.

Thank you to Iwanami Shoten for generously providing images of Zenchiku's *Rokurin Ichiro*.

Very special thanks to Jo Kondo for two decades of support, and without whom I never would have come to Japan in the first place.

Finally, and most importantly, for decades of support in every conceivable way, I want to thank my partner, Hiroshi, and also our beloved cats, Tamon and Nyoro.

Introduction

0.1 'Contemporary' music

This is primarily a book about music and sound, listened out through a filter of Japanese[1] aesthetic thought. It explores what value there might be in making or listening to music in the twenty-first century, amidst the social and economic pressures brought on by the pervasive political and environmental instability of this stage of capitalist Modernity.[2] This is also a book about Japanese philosophy and the aesthetics of nature, and a refutation of the myth that human society is somehow separate from nature – or that music (art in general) can exist separate from society, politics or the environment. Music, sound and art are part of the world and this world is a sounding world.

The musical tradition which is the focus of much (though not all) of the text is what is generally known as 'contemporary music' or 'new music' (not to be confused with 'modern music', which precedes

[1] 'Japan' and 'Japanese' are linguistic symbols which can mean a huge variety of things to different people, and the nation state under that name controls territories now that until the early 1970s it did not (and it did control a great deal of territory in the early 1940s that it does not control now). No word's meaning is stable. All uses of 'Japan' in this book, then, are used in the knowledge that it names a fluid category and applies in general more to the language and the cultural and philosophical world developed through that language than the state which shares its name.

[2] Throughout this book, Modern (when capitalized) will refer to the historical Modern era – beginning with the Enlightenment and continuing to the present (2025 at the time of writing). Unless clearly indicated, it does *not* refer to the art- and musico-historical period after Romanticism and followed by post-modernism. Similarly, Modernism (capitalized) refers to the set of ideas flowing from the Enlightenment which includes anthropocentrism ('Man is the measure of all things' and artistic anthropocentrisms, such as perspective drawing) and the myth of progress (infinite growth and infinite improvement).

it, though the border between the genres is very porous).[3] Federico Campagna notes that 'encountering a civilization that calls itself Contemporary is a good indicator of a world at the tail end of its own narration, unconsciously readying itself for an incoming Middle Age – since trauma operates not only projectively, conditioning what happens afterwards, but also retrospectively: it already haunts a subject who is readying themselves to recognize it'.[4] Whether it is called 'contemporary' or 'new', this genre of music's self-proclamation of currency and relevance is a symptom of the suppressed knowledge of the genre's ephemerality. (That said, ephemerality is not necessarily a negative characteristic.)

The world of 'new music' is a microcosm of the collapsing social and life-supporting environmental systems caused by the Western and Westernized cultures and societies in which the genre takes root. Marianna Ritchey's book *Composing Capital: Classical Music in the Neoliberal Era*[5] is a detailed look at how intertwined both traditional classical music and newly composed music are with the neoliberal, capitalist-Modernist regime under which we live. One of her case studies is a site-specific opera which enacted gentrification in Los Angeles (and was performed in a fleet of dozens of cars); another chapter focusses on the requirement of contemporary musicians to be entrepreneurs and self-promoting micro-capitalists in which all of their artistic choices inevitably become subsidiary to financial ones. Though she focusses on examples from the United States, her conclusions are generally applicable to all capitalist economies in which 'classical' music is used

[3] A good overview of music since 1945 can be found in Paul Griffiths, *Modern Music and After*, 3rd edn. (Oxford: Oxford University Press, 2010). An excellent study of post-1989 music is Tim Rutherford-Johnson, *Music After the Fall: Modern Composition and Culture Since 1989* (Oakland: University of California Press, 2017). A detailed study of the sub-genre of contemporary music which is called experimental music can be found in Jennie Gottschalk, *Experimental Music since 1970* (London: Bloomsbury, 2016).

[4] Federico Campagna, *Prophetic Culture: Recreation For Adolescents* (London: Bloomsbury, 2021), 23.

[5] Marianna Ritchey, *Composing Capital: Classical Music in the Neoliberal Era* (Chicago: University of Chicago Press, 2019).

as symbolic of sophistication, prestige and worldliness by governments and corporations.

Music and sound are not themselves problematic – the issue is how they are instrumentalized in the capitalist-Modern societies in which we almost all, at the end of the first quarter of the twenty-first century of the common era, live. If there is an answer to be found for the question of why one might make or listen to music that is not seductive or easy or relaxing (or not just those, or not immediately, obviously those), that answer perhaps lies outside of capitalist Modernism.

0.2 Past ways of being

The famous opening line of L. P. Hartley's *The Go-Between* (1953) is 'The past is a foreign country: they do things differently there'.[6] It has become a cliché because it speaks to an obvious truth: the way societies were constructed, how people thought of themselves in relation to the cosmos, what was important to them and so on was different in the past in the same way – and very often to a much more significant extent – than various societies in the present are different from each other. How past societies treated music, poetry and the arts was also very different to how it is treated now. One of the aims of this book is to begin to reimagine the place of music in society through reference to one of these models from the past, namely mediaeval Japan.

This approach is itself a traditional one: prior to the myth of progress propagated by capitalist-Modernism, almost all societies believed in a prior Golden Age which was superior to the present, to which we can never return, the traces of which we should try to emulate. In the present, there are also many scholars and artists who have devoted their careers to bringing aspects of the thought of the past into dialogue with that of the present in order to move beyond a felt blockage in

[6] L. P. Hartley, *The Go-Between* (1953; repr., London: Penguin, 1997), 5.

the cyclical flow of time. Some of the scholars whose names appear scattered throughout this book – whose work might not be related to music or whose work touches upon music of entirely different kinds than are treated in this volume – are anthropologists. For example, David Graeber's anarchist methodology,[7] his polemical essays as well as his extremely wide-ranging historical work show how diverse political and social polities have been, and how no system – however seemingly powerful – is ever unchangeable. Without such an understanding of other ways of organizing society, and without believing that the current system of organization can be changed, any project (such as the present book) which looks back to ideas from the past could only be reactionary nostalgia.

Within any given society, the shift from one age to another – one cosmology to another – necessarily involves the suppression (if not the outright repression) of both the previous age's cosmology and the people who kept that cosmological knowledge. In the shift from the mediaeval period to the early Modern period in Europe, for example, non-rationalist, non-scientific beliefs and practices had to be suppressed in order for the new scientific age to take hold. These suppressed beliefs and practices – by and large the folk wisdom and herbal medicines practiced by experienced elder women – necessitated the creation of the figure of the witch, who could then be demonized and their embodied knowledge defamed.[8] Huge amounts of oral knowledge were lost in this transition to the Modern age, most of it gone forever, although some survives in folk wisdom and stories.

In Japan, the transition to Modernity effectively happened later, in the mid-nineteenth century. In a very top-down approach to Modernization, the Meiji government (1868–1912) largely imitated the Prussian model of a state, quickly building up their industrial

[7] David Graeber, *Fragments of an Anarchist Anthropology* (Chicago: Prickly Paradigm Press, 2004).

[8] Silvia Federici, *Caliban and the Witch: Women, the Body and Primitive Accumulation* (New York: Autonomedia, 2004).

capacity to a level which allowed them to defeat a European power, Russia, in the Russo-Japanese War of 1904–05. Early modern Japan – the Edo period (1603–1868) – had been a much more literate society than mediaeval Europe, and so at least some portion of the embodied knowledge which was being suppressed – or in many cases, simply forgotten – in the mad rush to catch up to Europe was retained in writing. In addition, there was a tradition of jealously-kept secrecy surrounding the artistic lineages of mediaeval and early modern Japan,[9] which ensured that the most highly-prized teachings of earlier generations were maintained and recopied with care (though multiple natural disasters and the American firebombings of Japan in the Second World War mean that not all highly-regarded documents have survived to the present).

Despite this book's focus on Japanese thought, it is not limited to Japanese, East Asian or other non-Western thought to notice that, in seventeenth-century English poet John Donne's words, 'No man is an Iland, intire of itselfe'. And despite early modern Japan's policies of self-isolation, no culture or nation is an island entire of itself either. As all phenomena interpenetrate and are reflected in each other, all cultures and subcultures are influenced by and reflect all others. Though studies of orientalism and colonialism within experimental music have been important topics of discussion in the past decades,[10] decolonial action by classical music institutions has often seemed to be limited to a tokenistic and reactionary expansion of performed music to include composers from non-Western countries who are nonetheless making music according to Modernist, Westernized paradigms, music which

[9] Bernhard Scheid and Mark Teeuwen, eds, *The Culture of Secrecy in Japanese Religion* (London: Routledge, 2015); see especially Susan Blakeley Klein, 'Esotericism in Noh commentaries and plays Konparu Zenchiku's Meishukushū and Kakitsubata', 229–54.

[10] See, for example, David Hesmondhalgh and Georgina Born, eds, *Western Music and Its Others: Difference, Representation, and Appropriation in Music* (Berkeley: University of California Press, 2000); Tobias Janz and Chien-Chang Yang, eds, *Decentering Musical Modernity: Perspectives on East Asian and European Music History* (Bielefeld: transcript, 2019); and Christian Utz, *Musical Composition in the Context of Globalization: New Perspectives on Music History of the 20th and 21st Century* (Bielefeld: transcript, 2021).

will easily fit into existing capitalist structures of concert promotion and music distribution. This book is certainly very interested in decentring Modern Western paradigms,[11] though not at the superficial level of the nationalities or personal identities of artists. Nor does it take the Modern Western concept of 'music' as read: Rather, the project of this book is to question what music and sound conceptually are within a Japanese aesthetic framework, and from within that framework listen to (interpret) a variety of musics.

Thus, one of the projects of this book is to propose a way of listening which is not instrumentalized or goal driven in the manner that all activities under capitalist Modernity almost inescapably are. It focusses on sources within a tradition of written aesthetics of sound, music and performance that predates the turn to Modernity by many centuries – or millennia, if one stretches the Buddhist influences back to the time of the Buddha – and one that is geographically and intellectually widely separated from the place in which Modernity arose. By concentrating on sources from the Kamakura (1185–1333) and Muromachi (1336–1573) periods, periods marked by war, severe natural disasters, political and social upheaval (including, for example, a *shōgun* taking in and educating a young *sarugaku* nō [猿楽能] actor – a class of people previously considered to be low-class illiterates – as a *chigo* [稚児]),[12] ways of being – ways of interpreting, ways of creating – in an uncertain world might be recovered from which new ways of listening for our own period of radical uncertainty might arise.

11 It is inappropriate to use a word such as 'decolonial' to describe a book about Japanese thought, given Japan's historical and continuing status as an imperial power, especially given Zen Buddhism's – and some members of the Kyoto School's – support for Japanese colonialism and warmongering in the first half of the twentieth century.

12 Zeami's status (from around age 12) as a *chigo* – a beautiful adolescent acolyte and assumed sexual servant – to the Shōgun Ashikaga Yoshimitsu (足利義満; from around age 17) is not absolutely ascertainable but is considered highly likely by many scholars. He was, without any doubt, taken in to and educated in Yoshimitsu's court. Matsuoka Shinpei, *Embodied Performance: Warriors, Dancers, and the Origins of Noh Theater*, trans. Janet Goff (New York: Columbia University Press, 2024), 152–3.

0.3 Ground

It is important to recognize that works of the past – artistic works, as well as philosophical ones – are indeed of the past, and that there is an undeniable gap of understanding that can never fully be bridged. Whatever the undeniable merits of, for example, the early music movement in recovering older ways of making, maintaining and playing instruments from the early Modern era, we cannot possibly fully conceive of the embodied understanding of music that people in that time had. As Jo Kondo (近藤譲; b. 1947) points out, 'there is no possibility for us in the modern era to physically experience that music with the body of someone within that musical culture; we cannot listen with their ears'.[13] However much we might wish it otherwise, our ears have heard fragments of Mozart in car commercials, bits of Beethoven reworked into disco songs or film soundtracks and Puccini arias sung in stadia for audiences of billions: how can these same ears listen (by which I mean interpret and understand sound) in the same way as Mozart's, Beethoven's or Puccini's (especially considering the unique, utterly personal physical differences that distinguish every individual's ears from everyone else's)? This example is of Western classical musicians of today working with Western classical music of the past; the distance is even greater when the ideas in question are from outside one's professional or scholarly training and cultural sphere. But that is obvious; it is more important to note that, even within the same cultural and linguistic tradition, it is still impossible to 'listen with their ears', to read with their eyes or interpret with their minds.

Nevertheless, this book will weave its net of ideas out of three principal strands of historical thought. The first two are the aesthetics of early nō (能) theatre, and the identity of listening, composing and interpreting. Both of these ideas are ultimately rooted in Buddhist

[13] Jo Kondo, *Homo audiens*, trans. Daryl Jamieson (Cologne: MusikTexte, 2022), 31.

philosophy and aesthetics, which, in manifestations from both the mediaeval period and the twentieth century, forms the third strand. Thus woven, the net will envelop and shape the interpretations of 'new' or 'contemporary' experimental music I offer as practical case studies of the relevance of these ideas of the past for musical practitioners today. And, *vice versa*, in experimental music we will find a rich seam of contemporary applications and practical examples of the meaningfulness and relevance of Japanese traditions of aesthetics and Buddhist philosophy.

0.3.1 Nō theatre and creative interpretation

Nō – the Japanese music-theatre art which was refined into existence out of a number of other musical, dramatic, dance and comic traditions in the late fourteenth and early fifteenth centuries by Zeami Motokiyo (世阿弥元清; *c.*1363–*c.*1443), his father Kan'ami Kiyotsugu (観阿弥清次; 1333–84) and his son-in-law Konparu Zenchiku (金春禅竹; 1405–*c.*1470) – is the central axis around which this book turns. Zeami is well-known in Japan and abroad, and while Zenchiku is well-known among nō scholars and aficionados, he is perhaps less well-known in general. It is Zenchiku's thought and methodology, though, which are of principal importance for this volume. *Waka* (和歌; Japanese poetry or song), and specifically *tanka* (短歌; literally short poem or song, referring to verses in semantic units of 5-7-5-7-7 morae), the principal form of *waka* for a millennium, were vitally important to the development of nō aesthetics as well. Both Zeami and Zenchiku were trained under master poets who are still revered today: Zeami's *waka* tutor was Nijō Yoshimoto (二条良基; 1320–88); Zenchiku's was Shōtetsu (正徹; 1381–1459). Zenchiku also wrote of the fundamental unity in his aesthetics of poetry and dance – both of which are, of course, also musical – with his phrase *kabu isshin* (歌舞一心; literally song-dance-one-mind).

Zenchiku's approach to the theorization of nō has been described by scholar Noel Pinnington as 'creative misinterpretation'.[14] It is not, I think, meant to be a critique (though I may myself be misinterpreting Pinnington here). At any rate, I will take it positively and as a guide for what an artist-scholar can have licence to do that might cause an intellectual historian to hesitate. While I do, to the extent possible, understand the sources I draw from, the intent in this book is not principally to present a picture of what these ideas meant to the people who wrote them, or what the original readers or listeners might have understood by them. Rather, the reason for excavating ideas from pre-Modern philosophy, aesthetics and artistic practice is to see which ones might be generative – as antitheses to test ideas against, or as bases for new music and sound work – in the present moment. This book, therefore, is not meant as an exegesis of any philosophy in particular, but rather as a set of possibilities for the interpretation and creation of music and sound and related art works in the past, and which might be useful again in the present.

0.3.2 Listening as interpretation

Kondo, invoking Roland Barthes' famous essay 'The Death of the Author',[15] similarly insists that a musical text is empty of intrinsic meaning – and certainly devoid of authoritative meaning handed down by a composer – but instead affords a wide range of creative interpretations (not absolutely any interpretation, but any which can be coherently defended).[16] Interpreting non-verbal musical texts affords a much wider range of reasonable possibilities than does interpreting textual sources, but one only needs to compare two or more translations

[14] Noel Pinnington, *Traces in the Way: Michi and the Writings of Komparu Zenchiku* (Ithaca: Cornell University Press, 2006), 103.

[15] Roland Barthes, *Image Music Text*, trans. Stephen Heath (London: Fontana Press, 1977), 142–8.

[16] Kondo, *Homo audiens*, 81*ff*.

of any text to see how widely interpretations of texts can diverge, especially when dealing with matters that are inherently difficult to write about with clarity, such as spiritual experiences or music (Zeami and, especially, Zenchiku, wrote frequently about both). In this text, I offer creative interpretations[17] of Zenchiku's and Zeami's writings, and of the works of many new music composers' works, but always within parameters of defensible readings. I do this not only because it is my 'right' as an interpreter,[18] but also because it is how Zenchiku himself treated the texts of his teacher, Zeami.[19]

There is no hierarchy in Kondo's 'right' of interpretation.[20] He insists that the audience has as much right to deeply listen and offer their interpretation of a piece of music as does the performer who develops an interpretation from reading a score and then physically embodying that score in living sound. Likewise, the performer has no lesser a right to interpret the meaning of the score than the composer who wrote it down. The reason for this – beyond Barthes' observation that any text (including any musical text) 'is a tissue of quotations drawn from the innumerable centres of culture'[21] – is that the three participants in the ersatz hierarchy of composer (active giver)—performer (medium)—audience (passive receiver) are all fundamentally *listeners* (Kondo's *homo audiens*). The composer *listens to* sounds conjured in their head, or at their instrument, or at their digital audio workstation, or in the outside world. The score – which can be defined broadly as any instruction or set of instructions

[17] I have chosen to omit Pinnington's 'mis' from my 'interpretations'.

[18] Kondo, *Homo audiens*, 97.

[19] We have no writings of Kan'ami's – presumably he was not literate, or not literate enough to write his aesthetic ideas down – but we know that many of Zeami's plays are rewritings of Kan'ami's, so at least in his plays, we know that Zeami also was a creative reinterpreter of his father-*cum*-teacher.

[20] Lack of hierarchy is axiomatically anarchistic, and Kondo's invocation of it reflects Graeber's concept of 'everyday' or 'baseline' communism which, he claims, 'is the ground of all human social life'. David Graeber, *Debt: The First 5000 Years* (Hoboken: Melville House, 2011), 101.

[21] Barthes, *Image Music Text*, 146.

on how to realize a piece of music, whether written down or not – is a trace of those sounds which they *listened out* of the world. That trace (the score) is then *listened to* by the performer (who can also be the composer), who, whether an instrument is in hand or not, reads it as much with their ears as their eyes, hearing the sounds physically and/or mentally. The interpretation they develop is through consideration of the sound through *listening*, and the performance is an enactment of a particular interpretation at a particular time and in a particular place. Whether that performance is in a rehearsal alone, in a studio with other musicians and/or audio engineers, or on stage with a live audience, the interpretation is done through listening. And, etymologically, the audience is interpreting through listening as well.

Because all of these actions are non-dually unified through listening, we can reformulate – and, in doing so, eliminate – the composer—performer—audience hierarchy. If composing is an act of *listening* sounds *out*[22] – that is, of attending to particular sounds from among the myriad sounds that surround us at all times – and recording (on paper, with audio recording equipment or memorizing) a trace of those listened-out sounds, we can divide the act of composition into a creative act (the listening out) and a technical skill (the recording of those sounds for future reference). An audience member in a concert hall, for example, is also presented with myriad sounds – including all the sounds of the instruments on stage, but also the coughing or rustling of audience members or, perhaps, the clatter of staff in the lobby. The audience member also focusses their attention on particular sounds, thus listening out – composing – their own unique musical event. This event will be similar to but to some degree different from the event as perceived in every other audience member's listening experience, and in this sense, every audience member is their own composer of that particular performance – a unique musical event is manifest in the place

[22] To 'listen out' (*kikidasu* 聴き出す) is a keyword of Kondo's. Kondo, *Homo audiens*, 107*ff*.

between them and the performers, who are also listening out a unique version of the musical work around them from their unique places. This is no different if the listening occurs in a concert hall or walking down the street, whether the object is so-called 'music' or 'sound'. Just as composers and performers are listeners, audience members and performers are also composers.

As long as your ears are open, you are, by focussing on some sounds and filtering out others, always composing. The only difference with a composer so-called is that they have practiced the skill of recording their compositions.[23] As such, in this book, the word 'listener' is always inclusive of composers, performers and interpreters of sound and music, and 'listening' is likewise always inclusive of composing, performing and interpreting. This is sometimes mentioned directly in the main text when emphasis for the particular point being made seems necessary, but 'listener' and 'listening' can be read in the most inclusive way whenever these words appear in this book.

0.3.3 Buddhism and the Kyoto School

The third strand of the net is Buddhism. In this book, unless otherwise stated, the word 'Buddhism' refers only to Mahāyāna Buddhism (Jp. *daijō bukkyō* 大乗仏教) as practiced on the main islands of the Japanese archipelago and, usually, in the Japanese language. Mahāyāna is one of the two principal branches of Buddhism, and most East Asian Buddhist sects are Mahāyāna.

Dōgen (道元; 1200–53), the founder of the Japanese school of Sōtō (曹洞宗; Ch. Cáodòng Zōng) Zen (禅; Ch. Chán) Buddhism, is the foremost representative of mediaeval Buddhism in this book. Trained as a Tendai (天台; Ch. Tiāntāi) monk, he went to China to

[23] A further, non-musical analogy: every time you speak you are 'writing' in that you are bringing forth unique combinations of words into being. Whether you record those words on paper is the difference between writing (which everyone does) and being a writer (which almost everyone also does, but less frequently than professional writers do).

study and brought Sōtō Zen back to Japan. His collection of sermons, the *Shōbōgenzō* (正法眼蔵), is written in language that affords an unusually wide range of interpretations, and thus the many English-language translations can be surprisingly different.[24]

Aside from Dōgen and his Sōtō Zen school, figures, texts and ideas from the Tendai, Kegon (華厳; Ch. Huáyán; En. Flower Garland) and Shingon (真言; En. True Word) schools of Buddhism will be discussed. Most of these schools are on the border between exoteric and esoteric, with Shingon considered to be fully esoteric; these schools were all influential on the development of Zen (Chán) in both Japan and China.

In the early twentieth century, a loose grouping and, later, lineage of philosophers developed around the person of Nishida Kitarō (西田幾多郎; 1870–1945). These philosophers came to be known as the Kyoto School, after Kyoto University where Nishida taught the second generation of the School. If it can be said that there is a common thread among that diverse group of philosophers, it is that most of them were engaged in bringing concepts from Buddhism into dialogue with ideas in continental European philosophy. For some, including Nishida himself, this was more implicit, but in later generations, such as in the work of Nishida's student Nishitani Keiji (西谷啓治; 1900–90), the intercultural and interfaith dialogue between Japanese and Continental,

[24] Translations of the title *Shōbōgenzō* in English include literal versions – *e.g.*, Tanahashi Kazuaki's *Treasury of the True Dharma Eye* (Dōgen, *Treasury of the True Dharma Eye: Zen Master Dogen's Shobo Genzo*, ed. Tanahashi Kazuaki [Boston: Shambala, 2010]), and Nishijima and Cross's open source version *The True Dharma-Eye Treasury* (Dōgen, *The True Dharma-Eye Treasury*, trans. Gudo Wafu Nishijima and Chodo Cross [1994–99; repr., Berkeley: Numata Center for Buddhist Translation and Research, 2007]) – and my preferred translation of the title, Rein Raud's *The Core Transmission* (Rein Raud, et al., *Forgetting the Self* [Tallinn: Haus galeriis, 2024]). Raud has only published excerpts rather than a full translation of *Shōbōgenzō*, but where he has published a version of a particular passage, I will in general use that as the basis of my English version in this book. Otherwise, I use Tanahashi's.

Because of this diversity of translations, and the lack of uniformity among translated titles, the Japanese titles for Dōgen's writings will be used throughout this book. I will give an English title on the first mention of each fascicle, but thereafter use the Japanese. On a related note, translations which do not have citations are by me; if substantive reference was made to an existing English translation, this is noted in the citation with the words 'translation modified'.

Buddhist and Abrahamic traditions was made explicit. In this volume, the Kyoto School lineage represented by Nishida and Nishitani, and especially Nishitani's student Ueda Shizuteru (上田閑照; 1926–2019), will constitute the principal voice representing contemporary Japanese Buddhist (or Buddhist-influenced) philosophy and aesthetics.

0.3.4 John Cage and experimental music

The net woven of the previous three threads – nō, creative non-hierarchical listening out and Buddhist philosophy – provides the theoretical cradle in which the interpretation of a variety of experimental music case studies lies. Experimental music was famously defined by the American composer John Cage (1912–92) in 1959 as 'composing in such a way that what one does is indeterminate of its performance'.[25] I contend (in further detail in Chapter 4) that 'new music' and 'contemporary music', however unsatisfactory these labels are, can be subdivided, roughly, into two strands – avant-garde composers (for whom sound is material to be manipulated) and experimental ones (for whom music is essentially listening, and composition is not goal-directed or artificially structured). Kondo, given the focus above on his ideas about listening and the right to interpretation, is an experimentalist, as is Cage himself. Cage made use of many Buddhist ideas, as well as the Chinese Book of Changes (Ch. Zhōuyì 周易; Jp. Shūeki; also known as the Yìjīng 易經; Jp. Ekikyō), Indian aesthetics and Christian mysticism. His ideas and writings are thus a clear starting point for any discussion of an aesthetics of music in relation to Buddhist philosophy.

Like Cage's music, Zenchiku's nō was heavily influenced by his philosophical and religious milieu, which was deeply informed by Buddhist, Confucian and local *kami* (神) worshipping traditions. In his creative interpretations of his mentor Zeami's treatises, as well as Buddhist, Confucian and Japanese classics, Zenchiku can also be read

[25] John Cage, *Silence* (1961; repr. Middletown: Wesleyan University Press, 2011), 69.

as an experimentalist. It is from this perspective that this book seeks to make Zenchiku's writings relevant for experimental listeners (and viewers) in the twenty-first century.

0.4 Superstructure

This book is in seven chapters, each of which delves into a key philosophical and/or aesthetic concept from the Japanese tradition. Each also contains at least one case study, wherein musical examples – mostly, but not exclusively, from the tradition of post-Cagean experimentalism – are discussed in the light of that chapter's key ideas. The intention of alternating between philosophical–aesthetic theories and interpretive practice is to illustrate, first and foremost, the relevance of the ideas to the practice of listening and also to show the applicability of the ideas to a wide variety of musics.

Though some of the musical examples are by Japanese composers, or composers who have publicly stated that they engage in some form of Buddhist practice, one of my central contentions is that all music – all sound – can be listened to from the standpoint of an experimental listening approach informed by these ideas from Japanese aesthetics. Therefore, I have deliberately selected as case studies many pieces which are by composers who are not explicitly engaged with the ideas presented in the book. Per Kondo's right of interpretation, I claim the right to interpret these composers' pieces in ways which they may not have expected or intended, but which are, I hope, illuminating.

The overall form of the book is meant to illustrate the concept that artistic practice is rooted in an embodied understanding of philosophical and spiritual ideas. Therefore, the earlier chapters are denser with explanations of Buddhist philosophy (the theory), which gradually gives way to more essayistic and expressive writing in the final chapters (the practice). Reflecting the Buddhist and nō idea of cyclical time, and the related idea of returning to the conventional world after playing in the hollow world, the afterword (the end) is a return to the personal reflection of the preface (the beginning).

The main argument of the book begins in Chapter 1 with an exploration of the idea of silence. As John Cage famously showed, true silence (absolute lack of sound) is an impossibility. Life *is* sound, and as long as we are alive, we will be hearing something. From this, I argue that since 'silence' cannot truly refer to a complete absence of sound, it could instead be redefined as unintended sound; unlistened-to sound; obscured, repressed or oppressed sound. This chapter also begins to explore the Buddhist idea of emptiness and question whether silence can be conceived of as a kind of emptiness. I begin to flesh out the argument that all sounds are interesting (which Cage also claimed) and that all sounds are valuable and important. Finally, the exploration of silence and emptiness will conclude with a look at the idea of ruination, drawing on Kondo's interpretation of Cage's aesthetics of 'ruined' sound.

From this there is a discussion of the post-Cagean use of silence in music, with a focus on the aesthetics of the Wandelweiser collective of composers (specific examples of which will be explored in later chapters). In addition to this, two musical case studies are analysed in greater detail. The first is *Water Piece* (1964) by Ono Yoko (b. 1933), probably the most well-known member of the Fluxus movement of post-Cagean radical artists. Through an analysis of this text score, the timbral qualities of musical silence are considered, as well as the effectiveness of musical silence as a metaphor for emptiness. The second piece is concert-music composer Evan Johnson's (b. 1980) piece *mes pleurants* for piano solo (2020), which is analysed in terms of an aesthetic – and compositional technique – of ruination.

Chapter 2 continues to develop the idea of emptiness introduced in Chapter 1 through an examination of the ontology and aesthetics of the Kyoto School. Nishida's *basho* (場所; En. place) of absolute nothingness is investigated as a twentieth-century iteration of the concept of emptiness. From there, the chapter looks at Ueda Shizuteru's approaches to language, especially its generative and creative potential. The chapter emphasizes Ueda's threefold approach to classifying language: sign, symbol and hollow. Hollow words are words (or usually combinations of words) which afford opening a new creative place, a glimpse into the limitless 'hollow expanse' beyond conventional reality (a further development of the concept of emptiness).

The centrepiece of Chapter 2 is the application of this idea of hollow words and hollow language to sounds, that is hollow sounds. Bracketing the debate about the extent to which music is a language (which will be addressed from a Buddhist perspective in Chapter 7), this chapter will show that sounds can be interpreted using Ueda's three linguistic categories, and that hollow sounds, like Ueda's hollow words, afford being interpreted as having a soteriological function as triggers for awakening. Developing this idea of hollow sounds, I will then show how beautiful obscurity (*yūgen* 幽玄) in language and music is used as a key aesthetic concept by Zeami, one which is further developed by Zenchiku into a spiritual idea linking words, music and nonhuman sounds. Returning to the twenty-first century and Ueda's thought, I will explain his idea of creativity and play in the hollow expanse, using the example of the Ten Ox Pictures. This chapter's case study, Cassandra Miller's (b. 1976) *Duet* for cello and orchestra (2015), illustrates Ueda's idea of 'playing in the hollow expanse' in its dialogic interplay between the two musical figures of the solo cellist and orchestra.

Having focussed on emptiness, the hollow and the *basho* of absolute nothingness in the first two chapters, Chapter 3 moves us on to discuss the importance of place in conventional reality and in art. This discussion of place begins with the poet Fujiwara no Shunzei's (藤原俊成; 1114–1204, also pronounced Toshinari) reading of the topic of places in the Japanese poetic tradition – *utamakura* (歌枕) – through a Buddhist lens. He argues, in a way that is resonant with Ueda's understanding of the function of language, that poetic language adds a palimpsestic layer of cultural connotative meaning atop the raw physical reality of sensory data received when you go to a place which has been described in a poem. *Utamakura* have a long history in Japanese poetry, and there are many *utamakura* places throughout Japan. Nō as a genre is indebted to this *utamakura* tradition, which was already more than half a millennium old by the time of Zeami and Zenchiku. Many nō plays are based on these *utamakura* poems and are set in these places. To widen the inquiry, this chapter also discusses James and Eleanor Gibson's theory of ecological perception in relation to the uniqueness of place and the multiplicity of interpretations each place affords, before ending with a short discussion of mediaeval Japanese Yin-Yang geomancy (*onmyōdō* 陰陽道).

There are two musical case studies in Chapter 3. The first, with an interpretation drawing on Shunzei's palimpsest-like theory of *utamakura*, looks at composer-guitarist Sugimoto Taku's (杉本拓; b. 1965) 2021 (COVID 19 lockdown-era) performance for electric guitar performed outdoors titled *May (Tama)*. The second is Wandelweiser-associated composer Michael Pisaro-Liu's (b. 1961) piece for solo piano and 4-channel field recording *Fields have ears (1)* (2008). This piece is analysed in light of ecological perception and the concept of hollow sounds.

Building on the aesthetics of place in the previous chapter, Chapter 4 widens the discussion from the aesthetics of individual places to an aesthetics of nature as a conceptual whole. It begins, though, with a discussion of the difference between avant-garde (speaking, discursive) and experimental (listening) approaches to composition. From there, drawing on writers such as Tim Ingold and Gordon White, the discussion returns to place in order to explore the difference between the abstract concept of 'space' and the concrete concept of 'place'. This section is capped by a discussion of field recording artist Tsunoda Toshiya's (角田俊也; b. 1964) own reflections on this distinction, and a case study of selected tracks from his mammoth collection *Extract From Field Recording Archive* (2019).

The second half of Chapter 4 returns to the importance of place for nō and the importance of the active audience. It reimagines *mugen* nō's (夢幻能) secondary character, the *waki* (ワキ), as a kind of experimental listener, who interacts with the *utamakura* place and the *utamakura* poetry about the place to manifest the entirety of the on-stage drama. It also brings in a nostalgic essay by Nishitani in which he re-encounters a landscape of his childhood in a similar manner. The chapter ends with a discussion of field recording artist Sam Dunscombe's 2023 album *Two Forests / Oceanic*.

Chapter 5 focusses on the practice of soundwalking. First conceived as part of the World Soundscape Project in the early 1970s by Hildegard Westerkamp (b. 1946), soundwalking refers to a way of moving through the world focussing on sounds which would otherwise be ignored. This listening practice is reexamined through the lens of Kondo's idea of 'purposeless' listening. From Kondo's Kegon Buddhist-derived idea that sounds, too, are living beings, I examine whether an ethics of care can be derived from a purposeless listening practice, and whether purposeless listening supports and deepens such an ethics. This chapter includes the most thorough discussion of Japanese aesthetics of nature in this volume, drawing on a variety of mediaeval sources, principally Dōgen. I will explore the queer (ambiguous, obscure) nature of sound, its ephemerality and probe the connections between these ideas and the ultimate nō aesthetic of *yūgen*.

The first of this chapter's two musical case studies is by Pauline Oliveros (1932–2016), a short text piece called 'Native' from her 1971 collection of *Sonic Meditations*. It is examined as a score of soundwalking and silence. The second case study is of an early work by Jo Kondo, his 1970 piece for clarinet and field recording *Summer Days*. The work is interpreted as an exploration of the other, the nonhuman and the environment through the medium of recording, as well as a work of dialogue with the past which resembles the dialogue between *shite* (シテ, the principal actor) and *waki* in *nō*.

Zenchiku, whose theories of nō are peppered throughout the entirety of the book, is the focus of the penultimate Chapter 6. With Zenchiku as an early example of a soteriological practice and theory of creative experimental listening, this chapter asks how we can make an art rooted in the ethical concepts explored in Chapter 5. The chapter discusses how Zenchiku draws on a syncretic mix of Buddhist, Confucian and *kami* worshipping philosophies and practices to enrich his soteriological music theatre works. It also explores Zenchiku's two major theoretical works – *Six Circles One Dewdrop* (*Rokurin ichiro* 六輪一露) and *Meishukushū* (明宿集). I will show what value these can have for contemporary artists looking for a way to reconnect with something real, rooted, non-anthropocentric and non-instrumentalized.

In the vein of this chapter focussing on nō, the first two musical case studies will be music theatre works. Firstly, it is only appropriate to discuss one of Zenchiku's plays, *Tatsuta* (龍田), in some detail to interrogate how Zenchiku's theories are realized on stage, in what is assumed to be an early work (dating, and even precise attribution of authorship, cannot be done with absolute confidence for early nō repertoire). The second example will be the pantomime from Hector Berlioz' (1803–69) *Les Troyens* (based on the pre-Modern cosmology of Vergil's *Aeneid*). The chapter ends with a discussion of the nō-like qualities of Apichatpong Weerasethakul's (อภิชาติพงศ์ วีระเศรษฐกุล; b. 1970) 2004 film *Sud pralad* (สัตว์ประหลาด, En. Tropical Malady), the soundscape of which, in its second half, is mostly field recordings of the Thai jungle with almost no spoken (human) dialogue.

The seventh and concluding chapter is divided into seven short sections, each named and themed after Zenchiku's six circles and one dewdrop. The first – *jurin* (寿輪; En. circle of life) – is a more creative assembly of ideas, including a discussion of the inherent emptiness of – and thus a certain kind of equality between – both spoken language and musical sounds from a Buddhist-mythological perspective. Section 2 – *shurin* (竪輪; En. circle of arising) – acts as a recapitulation of the ideas of rootedness and place and a discussion of the usefulness of recovering – rescuing – ideas from the pre-Modern past in order to have them available for use in the present and post-Modern future. Chapter 7's two case studies are in Section 3 – *jūrin* (住輪; En. circle of abiding). Firstly, Frank Denyer's (b. 1943) *Screens* (2018) is analysed as a piece of music theatre embodying a present-day version of *yūgen* which is both original and congruent with nō theory. The second case study looks at Wandelweiser-associated composer Eva-Maria Houben's (b. 1955) *on the periphery* (2021).

Sections 4 and 5 of Chapter 7 offer concluding statements from different perspectives. Section 4 – *zōrin* (像輪; En. circle of phenomenal forms) – addresses the role of listening to and creating art amidst the ever-worsening environmental crisis. It also addresses the subtle but crucial differences between a Buddhist ethics based on the inherent buddha nature of all things and contemporary Western philosophies of New Materialism. Section 5 – *harin* (破輪; En. circle of breaking) – looks at how the ethics of care that is fostered by purposeless listening can manifest politically. Section 6 – *kūrin* (空輪; En. circle of emptiness) – is, perhaps predictably, (almost) blank, while Section ∞ (which, while ordinally seventh is adamantly not Section 7) – *ichiro* (一露; En. one dewdrop) – offers an anecdote about overcoming the duality of sound and silence.

1

Silences and hollowness

Sound arises out of silence; all phenomena arise from the hollow expanse.

Every sound is a being of limitless possibilities, and though there are a near infinite number of sounds, even the most musically and sonically attentive people will ignore most of the sounds that are happening within their range of hearing. There are simply too many sounds; attending to all of them would be impossible. And those sounds that we do interact with can be interpreted in nearly limitless ways. Which is not to say that all ways are valid, but also not to say that any particular approach is more valid than others. Within a particular culture or tradition of attentive listening, understanding and interpretation, some interpretations will be considered more valid, more appropriate than others. But that stems from an anthropocentric, cultural-specific imposition on other humans. What first of the sounds themselves?

Those last three words are as evocative as a Proustian madeleine for myself, and surely for others steeped in the American experimental music tradition. John Cage and the composers and sound artists in Cage's orbit often invoked 'the sounds themselves'; Cage claimed in the 1958 lecture 'Composition as Process' that the way of composing he was striving towards was 'a composing of sounds within a universe predicated upon the sounds themselves rather than upon the mind which can envisage their coming into being'.[1] Catherine Costello Hirata

[1] Cage, *Silence*, 27–8.

notes that the phrase 'the sounds themselves' has a multiplicity of interpretations, though she says that for Cage and his colleagues such as Morton Feldman (1926–87), '"the sounds themselves" usually seems to refer to this idea of hearing sounds in a composition just as we would hear them were they not in the composition'.[2] Malcolm Riddoch links the thought of European *musique concrète* composers such as Pierre Schaeffer (1910–95) with Cage's, writing that 'what binds these disparate musical imaginaries together is a phenomenological shift away from traditional conceptual notions of musicality and toward focusing on the concrete and immediate experience and manipulation of actual sounds as they are heard in the world'[3] (though we will come back to the question of whether Cage's conception is inclusive of 'manipulation' of sounds).

Hearing sounds themselves 'just as we would hear them were they not in the composition', attending to the 'concrete and immediate experience . . . of actual sounds as they are heard in the world': these conceptions still both centre the listener as a human being, as if the sounds themselves are ever-present and eternal, just waiting for an attentive listening human to lend their ears for a quick bit of audition. In this opening chapter, I want to focus on the ground of sounding being in silence, as a specific manifestation of the Buddhist idea that all phenomena – including, of course, human beings – are grounded in emptiness (i.e. nothingness, or the hollow expanse). How does it change our relationship to sounds when we recognize them as beings just as we are, beings which arise from the disorientingly limitless possibilities of the hollow expanse and to which they, like all things, are destined to return sooner or later?

[2] Catherine Costello Hirata, 'The Sounds of the Sounds Themselves: Analyzing the Early Music of Morton Feldman', *Perspectives of New Music* 34, no. 1 (1996): 22n5.

[3] Malcolm Riddoch, 'Imagining the Sounds Themselves', in *The Oxford Handbook of Sound and Imagination* vol. 1, ed. Mark Grimshaw-Aagaard, Mads Walther-Hansen, and Martin Knakkergaard (Oxford: Oxford University Press, 2019), 57. https://doi.org/10.1093/oxfordhb/9780190460167.013.3.

1.1 The hollow expanse

Śūnyatā (Jp. *kū* 空) is the Sanskrit word for the Buddhist concept that has often been translated as void or nothingness, though emptiness is my preferred translation.[4] In Buddhist cosmology, *śūnyatā* is one of the five (or six) elements, along with air, fire, water and earth (and, within esoteric Buddhism, consciousness is a sixth element). Unlike the words nothingness or emptiness in English, which connote a negative lack of something, Buddhist emptiness signifies a pregnant place of limitless possibilities that have yet to take shape. It can be conceived of as a kind of primordial sea of potential phenomena, waiting for a golden spark to initiate the arising of particular phenomena. In Kegon (華厳, Ch. Huáyán) Buddhism, this metaphor of the sea is frequently used, and the golden spark, or wave, is sometimes pictured as moonlight. Huáyán master Lǐ Tōngxuán (李通玄, 635–730) uses this metaphor: 'The Sea of Emptiness, windstill. And yet, of itself, a glimmering golden wave arises.'[5] That image of the golden wave can be understood as a wave reflecting moonlight, and the whole phrase can be understood as an illustration of coming to an awakening (the glint of moonlight) of the relationship between the phenomena of humanity's perceived conventional reality (the wave) and the surrounding ground of generative emptiness (the endless deep ocean). As the wave on its surface is only a fraction of the entire ocean, what we perceive as reality is only ever a tiny fraction of the possible realities that could (or do) manifest.

Mahāyāna Buddhist ontology is not negative or nihilistic, nor does it deny matter. The concept of the inherent emptiness of all things

[4] When referencing the historical Buddhist concept, I will use 'emptiness'. In referring to more contemporary theorizations of emptiness, I will use 'hollowness', or sometimes 'nothingness', as appropriate for the thinker being discussed.

[5] '性海無風、金波自涌。' Zeami Motokiyo and Konparu Zenchiku, *Zeami Zenchiku*, ed. Omote Akira and Katō Shūichi (Tokyo: Iwanami Shoten, 1974), 325. 'Ocean of Thusness', 'Suchness', or 'Original Nature' would be more traditional, less poetic translations of '性海'. 'windstill' is an English coinage of Hildegard Westerkamp's (see Chapter 5), heard in her iconic soundscape composition *Kits Beach Soundwalk* (1988), derived – one assumes – from the German *windstill*, meaning 'without wind'.

is rooted in empirical knowledge: all individuated phenomena are individuated by human observers based on the biases of their senses (which cannot sense all phenomena) and cultural traditions. For example, we are disposed to call a particular group of cells enclosed in skin a 'human' despite a significant portion of the cells within the skin not having human DNA. We could just as accurately classify these cells into separate emergent phenomena rather than naming them a single 'human being', but by both social convention and for evolutionary biological reasons, we generally choose the latter.

What we conventionally call 'music' is an empty, hollow phenomenon like any other. By tradition and convention – and, of course, different cultures and subcultures have different traditions and conventions – we choose to call some sounds music and others language and others noise. The 171 consecutive rhythmically identical repetitions of A_5 that Jürg Frey (b. 1953) writes in *pianist, alone* (1998–2004) may be considered as 'music' by some and not by others. That same A_5 in a Beethoven piano sonata, or a nō play by Zenchiku, or played on a bone flute, or whistled by a bird would be considered as music by some and not by others. The note by itself – a single note – played on a piano might not be considered 'music' by someone who would consider it music if it were played in the context of the Beethoven or Frey pieces.

When does an A_5 on a piano become music, and when is it just a sound? For some it is always both, for others, melody, harmony or rhythm is a requirement of music, and a single note has, at most, only rhythm.[6] Likewise, when does a cell become part of a human being? Does it require human DNA, or just to be present within the skin sac of a human? When is a wave a wave and not merely the ocean, or is it always both? Perspective, culture, education and beliefs will affect the

6 Rhythm here can be understood as duration, but it can also be understood as the 884 repetitions per second that a given waveform must repeat in order to be perceived as A_5. *cf* Daniel K. L. Chua and Alexander Rehding, *Alien Listening: Voyager's Golden Record and Music from Earth* (New York: Zone Books, 2021).

answers different people give. This is the (or, at least, a) meaning of emptiness in Buddhism: no phenomenon can ever have a single, fixed identity; any object's identity is always co-created by the subject which perceives it, and every object is equally a subject which is perceiving (in its way) and interpreting (classifying) all other sensible objects, including the original perceiving subject.

Sounds are beings perceiving us listeners just as much as we are perceiving them as sounds. Dōgen, in the '*Zenki*' (Jp. 全機, Undivided Activity) fascicle of *Shōbōgenzō*, writes

> Life is just like riding in a boat. You raise the sail, and you steer. Although you maneuver the sail and the pole, the boat gives you a ride, and without the boat you couldn't ride. But you ride in the boat, and your riding makes the boat what it is. Investigate a moment like this. At just such a moment there is nothing but the world of the boat. The sky, the water, and the shore all become conditions of the boat, which is not the same as conditions that are not the boat's.[7]

For a sound, all things exist in relation to – become conditions of – the sound. As listeners, all things necessarily exist in relation to ourselves, and the listened-to sound only exists in relationship to us. But from the point of view of the sound, we only exist in relationship to it. It is a reciprocal and equal relationship. Likewise, each note in a melody, each note in a chord, each voice in a choir and so on; these all exist only in relationship to – are conditions of – one another.

1.1.1 Moonlight reflected in water

Chéngguān (澄観, *c.* 738–*c.* 839; Jp. Chōkan), the fourth patriarch of Huáyán Buddhism, distinguished four progressive understandings of the relationship between phenomena (conventionally perceived things in the world; Jp. *ji* 事) and limitless emptiness (what is called in the

[7] Dōgen, *Shōbōgenzō*, ed. Mizuno Yaoko (Tokyo: Iwanami, 1990), vol. 2, 83–4; Dōgen, *Treasury*, ed. Tanahashi, 451; translation modified.

Huáyán school principle; Jp. *ri* 理) interact. He elucidated these four levels of understanding with the metaphor of waves (phenomena or *ji*, i.e. conventional reality) on the ocean (principle or *ri*, i.e. limitless emptiness). The first level of understanding is the 'universe as phenomena (Jp. *jihokkai* 事法界)' in which the waves on the ocean (phenomena) look as though they exist in-and-of themselves. Second is the 'universe as principle (Jp. *rihokkai* 理法界)', where the universe is understood as emptiness (principle or *ri*) and the waves (phenomena or *ji*) are not seen as separate from the ocean (emptiness or *ri*). Third is the 'universe as the unimpeded interpenetration of principle and phenomena (Jp. *riji muge hokkai* 理事無礙法界)', in which the waves and the ocean are understood as both interdependent and distinct from one another. The fourth and most advanced level of understanding is the 'universe as the unimpeded interpenetration of phenomena and phenomena (Jp. *jiji muge hokkai* 事事無礙法界)' – which is the understanding of the universe described above in relation to the quotation from Dōgen's '*Zenki*' – that waves (phenomena or *ji*) and ocean (emptiness, principle or *ri*) are absolutely dependent on each other (interpenetrating), and that everything exists as pure relationship, without the possibility of an intrinsic individual identity.[8]

This metaphor of the waves and the ocean is a common one in Huáyán/Kegon Buddhism. Kegon was influenced by Daoism, and it in turn had a strong influence on Chán (禅, Jp. Zen), and thus the metaphor has remained in use even after Kegon became much less of an influential sect in both China and Japan. Another important image that is often used in Kegon and Zen discussions of reality (as well as in visual artworks) is that of the moon, especially the image of the moon reflected on the surface of water or in waves (as in the Lǐ Tōngxuán quotation above).

8 Richard Bowring, *Religious Traditions of Japan 500–1600* (Cambridge: Cambridge University Press, 2005), 105.

One popular story employing this motif is called *Catching the Moon's Reflection* (Jp. *enkō sokugetsu* 猿猴捉月). This is a Chinese Buddhist parable of a tribe of monkeys who, having become fascinated with the reflection of the moon in a pond, work collectively trying to fish it out. Not unlike Plato's cave parable, the monkeys symbolize the unenlightened mind grasping at – becoming attached to – reflections of reality (in other words conventional phenomena) rather than ultimate reality (the absolute). The Japanese story of Lady Chiyono (千代野) also uses this trope. Chiyono was a Zen nun, possibly the founder of what became Kyoto's most important Zen nunneries, Keiaiji (景愛寺),[9] though some scholars dispute the identification of the nun in the story with the temple's founder (the two may have shared the birth name Chiyono).[10] She is said to have been struggling with her meditation practice when one evening, while carrying a bucket of water, she noticed the reflection of the moon in the bucket. Suddenly, the bottom of the bucket broke, the water gushing out over the path where she walked. Of course, the image of the moon disappeared with the water, prompting a sudden awakening to the inherent impermanence and emptiness of all phenomena. The following poem about the experience is attributed to her:

> とにかくにたくみし桶の底ぬけて水たまらねば月もやどらず[11]
> *tonikaku ni takumishi oke no soko nukete mizu tamaraneba tsuki mo yadorazu*
> In any case, when the bottom of the bucket gives way, it holds neither water nor the moon[12]

[9] Kamei Shin, '*Kieyuku Tsuki:* Chiyo nōhime shichihenge monogatari *no shohon*', *Bunken tankyū* 39 (2001): 68.

[10] Yusa Michiko, 'Japanese Buddhism and Women: The Lotus, Amida, and Awakening', in *The Dao Companion to Japanese Buddhist Philosophy*, ed. Gereon Kopf (Dordrecht: Springer, 2019), 119–20.

[11] Nishiyama Mika, 'Keiaiji, Hōji'in Monzeki', in *Amamonzeki, A Hidden Heritage: Treasures of the Japanese Imperial Convents*, ed. Patricia Fister and Monica Bethe (Chicago: Paragon Book Gallery, 2009), 61.

[12] Translation mine. Alternative translations are in Nishiyama, 'Keiaiji', 61, and Yusa, 'Japanese Buddhism and Women', 119.

This story was well-known and often referenced in art, by well-known artists such as Hakuin Ekaku (白隠慧鶴; 1686–1769) and Maruyama Ōkyo (円山応挙; 1733–95).

1.1.2 Yoko Ono's *Water Piece*

The stories of Lady Chiyono's awakening to emptiness and the tribe of monkeys attempting to capture the moon are also clearly referenced by Yoko Ono in her *Water Piece*, which can be found in her 1964 collection *Grapefruit*. It is a text score, which is a set of instructions for a piece of music written entirely in plain language rather than using Western musical staff notation. Ono's text score reads in full:

> Steal a moon on the water with a bucket.
> Keep stealing until no moon is seen on
> the water.[13]

The verb steal is of key importance. While on the surface, employing the most common meaning of 'steal' (to take something without permission), the idea of stealing the moon is an impossible instruction which clearly alludes to the foolishness of the monkey tribe's attachment to conventional reality and ignorance of ultimate reality,[14] 'to steal' can also mean 'to move quietly'. Interpreting Ono's text score with both meanings of steal feels more apt, and performing the piece in this manner also results in a much slower, more deliberate and nearly silent soundworld than a frantic attempt to capture and remove the image of the moon. Like the chanting of a mantra, the quiet, deliberate, concentrated repetition of 'stealing a moon' increasingly loses its conventional meaning over time and becomes more and more a meditative practice affording the awakening of an interpreter (performer or audience).

13 Ono Yoko, *Grapefruit* (1964; repr. New York: Simon & Schuster, 2000), n.p.

14 We will revisit the meanings of the terms 'conventional' and 'ultimate reality' in the next chapter.

As the first instruction references the 'Catching the Moon's Reflection' parable, the second obliquely refers to Lady Chiyono. The condition for finishing the piece is entirely out of the control of the performer, since – on the surface reading, in other words in conventional reality – the series of actions is potentially endless: If the 'water' is a body of water much bigger than a backyard swimming pool it is hard to imagine a performer being able to reduce the amount of water to zero so that no moon remains. On this reading, the performer either has to scoop out all the water and, presumably, scatter it somewhere where it will be absorbed or drain away, eliminating the reflection anywhere but the surface of the water in the bucket. But carrying away a moon on the surface of the bucket cannot be the end-state; in the Chiyono story this is just the starting point, prior to her awakening. For an awakening to occur, the endpoint of *Water Piece* has to be outside of the control of the interpreter. Two possibilities occur to me (though undoubtedly there will be other interpretations). The first is that a cloud obscures the celestial moon, or the moon changes position (or sets), so that no moon is reflected on the surface of the water. This case affords being interpreted as awakening to the transience of conventional phenomena, which is the realization of Lady Chiyono had after the accident with the bucket caused her moon to disappear. The second possibility is that the distinction between moon and waves, light and water, dissolves in the mantric practice of repetitive action; the moons on the water and in the bucket are transient phenomena, reflections of a truer reality: the moon is not on the water, nor is it in the sky. Rather, the moon and water are both empty phenomena with no intrinsic identity. There never was a moon on the water at all.

As Kristofer Svensson points out in his discussion of Ono's even more silent 1963 piece *Tape Piece I: Stone Piece* – the text score of which reads, in full, 'Take the sound of the stone aging.'[15] – the quality of the silence matters greatly for a piece like this to effectively afford

[15] Ono, *Grapefruit*, n.p.

interpretation as an *upāya* (Jp. *hōben* 方便), a Sanskrit term meaning a tool for leading people to awakening.[16] They contrast the silences of John Cage's *4'33"* (1952) and *Stone Piece*, saying that what Cage's piece allows is for the background, ambient sounds of wherever the piece is listened out to move to the foreground, drawing the listeners' attention to those sounds which are conventionally ignored. Ono's *Stone Piece*, on the other hand, forces our attention to the sound of aging stone, a sound which is not perceptible by human ears or on a human timescale (i.e. rhythm). Thus attuned to a sound which is not audible (to humans), the vague ambient background sounds are, without 'being released of [their] vagueness, . . . pushed to the foreground *as background*'.[17]

Though the stealing of a moon on the water is not as purely silent as either *Stone Piece* or *4'33"*, in *Water Piece*, the rhythm of the repetitive 'keep stealing' is left to the discretion of the interpreter. This certainly affords – and, considering the definition of 'steal' as 'surreptitious movement', encourages – an interpretation of *Water Piece* as having wide and irregular repetitions of the act of stealing the water in which the moon's reflection abides with a bucket. An interpretation of *Water Piece* which reads 'steal' as both 'take' and 'stealthily move' allows for long and unpredictable silences in which the background sounds are 'pushed to the foreground *as background*', and is an interpretation which affords being an *upāya*.

1.2 Silence

The importance of silence – not absolute lack of sound, but rather vague background sounds 'pushed to the foreground *as background*' – as sonic *upāya* for human interpreters notwithstanding, there can also

16 Kristofer Svensson, 'A Buddhist Musical Poetics', in *Intimating Emptiness* (Blogspot, 2015).

17 In this formulation, Svensson is quoting Martin Seel, *Aesthetics of appearing* (Stanford: Stanford University Press, 2005), 148.

be great importance in foregrounding those background sounds in our attention.

Silence has always been a defining parameter of music. There can be no music without silence, at the very least preceding and following any musical piece, framing the music, separating it from other, contingent sounds. In most cases, there are also points of silence used within pieces for rhythmic or rhetorical dramatic effect, or (in longer pieces for more than one player) for the practical reason of giving each performer a bit of a break.

Svensson makes a useful distinction between 'musical silence' and 'silence-as-emptiness'.[18] A musical silence is one which is used rhetorically as part of the musical structure. It builds tension and aims to create in the listener a sense of anticipation about what will occur after the silence – how the silence (intended to be heard as blank void, *nihilo*) will be broken. 'General pauses' of this type occur throughout the Western art-music canon: for example between the majestic opening chords of Mozart's *Die Zauberflöte*, the sea of rests from which arise spare staccato chords in Variation XIII of Beethoven's *Diabelli Variations*, the grandeur of the long pauses alternating with six massed-orchestral chords at the end of Sibelius' fifth symphony. All of these – and countless more – examples of silences function as rhetoric, silence as musical material: they are coloured by the sounds which came before and by desire for the sounds to come. In other words, like the moments without sound which frame the beginning and end of a piece, these pauses are conceived of as negative spaces, rhythmic spaces defined by a present lack of sound, memories of past sounds and anticipatory longing for future sounds. Crucially, the memory of past sounds and longing for future sounds work together: In these rhetorical silences, there is always an expectation that there will be a logical connection between the sounds preceding and following the silence.[19] Thus, the

[18] Svensson, 'A Buddhist Musical Poetics'.

[19] 'Logic' is here defined by the genre and tradition of the piece in question, whatever it is.

silences become placeholders; they cannot merely be silences in and of themselves.[20]

Silence-as-emptiness, on the other hand, is not silence as void or *nihilo*, but emptiness in the Buddhist form discussed above: limitless and generative, an open place of creativity and play. A silence such as this cannot be too short; it must be at least long enough for the listener to perceive that the silence is not silent at all; there are always other sounds outside the artificial frame of 'music', as there are always other phenomena outside of what any one person tends to attend to (or are physiologically able to attend to). Silence-as-emptiness, as noted above, cannot be independent of surrounding sounds, whether they are intentional (musical) or unintentional (ambient background) sounds. But they need to be long enough that the intentional (musical) sounds no longer hold an anticipatory grip on the listener's sense of what sounds might come, what sounds might be musical.

One of the principal movements in the late twentieth and early twenty-first centuries exploring silences-as-emptiness is the Wandelweiser composers collective, a group founded by Antoine Beuger (b. 1955) and Burkhard Schlothauer (b. 1957) in 1992 and comprising thirty-three composers (at the time of writing in late 2025) such as Jürg Frey, Eva-Maria Houben and Michael Pisaro-Liu.[21] Frey, in a short 1998 text called 'The Architecture of Silence', explains his attitude to silence:

> There are pieces in which the absence of sound has become a fundamental feature. The silence is not uninfluenced by the sounds which were previously heard. These sounds make the silence possible by their ceasing and give it a glimmer of content. As the space of silence

[20] Not that any phenomenon can literally be in and of itself, but in this case the silences cannot easily be understood, even in conventional reality, as independent of the surrounding musical material any more than any particular note of a melody can be heard as independent from the other notes in a melody.

[21] See https://wandelweiser.de/ as well as an introductory article by Nicholas Melia and James Saunders ('Introduction: What is Wandelweiser?', *Contemporary Music Review* 30, no. 6 (2011): 445–8) and an insider's history of the first 17 years of Wandelweiser by Pisaro-Liu. Michael Pisaro-Liu, 'Wandelweiser', *wandelweiser*, 2009 https://wandelweiser.de/_texte/erstw-engl.html.

> stretches itself out, the sounds weaken in our memory. This is the long breath between the time of sound and the space of silence created. Silence can also be present in the sounds. In order to have silence in sounds, one must let go of everything which gets in the way of this silence. This sound is a sound without the idea of what it can mean or how it should be used. This sound achieves a hint of permeability, which otherwise belongs only to silence.[22]

What Frey is describing here with the idea of 'a sound without the idea of what it can mean or how it should be used' is akin to the emptiness of – 'silence . . . present in' – sound, made possible by long durations of silence, an aesthetic deeply and richly explored by many of the Wandelweiser composers. Beuger acknowledges this strain of Wandelweiser composition as being with the 'event' (in philosopher Alain Badiou's terms) of John Cage's *4'33"*.[23] Similarly, Pisaro-Liu writes that for himself and Wandelweiser-adjacent composer Kunsu Shim (b. 1958) '*4'33"* was seen not as a joke or a Zen kōan [公案] or a philosophical statement: it was heard as music. It was also viewed as unfinished work in the best sense: it created new possibilities for the combination (and understanding) of sound and silence.'[24]

Cage's *4'33"* can be interpreted as encouraging listeners to attend to background sounds, unintentional sounds – overlooked voices – with the same concentrated listening we give to intentional, socially accepted sounds. In a 1954 letter to Helen Wolff (mother of his colleague Christian Wolff [b. 1934]), Cage says that 'What we hear [when we listen to *4'33"*] is determined by our own emptiness, our own receptivity; we receive to the extent we are empty to do so.'[25] In this, Cage seems to be pointing to

[22] Jürg Frey, 'The Architecture of Silence', *wandelweiser*, 1998. https://wandelweiser.de/_juerg-frey/texts-e.html#THE.

[23] Nicholas Melia, 'Stille Musik—Wandelweiser and the Voices of Ontological Silence', *Contemporary Music Review* 30, no. 6: 475, 488, https://doi.org/10.1080/07494467.2011.676897.

[24] Pisaro-Liu, 'Wandelweiser'.

[25] John Cage, *The Selected Letters of John Cage*, ed. Laura Kuhn (Middletown: Wesleyan University Press, 2016), 176.

emptiness as a kind of 'lack', a conceptual void which needs to be filled by something. But regardless of how Cage listened to his own piece at the time of its composition, he acknowledges the key point about interpretation, which is that each interpreter has absolute freedom to interpret: Later in the same letter, he writes that *4'33"* 'will be received in unpredictable ways'. I feel free to interpret emptiness not as a lack but a limitless field of openness and possibility, and, in that vein, I interpret *4'33"* as being about background, small, overlooked sounds, a perceivable manifestation of emptiness within the conventional reality of the phenomenal world, which manifests not just the background sounds within silences, but also, per Frey, the silence (emptiness) within sounds. For a variety of aesthetic and political reasons which will be discussed further throughout the rest of this book, there is an imperative not to retreat into contemplative silences but to be active listeners to the silenced.

1.3 Creative misinterpretation

Performing *4'33"* is one way of attuning oneself to the small sounds of the overlooked. Done every day – which Cage said he did[26] – it can become something like a religious practice. Even when moving through the world without explicitly concentrating on listening, a regular practitioner of concentrated, deep listening (which naturally can be done without explicitly choosing to 'perform' or 'interpret' *4'33"* or any other composer's listening exercises) can become more aware of the voices of others – including nonhuman others – that are not typically attended to within capitalist Modernity. There are potentially as many understandings of *4'33"* as there are interpreters, and for each interpreter, as many understandings of the work as there

[26] Kay Larson, *Where the Heart Beats: John Cage, Zen Buddhism, and the Inner Life of Artists* (London: Penguin Press, 2012), 276.

are performances of it. This affordance of a constellation of possible interpretations is one aspect of what makes *4'33"* postmodern art, rather than a modernist 'world-unto-itself', in the terms of curator and theorist Nicolas Bourriaud.[27]

Within the monotheistic Western tradition, the model of communication between a creator (Creator) and their audience is often held to be hierarchical, with the (Absolute) creator as the sender of a message (a Truth) which should be received by the audience. That audience is meant to understand the received message as it was sent, without interpreting or deviating from the creator's intentions. Despite many people wanting to cling to the uncomplicated (false) certainties promised by this model of transmission of (artistic) truth from creator to receiver, it seems much less tenable in the twenty-first century west. This is thanks in part to Roland Barthes' 'death of the author',[28] but also to experimental artists and musicians, such as Cage, whose practice eschews intentionality or purpose in creation.[29]

If Cage had any intention when he wrote *4'33"*, it was to force audiences to interpret for themselves (this, of course, is my own interpretation, not Cage's – and, as per Barthes, Cage's own interpretation of his own work would not be of any greater value than my interpretation, or yours). This idea of the 'freedom of interpretation', to borrow Kondo's phrase,[30] was not a new discovery of the French post-modernists, however. If it had to be rediscovered in the post-Enlightenment Modern world, in times past and around the world the notion of *author*ship and the *author*ity of a creator's intentions for a work were simply foreign. In Japanese poetics, though generally authors' names are recorded and known, a central feature of that intertextual tradition is borrowing entire lines (up to half of a

[27] Nicolas Bourriaud, *The Exform* (London: Verso, 2016), 63.

[28] Barthes, *Image Music Text*, 142*ff*.

[29] Jo Kondo explores the history of the idea of music as a language of the feelings through which the composer can 'touch' the audience: Kondo, *Homo audiens*, 53*ff*.

[30] Ibid., 81.

poem) from another poet and recontextualizing them. Some of these phrases became standard tropes, but a poet's skill lay not in avoiding repetition as 'cliche', but in shifting – reinterpreting – the meaning of set phrases. These oft-repeated words and phrases were known as *makura kotaba* (枕詞, literally meaning pillow words) or *utamakura* (歌枕, literally poem pillows); these respectively were set phrases and place names, both associated with a constellation of meanings which built up over centuries of poetic practice (see Section 3.2 for further detail).

The world of nō theatre is closely related to the world of poetry: The climax of the first act of many plays is centred around the chanting of a famous poem about the location in which the nō is set.[31] Zeami was the first actor of what was then called *sarugaku* nō to theorize about the art form, how to act, how to sing, how to dance, how to compose music for the stage and how to write a play. Many of his plays were radical reinterpretations of his father Kan'ami's works. One example of this tendency is *Tōru* (融), a play based on Kan'ami's demon play *Tōru no otodo* (融の大臣), which Zeami turns into an exploration of the elegance of the titular Heian aristocrat.[32] Zeami's treatises were subject to the same kind of radical reinterpretation by his artistic heir and son-in-law Konparu Zenchiku, whose artistic purpose (which we will explore in greater depth in Chapter 6) was much more spiritually inclined than Zeami's more practical, worldly outlook. This difference meant that Zenchiku repurposed Zeami's theoretical and artistic legacy through what Noel Pinnington calls Zenchiku's 'creative misreading' of Zeami's texts, and indeed makes the point that 'creative interpretation' was a standard intellectual technique of the late mediaeval period in Japan.[33]

[31] Zeami calls this a *tsumedokoro* (詰め所) in his treatise *Fūshikaden* (風姿花伝, Transmitting the flower through effects and attitudes) written in 1400. *Zeami Zenchiku*, 47; Zeami Motokiyo, *Performance Notes*, trans. Tom Hare (New York: Columbia University Press, 2008), 57.

[32] Paul S. Atkins, 'Depictions of the Kawara-no-in in Medieval Japanese Nō Drama', *Asian Theatre Journal* 27, no. 1 (2010): 10; see also Daryl Jamieson, 'Spirit of Place: Zeami's *Tōru* and the Poetic Manifestation of *Mugen*', *Japanese Studies* 42, no. 2 (2022): 137–53.

[33] Pinnington, *Traces in the Way*, 103.

The spirit of this mediaeval Japanese approach to sources – meticulous sourcing of quotations from preceding scholarship, but not being constrained to the use of those words in the way the original author likely intended them – is fully in line with the post-modern Barthesian death of the author: How can we be bound by the intention of the author if the author's intention can never be fully known in any case, even to the author themself? Furthermore, and most crucially for this book, it is also congruent with the style of experimental music called 'listening composition' (*kiku sakkyoku* 聴く作曲) by Kondo[34] in which attending to each sound is the only structuring principle of a composition (eschewing all other artificial musical structures such as chord progressions, musical forms, etc.). 'Listening composition' takes sounds as they are, really listens to them (and to the extent possible, does not impose on sounds the composer's preconceived ideas about how sounds are 'supposed' to be combined into a 'piece of music'); it is a process of creation which treats the sounds respectfully as fellow beings in the world, not as inanimate dots signifying sonic material to be pushed around a page or computer screen.[35] Cage's fellow listening composer Morton Feldman once said, in response to a question about composition technique put to him by the avant-garde German composer Karlheinz Stockhausen (1928–2007),

> My past experience was not to 'meddle' with the material, but use my concentration as a guide to what might transpire. I mentioned this to Stockhausen once when he had asked me what my secret was. 'I don't push the sounds around.' Stockhausen mulled this over and asked: 'Not even a little bit?'[36]

[34] Kondō Jō, *Mimi no shikō* (Tokyo: Seidosha, 1985), 153–74; Kondo, *Homo audiens*, 67–82.

[35] This is not an attitude to sound limited to composers associated with the New York School like Cage and their artistic descendants like Kondo and the Wandelweiser group. Icelandic composer Bára Gísladóttir (b. 1989) has described a similar attitude to the life of sounds: 'It's very important to me the idea of sound being treated as something alive. The feeling of sound as something sterile is extremely depressing. It's so important to remember the life in everything, and not only in humans.' Tim Rutherford-Johnson, liner notes for *Bára Gísladóttir: Orchestral Works* (Copenhagen: Dacapo Records, 2024), 12.

[36] Morton Feldman, *Give My Regards to Eighth Street: Collected Writings of Morton Feldman*, ed. Bernard Harper Friedman (Cambridge: Exact Change, 2000), 143.

Feldman here articulates the conceptual difference, not only between listening composition and speaking composition, but the difference alluded to earlier between the *musique concrète* composers – who used the 'sounds themselves' as material to be manipulated – and the Cagean and post-Cagean experimental composers – who did not use sounds, but rather listened out open places wherein sounds could sound as themselves.

But listening composition as a technique is not limited to what is traditionally called 'composition'. Listening with respect to sounds as fellow beings in the world, not pushing them around to fit your preconceptions (in other words, bracketing your preconceived notions about what music is or can be), and framing those sounds listened to with concentration and respect with a beginning and end (which is not to say adding rhetorical flourishes to indicate starting and stopping points, but merely – as with *4'33"* – defining starting and stopping points for the period of concentrated listening): all this is composition, which is to say listening, whether you then write down the results of your listening on paper, record them, or whether the sounds just leave a trace of themselves in your memory. By listening to anything at any time with concentration and due respect, you are composing an experience, and you are practicing listening composition, regardless of the 'intention' or not of whomever is creating the sounds. You can practice listening composition not only with the sounds of (so-called) nature, with John Cage's *4'33"*, with Feldman's or Frey's piano pieces, but also with Beethoven's, Zeami's or Public Enemy's. The composer of a piece has no authority over how you listen to – that is interpret – it.

1.4 Ruins

Future of Museums is the signature dessert of Kyoto pâtissier Kakimoto Akihiro (垣本晃宏). The dish is constructed to order, the empty glass receiving cacao streusel, celery butter cream, chocolate mousse, caramel ice cream, chocolate sponge biscuits, caramelized almonds, grapefruit sauce and topped with a thin disc of chocolate which covers the glass, a leaf-shaped chocolate tuile and a frond of dill. Served alongside is a vial of hot grapefruit sauce which the diner can pour over the chocolate topping, thus melting it and allowing access to the various creams, biscuits and crunchy crumble inside.[37] From emptiness to form, the dessert is manifest out from various unusual components (notably, for a dark chocolate-based dessert, celery, grapefruit and dill). Though of course all food must be destroyed as food in order to serve its function as food, notably this dessert must be ruined even before being eaten: in order to access the dessert, you must melt through the cold dill-garnished chocolate disc which covers the mouth of the glass by pouring the hot grapefruit sauce over it. Only after having broken through – having *ruined* the form of the dessert – can the diner eat, finally returning the glass to its empty state at the end of the meal.

The attentiveness of Kakimoto to unexpected combinations of flavours which – on their own – are not excessively unusual brings to mind Morton Feldman's late works, which are almost exclusively written for traditional combinations of instruments and instrumental techniques but nonetheless sound entirely novel. Composer Frank Denyer relates that one of Feldman's composition lessons at the State University of New York at Buffalo consisted of inviting students to his home, bringing them 'from shop to shop looking for fresh handmade pasta, genuine Italian tomatoes, a particular kind of cooking oil, various herbs and other ingredients he insisted were all essential', after which he slowly prepared the meal explaining the importance of each ingredient, the timing of each aspect of preparing the dish, and 'tasting continuously'. To the exasperation of the students, who were expecting a

[37] The recipe is available from Kakimoto Akihiro, 'Future Museum with Chocolate, Celery, and Grapefruit', *So Good* 24 (2020), https://www.sogoodmagazine.com/pastry-recipes/future-museum-chocolate-celery-grapefruit-akihiro-kakimoto/ (accessed 13 September 2025).

composition lesson, Feldman said 'I've taught you everything I know'.[38] High quality ingredients, treated with respect, arranged in an order which is attuned to their being-ness – attuned through attentive scent and taste (or listening) – is all (listening) composition is.

Fluxus-associated composer Shiomi Mieko (塩見允枝子; b. 1938) said that 'feeling duration itself is music',[39] in other words, attentive perception (i.e. listening, but also potentially including tasting, looking, smelling, touching) over a period of time (i.e. duration, rhythm) is music. Like Feldman's lesson, and like Alison Knowles' (1933–2025) famous 1962 text score *Proposition* (which reads in full 'Make a Salad' and conventionally includes the eating of the salad by the audience as part of the performance),[40] Kakimoto's *Future of Museums* can be read as a musical performance piece in which the audience is physically required to participate in the work. Of course, for any collection of perceptions (sounds) to be considered music, even works of common practice classical music, a listener (be that a composer, performer or audience member) must also participate actively in the assembling of sounds into an artistic order, whatever that means to them. The subjective nature of this is unavoidable; it is why some people would listen to Stockhausen, Wandelweiser, Kendrik Lamar or Ghanian drumming and say, for their own subjective reasons, 'this is not music' – and it isn't, for them, since they are not giving the music the attention needed for it to be perceived as music for them, by them.

But aside from the composition of the recipe – and the knowing nod to the art world in the title – it is because of the ruination (i.e. decomposition) of this dessert which affords its being read as an artwork. Though all things manifest from and return to emptiness, in the conventional world – and even more so under Modern capitalist

[38] Frank Denyer, *In The Margins of Composition* (London: Vision Edition, 2019), 84.

[39] Kakinuma Toshie, 'Oral History Interview with Shiomi Mieko', trans. Tomii Reiko (Kyoto City University of Arts, 2014).

[40] Alison Knowles, 'Proposition', in *Fluxus Performance Workbook*, ed. Ken Friedman, Owen Smith, and Lauren Sawchyn (Performance Research e-Publications, 2002), 69.

realism[41] – we have become adept at ignoring the emptiness. This willed ignorance is rather like the false lyricism of *cantabile* (sung style) melodic playing on a piano: A piano physically cannot sustain or increase the volume of any note once it is played, it can only decay, but a huge amount of classical and Romantic (roughly 1750–1900) piano music is predicated on the illusion that a piano can produce a smooth melodic flow. Ruins are an aesthetic reminder of the fundamental emptiness which grounds reality that Modernity wants to ignore.

Ruins are the traces of the past no longer functioning as originally intended, but which can and do function otherwise. As such, they are attractive in and of themselves for Romantics and post-moderns, those in reaction against (but often defined through their opposition to rather than their independence from) Classical or Modernist ontologies and conceptions of art. For Romantic and post-modern artists, the ruin is a reminder that nothing is permanent, that no artist or architect's intention can withstand time. But also that the ruin is itself a place where different times and spaces coexist,[42] and as such gives birth to ruination as a form of interpretation and composition.[43]

As Kondo points out, Cage's technique of ruination – the use of chance operations (imitating 'nature in her manner of operations', per Thomas Aquinas' phrase which was commonly used by Cage) to alter various properties of works such as Erik Satie's *Socrates* (which became Cage's *Cheap Imitation*) and James Joyce's *Finnegans Wake* (Cage's *Writing through Finnegans Wake*) – is essentially a Romantic one (while also being a romantic one, in that Cage only 'ruins' works which he loves; there would be no point in the active preservation

[41] Mark Fisher, *Capitalist Realism: Is There No Alternative?* (London: Zero Books, 2009).

[42] 'The predominance of multiplicity has the corollary of a heterochronic conception of time: beyond the 'pure presence' and momentariness that distinguish the modernist work as a world-unto-itself, contemporary art postulates multiple temporalities – a representation of time evoking the constellation'. Bourriaud, *Exform*, 63.

[43] See also Robert Ginsberg's *The Aesthetics of Ruins* (Rodopi: Amsterdam, 2004), especially the Chapter 2 'The Ruin as Form', 15–32.

– interpretation – of a past which is meaningless to you).[44] A ruin – which is both an interpretation of the original and also a derivative work itself – exhibits heterochronicity: it is in and of the past (in being an interpretation of the original), of the present (in being a work perceived in the present), while also manifesting the temporal process of deformation that extends from the original work's completion into the future of its eventual complete disintegration into emptiness. As pouring the hot grapefruit sauce onto the chocolate tuille in *Future of Museums* both 'ruins' the form of the dessert but also affords realizing its near-future functioning as a dessert while remaining as a trace of the form it had been, as mentally composing the scattered stones of a ruined monastery into an aesthetic form both recalls the building as it was and the further dissolution of the site in the fullness of time, so ruining a beloved piece of music or poem (as in the above-mentioned intertextual Japanese *waka* tradition) affords giving the audience a simultaneous experience of the past, present and future via the endless arising and extinguishing of all phenomena.

1.4.1 Evan Johnson's *mes pleurants*

Evan Johnson is a composer whose music delicately ruins the extremes of quantitative conventional reality within the embrace of affective emptiness. His recent music wells up intermittently, seeming to reach us (and sometimes not audibly reach us) though ambiguous means from some other dimension of spacetime.

Approaching Johnson's 2020 solo piano work *mes pleurants* from a traditionally musicological, score-based analyst's (or, indeed, a performer-interpreter's) point of view, the piece strikes you as incredibly complex and beautifully – but idiosyncratically – hand-written. The page overflows with detailed, non-standard markings that are unique to Johnson, indecipherable without the four pages of textual instructions

[44] Kondo, *Homo audiens*, 22–6.

which precede the thirteen-page score. Approaching it via audio – listening to the piece live in concert, or, perhaps, on the 2021 recording by the piece's dedicatee Ben Smith[45] – the piece feels like a faded trace of something ancient and powerful.

As with much of Johnson's music, the musical material in *mes pleurants* is a ruination (decomposition) of a late mediaeval work. In this case, three of the four movements (the second main movement and both of the shorter 'satellites') are based on Grimace's (*fl.* late fourteenth century) *Se Zephirus*, a *double balade* found in the *Chantilly Codex* written in a style reminiscent of Guillaume de Machaut (*c.*1300–77).[46] Johnson does not identify the source for the first main movement, titled '1-2', other than to indicate that it is also late mediaeval. The musical material, like the scattered stones of a fully-ruined mediaeval hall, is not immediately identifiable with the source (even when the source has been told to us by the composer), nor is the process by which the ruinations are accomplished. What is of greater aesthetic interest is the tangible weight of cultural history in these fragments. As Robert Ginsberg says of the repurposing of stones from ruined buildings for continued use by local people, 'Such pieces are a connection with the vaguely significant, a manifestation of roots in the locale. The celebrated ruin is part of our house, the owner might think, or, our house is part of the celebrated ruin.'[47] Likewise, Johnson's use of late-mediaeval found material declares his connection with deep Western European musical history; it makes him and Grimace part of each others' worlds, dissolving the boundaries of time and space which conventional thinking puts between them.

One of the notable aspects of this piece is how not all of the sounds are able to break through these boundaries. Johnson's notation is incredibly detailed, approaching a level akin to the scores of New Complexity composers such as Brian Ferneyhough's (b. 1943), but many of these

[45] Evan Johnson, *Lists, Little Stars: Piano Music 2003–2020* (London: all that dust, 2021).

[46] Elizabeth Eva Leach, 'The composer Grimace', *Musicology, Medieval to Modern* (2010), https://eeleach.blog/2010/12/29/the-composer-grimace/.

[47] Ginsberg, *Aesthetics of Ruins*, 185.

precisely indicated actions are intended to produce sounds so quiet as to be audible only by the performer, if at all. Some of these gestures include silently depressing keys, lifting keys, tapping keys and 'second-escapement attacks', where the piano key is first depressed halfway and only then (quietly) struck, thus limiting the kinetic force of the hammer striking the string. These sounds afford being heard – if at all – as muted, hushed or distanced. These effects are somewhat complicated – or potentially undermined – by the greatly increased intimacy of listening to a recording, wherein many more of these extremely quiet gestures do produce enough sound to be audible to listeners at home than would be in a live concert setting. Nevertheless, if the past-as-Johnson or Johnson-as-past is speaking to us, it is over a very dodgy (ruined) connection.

Like Cage's ruinations of the early twentieth-century modernist works that he loved, a sense of intimacy and love of each and every ruined fragment comes through in this piece. One element of the extremely detailed instructions to the performer is the expressive directions. Almost every note has a unique Romantic expression indication, for example '*quasi amoroso*' (somewhat lovingly), '*dolcissimo quasi "lirico"*' (very sweet, almost 'lyrically'), '*piacevole assolutamente privato*' (pleasantly, absolutely privately), '*apologetico*' (apologetically): These are all attached to single notes; '*apologetico*' is applied to a single note in the right hand while the left hand simultaneously plays another single note '*più intimo*' (somewhat intimately).

In an interview about another piece – 2023's *dust book* for viola d'amore – Johnson said that 'Virtually every event in this piece (and in most of my work more generally) has some sort of fissure, or crack, or instability, on a microscopic level—nothing is sustained for long without faltering, or without being in a continual state of incipient disintegration'.[48] For all the mathematical complexity of the rhythms and

[48] Another Timbre, 'Evan Johnson: Dust Book', *Another Timbre*, 2025, https://www.anothertimbre.com/products/evan-johnson-dust-book-marco-fusi-viola-damore.

precise gestural choreography of the fingers and feet, those Romantic expression marks, the various imprecisely measured fermatae, and the two surprising measures without precise rhythms in movement ii all combine to subvert (ruin) the veneer of modernist complexity. These freer, qualitative, subjective notations undermine the more modernist, scientific, precisely quantified, objective nature of the notation. These are the fissures or cracks through which the 'emptiness permeating everything' (also Johnson's words from that same interview) gets in.

That is not even to suggest that complex notation is in and of itself always precise and objective, that is, anti-freedom. In fact, the most complex music is arguably more free than standardly notated music – extreme precision is self-undermining, and New Complexity composers frequently exploit this contradiction. Greg Stuart, in an interview with Marianna Ritchey, points out that:

> It's absolutely not a form of 'control' over the player, but a real invitation to play—with the material, the act of reading, interpreting, technical challenges, etc. It's an invitation to make something, together. And by definition the composer doesn't know what the ultimate act of that play will look like. The piece is not realizable or knowable in the composer's mind alone. It requires interpretation.[49]

1.5 Emptiness of sound

As Shiomi Mieko said, 'feeling duration itself is music'. What we call pitch is just micro-repetitions of a sound (*i.e.* rhythm). If the same sound is repeated 884 times per second, a human with perfect pitch will name that sound 'A_5'. The same person might call two repetitions of that sound per second '120 BPM' (and some experimental music initiates would call 171 repetitions of that sound 'Jürg Frey's *pianist,*

[49] Marianna Ritchey and Greg Stuart, 'Accessibility and Instrumentality: A Conversation', *e-flux* 154 (2025).

alone'). We use two different categories – pitch and tempo – to describe different instantiations of rhythm, but in essence duration (i.e. rhythm) is all music – all sound – is. The fact that we have elaborate traditions of what constitutes sound versus noise is very much culturally and socially constructed. Like all other phenomena, we perceive sounds and assign higher value to certain sounds or combinations of sounds in the light of our own traditions and histories and biases. But all sounds are just manifestations of emptiness, arising for a particular duration and then extinguishing, with no inherent existence or meaning beyond what we as perceivers of – listeners to – that sound give it.

As in the Kegon Buddhist analogy of the waves on the sea, sounds are phenomena which are interpenetrated by silence, and all silences (and there are no true silences which are audible by humans since even in the most artificially quietened of all places we will at least hear the sound of our own bodies; to hear true silence is to no longer be alive[50]) are interpenetrated by sounds. Whether a given sound is heard or not, whether it manifests as a sound, as a noise, as music or as language is entirely dependent on the consciousness (attention) of a perceiver.

How does this affect how we understand the meaning of sound and music? In the next chapter, we will examine this question by looking at the place of art and music in a contemporary world view based in Kegon and Zen ontology through the aesthetics of the Kyoto School thinkers Nishida Kitarō and Ueda Shizuteru.

[50] It is important to note that hearing is just a specific form of touch, where vibrations are perceived through the ear drum rather than some other body part. Even those who are entirely deaf can 'hear' vibrations through their skin; some profoundly deaf people, such as the percussionist Evelyn Glennie, can hear differently in this way well enough not only to play music professionally, but to play ensemble music in which hearing is necessary for coordination with other musicians.

2

The twofold world

聞くままにまた心なき身にしあらばおのれなりけり軒の玉水[1]
Kiku mama ni mata kokoro naki mi ni shi araba onore narikeri noki no tamamizu
Listening without discrimination – I am the raindrop falling from the eaves

—Dōgen

2.1 Pure experience

An Inquiry into the Good (Zen no kenkyū 善の研究) by Nishida Kitarō begins with a definition of pure experience (*junsui keiken* 純粋経験) along with an example:

> To experience means to know facts just as they are, to know in accordance with facts by completely relinquishing one's own fabrications. What we usually refer to as experience is adulterated with some sort of thought, so by pure I am referring to the state of experience just as it is without the least addition of deliberative discrimination. The moment of seeing a colour or hearing a sound, for example, is prior not only to the thought that the colour or sound is the activity of an external object or that one is sensing it, but also to the judgement of what the colour or sound might be. In this regard, pure experience is

[1] Dōgen, 'Dōgen Zenji Wakashū', in *Dōgen Zenji Zenshū*, vol. 7, ed. Ōkubo Dōshū (Tokyo: Shunshū sha, 1990), 178.

> identical with direct experience. When one directly experiences one's own state of consciousness, there is not yet a subject or an object, and knowing and its object are completely unified. This is the most refined type of experience.[2]

Nishida's conception of pure experience draws on Western philosophers (notably William James, Henri Bergson, Wilhelm Wundt and Arthur Schopenhauer), but is also indebted to Buddhism through, at least, his decades of practical experiences of *zazen* (坐禅) sitting meditation. Dōgen's 'listening without discrimination' – my translation of *kokoro naki* (literally without the mind, or heart-mind) – is certainly a related concept. Both Dōgen and Nishida are describing an experience of the arbitrary distinction between a listener and what they are listening to dropping away, leaving only the experience of listening. The distinction is arbitrary because, as was discussed in Chapter 1, the definition of any phenomenon is entirely a product of human convention. The arbitrary phenomenon in question here – namely the belief that a listening subject and a listened-to object are distinct and independent phenomena – then, is just the product of the human mind reifying itself as something outside 'the world'.

In sound terms, Nishida's pure experience describes the moment of a listener listening to something before the listener thinks about it – interprets it – in any way. This listener is not categorizing the sound (music or noise?), nor are they thinking about the source (organ or car horn?), nor are they assigning value (good or bad?). Nishida puts it thus:

> when we become enraptured by exquisite music, forget ourselves and everything around us, and experience the universe as one melodious sound, true reality presents itself in the moment of direct experience. Should the thought arise that the music is the vibration of air or that one is listening to music, at that point one has already separated

[2] Nishida Kitarō, *An Inquiry into the Good*, trans. Masao Abe and Christopher Ives (1911. Trans. New Haven: Yale University Press, 1990), 3–4.

> oneself from true reality because that thought derives from reflection and thinking divorced from the true state of the reality of the music.[3]

In essence, then, pure experience, when applied to listening, is becoming lost in the soundworld. In the experience of being enveloped in sound, in becoming sound we, to borrow another phrase from Dōgen, 'forget the self'.[4]

Pure experience, and the dissolution of the subject-object divide, are among the foci of Nishida's early philosophical career. In his later career, his principal project was the development of the logic of place (*basho no ronri* 場所の論理). Although this reorientation of his thought stemmed from an attempt to overcome the subjective and psychological implications of a thought rooted in subjective experience, the logic of place doesn't erase the concept of pure experience; it merely shifts the focus from the subject prior to its self-consciousness as a subject to the *place* – the milieu – of that event which is the pure experience prior to the conscious separation of subject and object.

In his 1926 essay 'Basho'[5] in which his logic of place is introduced, Nishida identifies three *basho*: the *basho* of being, the *basho* of relative nothingness and the *basho* of absolute nothingness.[6] The *basho* of being (*yū no basho* 有の場所) is the standpoint of objective empiricism: sound itself – energy waves which are audible to our ears – exists objectively in the world. But this objective, scientistic *basho* excises the subject who hears, the listener, the experimenter. In order to understand empirical phenomena – in order for them to be sensed, felt, understood rather than simply exist – the *basho* of being

3 Ibid., 48.

4 This quotation is from '*Genjō Kōan*' (現成公案, The Challenge of Becoming-Immanent). Dōgen, *Shōbōgenzō*, vol. 1, 54; Dōgen, *Treasury*, 30.

5 Nishida Kitarō, 'Basho,' in *Place and Dialectic: Two Essays by Nishida Kitarō*, trans. John W. M. Krummel and Shigenori Nagatomo (Oxford: Oxford University Press, 2012), 49–102.

6 Much of this paragraph is a paraphrase of the lucid explanation in Thomas P. Kasulis, *Engaging Japanese Philosophy: A Short History* (Honolulu: University of Hawai'i Press, 2019), 464–8.

needs to be subsumed in the subjective *basho* of relative nothingness (*sōtaiteki mu* 相対的無): a sound is heard by a person, first as a pure experience, but then that person interprets that sound in the light of their knowledge, past, understanding and taste. In this subjective *basho*, objective phenomena not only exist (as they do in the *basho* of being), they relate to other phenomena in all their complexity, but also each in their own subjectivity.[7] But this *basho* is also wanting, since it leaves the subject as the arbiter of reality. And so Nishida posits a third *basho*, the *basho* of absolute nothingness (*zettai mu no basho* 絶対無の場所). Nishida's *basho* of absolute nothingness is, like the emptiness we discussed in Chapter 1, a limitless expanse pregnant with all possibilities, encompassing the *basho* of being (objectively existing phenomena), the *basho* of relative nothingness (all the subjective, contextual standpoints of objectively existing phenomena) and all non-existing (or not yet existing) phenomena, physical or conceptual. This is how he ultimately overcomes the subject-object divide, not for the instant of pure perceptual experience prior to cognition and reflection, but by grounding both objective and subjective experiences of sound (or any other event) in an empty field of limitless possibility.

How do we navigate this field, the *basho* of absolute nothingness? Because reality is grounded in the *basho* of absolute nothingness, phenomena are constantly arising and being extinguished, and reality is constantly being dynamically created. Every action[8] we take is creative: We create with every action, and we are reciprocally created by every action. This complex of acting on and being acted on, being subject and object, creating and being created means every action is a creative action.

[7] Ishihara and Miyahara explain that this 'basho refers not so much to the physical environment as to the space of meaning, such as the cultural, social, historical setting, one finds oneself in'. Yuko Ishihara and Katsunori Miyahara, 'Real Harmony of the Self: Enactivism and the Kyoto School', in *Considering, Questioning and Re-Imagining Harmony: Multicultural, Multihistorical and Multidisciplinary Reflections*, ed. Karyn Lai, Rick Benitez, and Chenyang Li (London: Bloomsbury, 2025), 177.

[8] I.e., action-intuition or performative intuition (*kōiteki chokkan* 行為的直観). Fujita notes that action-intuition bears some relationship with Marx's concept of praxis. Fujita Masakatsu, *Nishida Kitarō no shisaku sekai* (Tokyo: Iwanami, 2011), 176–8.

Every act of listening to sound (a phenomenon in the *basho* of being) is a creation (of intellectual and emotional responses in the *basho* of relative nothingness). With every act of listening, our reality subtly and slowly is reshaped by that objective sound and our subjective responses to it.[9] Reality, like the ever-changing rivers of Heraclitus (*fl.c.*500bce) and of Kamo-no-Chōmei (鴨長明; 1155–1216), is constantly in flux. It is not merely a creation; it is a co-creation that is constantly being recreated by all the phenomena within it. As Fujita summarizes: 'in this active and bodily context, reality manifests itself as something alive; and it is precisely thereupon that the objectivity of knowledge is based'.[10] The raindrop objectively exists; we listen to it strike the eaves; but if we are attuned to the *basho* of absolute nothingness and the contingency of such identities as 'raindrop' and 'self', the reality we co-create with that sound is one in which there is no firm separation between the listened-to sound of the rain on the eaves and the listener, us. We, like Dōgen, are the raindrop.

2.2 Sign, symbol and hollow

As Nishida's concept of pure experience relates closely to the no-mind (*mushin* 無心) of Zen practice, so does his *basho* of absolute nothingness resonate with the concept of emptiness we looked at in Chapter 1. Like the *basho* of absolute nothingness, which envelops and is the ground of the *basho* of being and the *basho* of relative nothingness, Mahāyāna Buddhist philosophy has, since at least the late-second-century

9 This includes listening to silence – theatre director Chris Goode points out that silence in a performative space (he uses Pinter as a paradigmatic example in English-language theatre) must be co-created between the performers and audience. It cannot be imposed on the audience: 'A silence . . . is produced communally'. Chris Goode, *The Forest and the Field: Changing Theatre in a Changing World* (London: Oberon Books, 2015), 74.

10 Fujita Masakatsu, 'The Development of Nishida Kitarō's Philosophy: Pure Experience, Place, Action-Intuition', in *The Oxford Handbook of Japanese Philosophy*, ed. Bret W. Davis (Oxford: Oxford University Press, 2019), 413.

Indian philosopher Nāgārjuna held to a twofold ontological model – conventional or provisional truth (Sk. *saṁvṛtisatya*; Jp. *zokutai* 俗諦) and ultimate or absolute truth (Sk. *paramārthasatya*; Jp. *shintai* 真諦). Collectively this model is called the doctrine of the two truths (Sk. *dvasatya*; Jp. *nitai* 二諦).

Third-generation Kyoto School philosopher Ueda Shizuteru – a scholar of Zen, Christian apophatic theology (e.g. Meister Eckhart) and Nishida Kitarō's philosophy – reframed the two truths doctrine as twofold-being-in-the-world (*nijū sekainai sonzai* 二重世界内存在). The world of conventional truth – what Nishida separated into the objective *basho* of being and subjective *basho* of relative nothingness – Ueda glosses as the 'real' world (jitsu *no sekai*「実」の世界) and the world of ultimate truth – Nishida's *basho* of absolute nothingness – is described by Ueda as the 'hollow' expanse (kyo *no sekai*「虚」の世界).

The conventional world (which is enveloped by the hollow expanse) is also called by Ueda a 'space of meaning' (*imi-kūkan* 意味空間). Ueda was interested in how the creative action identified by Nishida actually functioned in reality through speech acts. The pure experience theorized by Nishida – unmediated mutual perception between subject and object – is precognitive by definition. In order for pure experience, or any experience, to be communicated to others we need language. We can not have philosophy of any kind – let alone aesthetics, the philosophy of sensory experience – if we cannot communicate our experiences to others. Language – speech acts – are therefore necessary.

But language limits us. Ludwig Wittgenstein said in his 1921 book *Tractatus Logico-Philosophicus* that '*the limits of my language* mean the limits of my world'.[11] Similarly, Marshall McLuhan's famous phrase from his 1964 book *Understanding Media: The Extensions of Man* 'the medium is the message' suggests that any medium – such as a language – imposes restrictions, and the restrictions imposed by

[11] Ludwig Wittgenstein, *Tractatus Logico-Philosophicus* (London: Kegan Paul, Trench, Trubner & Co., 1922), §5.6.

any pervasive medium becomes (like ideology) invisible to the users of the medium.[12] Ueda's ontology is of a twofold-being-in-the-world, the ultimate reality of which is an absolutely limitless, absolutely unrestricted hollow expanse which enfolds a 'space of meaning' – it is in this place where language exists. Psychiatrist and philosopher Kimura Bin (木村敏; 1931–2021) points out that the word for language, *kotoba* (言葉), etymologically means 'a small part of *koto*', where *koto* means something like a Badiouan Event, and, ultimately, the Buddhist emptiness. Thus language discloses a small – and *only* a small – aspect of ultimate reality, which, for Kimura, 'explains the deepest distrust of verbal explanations in Zen Buddhism.[13] In order to understand how Ueda overcomes the limits of language with regard to expressing the ineffable hollowness which grounds all conventional reality – or, if not overcomes entirely, stretches those limits – and how that ultimately comes back to an understanding of art and sound (an aesthetics), we first need to understand Ueda's semiotics and his aesthetics of poetry.

Ueda identifies three semiotic functions of *words*: signs (*kigō* 記号), symbols (*shōchōgo* 象徴語) and hollow words (kyo*go* 「虚」語).[14] The first of these is signs. A word functions as a sign (a signifier) when, upon hearing the word, the listener perceives – manifests in their consciousness – a single concrete signified as unambiguously as possible (it is never completely unambiguous). Take the example of the moon. Upon hearing the word 'moon' (let us concentrate on oral linguistic expression rather than the written word in this book on sounds), if you interpret the word as a sign, an image of the moon will manifest in your consciousness. Simultaneously, as the image manifests, the word

[12] Marshall McLuhan, *Understanding Media* (1964. Repr. London: Routledge, 2001), 7*ff*.

[13] Kimura Bin, 'Self and Nature—An Interpretation of Schizophrenia', *Zen Buddhism Today* 6 (1988): 1–10.

[14] The following section is based on the first part of Ueda's essay collection *Kotoba* (言葉): Ueda Shizuteru, *Kotoba* (Tokyo: Iwanami shoten, 2008). The key passages are translated in Ueda Shizuteru, 'Language in a Twofold World', in *Japanese Philosophy: A Sourcebook*, ed. James Heisig, Thomas Kasulis, and John Maraldo (Honolulu: University of Hawai'i Press, 2011), 766–84.

itself as a phenomenon disappears, leaving you not with a linguistic phenomenon, but a phenomenon of consciousness manifested by language. There is roughly a 1:1 relationship between a word as a sign and the manifestation of an image.

Words understood as symbols are more complex. If a word as sign manifests a single phenomenon, then a word as symbol manifests an event in the listener's consciousness. An event here can mean anything from associations of the word in culture, history, subjective memory or a multiplicity of these. 'Moon' as a symbol might evoke an association with the autumn,[15] with loneliness,[16] with Buddhist awakening (per Chapter 1), scientific facts about the moon's history and geology or personal recollections of memorable nights spent under moonlight. Aside from when we are first learning words and each word is presented with a strict denotative meaning (i.e. as a sign), or in, for example, certain technical or scientific writing where the meanings of each term must be strictly defined and used accordingly, most of the time we are interpreting words in this symbolic way, simultaneous with or just after understanding the sign. Thus, when we hear a word, what manifests in our consciousness is not only the signified which the word denotatively points to, but also a constellation of connotative associations which function on socio-cultural levels as well as a personal level. Importantly, whether words are interpreted as signs and/or symbols, what manifests in the consciousness of the listener is something which is part of conventional reality, whether it's singular phenomenon, an event, an emotion or something else conventionally real.

Ueda's third level of semiotic interpretation, hollow words, are always functions of their context: They are words made strange or weird – magical or enchanted – by their unexpected juxtapositions or uses.

[15] As in Dōgen's famous poem:
春は花夏ほととぎす秋は月冬雪きえですずしかりけり (Dōgen, Wakashū, 158.)
haru wa hana natsu hototogisu aki wa tsuki, fuyu yuki kiede suzushi kari keri
In spring, the cherry blossom; in summer, the cuckoo; in autumn, the moon; in witer, the unmelted snow – how pure and refreshing.

[16] Which is itself associated with autumn, the cry of a stag looking for a mate, etc.

In poetry, Ueda's concept of hollow words is resonant with poet and theorist Fujiwara no Teika's (藤原定家; 1162–1241, also pronounced Sadaie) injunction to create 'new meanings with old diction', where the poetry manifests new meanings from hollow emptiness via unexpected and original combinations of words (but not to use neologisms or trendy, casual speech).[17] Through unexpected, novel uses of language in poetry and kōans – as well as in absurdist humour, among other possible places where hollow words are likely to occur – manifest things which are *not* conventionally real. When Teika writes that the lady of Uji Bridge brokenheartedly spreads the moonlight over half her bedding, the juxtaposition of the verb 'spread' and the object 'moonlight' is unexpected:[18] Words which are signs of conventionally real things are behaving in ways not congruent with conventional reality. But as the words-as-phenomena disappear and images manifest in the mind of the listener, what manifests is something conventionally impossible, and yet it has manifested. In so doing, in revealing that conventional reality is not the whole of ultimate reality – that so-called impossible phenomena can nonetheless be manifest – this phrase ('spreading moonlight'), these hollow words (or words hollowed out by emptiness) could, like the image of the moon spilling out of the bucket and disappearing did for Lady Chiyono, awaken the listener. This is what is meant by hollow words: they are words that *afford* an experience of awakening to the twofoldedness of reality. They do not describe the limitless hollowness/emptiness/nothingness of ultimate reality, as no human language can. They point towards it, as you can point with your finger to the moon without being able to touch it. As Ueda says,

17 Atkins's *Teika* is a good introduction to the poet and his poetics. Paul S. Atkins, *Teika* (Honolulu: University of Hawai'i Press, 2017).

18 さむしろや待つ夜の秋の風ふけて月をかたしく宇治の橋姫 (*Shinkokinshū* 420)
samushiro ya matsu yo no aki no kaze fukete tsuki wo katashiku uji no hashihime
the wind, this waiting night, darkens; spreading moonlight over half her small straw mat, the lady of Uji Bridge
Uji, an utamakura place name, can also be glossed as ushi (meaning 'sad'), enhancing the possible interpretations of the poem. Laurel Rasplica Rodd, Shinkokinshū (Leiden: Brill, 2015), 180.

'[c]ontravening the nihilistic desertification within the world that results from a toxic excess of meaning, such nonmeaningful words stir up the world and, supplying it with fresh air, promote a regeneration of meaning'.[19]

Ueda's division of standard language use into signs and symbols – and poetic, mystical-spiritual, absurd language used as hollow – mirrors not only his own twofold ontology, but also Nishida's. For the singular conception of the conventional world in Ueda's (and traditional Mahāyāna) thought, Nishida posits a *basho* of (objective) being as well as a *basho* of (subjective) relative nothingness (which is not 'a' *basho*, but rather each being's subjective point of view – Dōgen's point of view from the boat in Chapter 1 is the *basho* of that boat, for example). These two *basho* roughly correspond with Ueda's conception of the sign (objective, denotative language which describes what *is*) and symbol (subjective, connotative language, whose constellation of meanings is interpreted relative to the situation of the listener). Hollow words, then, similarly correspond to Nishida's *basho* of absolute nothingness, the creative, generative, ineffable place limitlessly unconstrained by what human minds think might be possible.

2.3 Hollow sounds

So that is how Ueda outlines the triple function of words, functions which are not inherent in the words themselves – nothing is inherent in anything – as any word can function in any of the three ways. But what about hollow sounds? How is this meaningful for music?

First of all, is music a language? If a language is a system of communicating precisely from one person to another, then no, it isn't. No music can communicate with the level of precision achieved by words. But what exactly is language, other than sounds that human

19 Ueda, 'Language in a Twofold World', 777.

cultures have collectively agreed are signs which point to particular signifieds? Consider this example from the canonical Buddhist sūtra, 'The Questions of the Kinnara King Druma' (Sk. *ma-kinnara-rāja-paripṛcchā-sūtra*, Ch. 伅真陀羅所問如來三昧經),[20] in which music and sound are a central focus. Here is an excerpt, in Fabio Rambelli's translation:

> All sounds (*onjō* 音声) emerge from empty space (*kyokū* 虚空). Sound has the nature of emptiness (*kyokūshō* 虚空性): when you finish hearing it, it disappears; after it disappears, it abides in emptiness. Therefore, all dharmas, whether they are taught or not, are emptiness. . . . All dharmas are like sound . . . . Sound is originally non-abiding anywhere . . . has no origin (*muuki* 無有起) and thus is not subject to extinction. Therefore, it is pure (*shōjō* 清浄) . . . and incorruptible (*muku* 無垢), like light (*kōmyō* 光明) and the mind (*shinjō* 心性) . . . . [Sound is thus] the condition of enlightenment (*shōi* 正位).[21]

The implication of this passage for the Buddhist understanding of sonic expression and interpretation is also well summarized by Rambelli:

> In short, King Druma adopts the standard doctrine of emptiness (*śūnyatā*) and transcendent wisdom (*prajñāpāramitā*), according to which discourses are simply voiced sounds (that is, signifiers); their signifieds are not inherent in those sounds and have no substantial reality. Druma then applies this doctrine to music and emphasizes that music is exactly the same as language. Because of its intrinsic evanescence and constitutive impermanence, music is a concrete example of emptiness in our experiential field.[22]

[20] Dharmachakra Translation Committee, 'The Questions of the Kinnara King Druma', *84000: Translating the Words of the Buddha*, 2020, Rev 2025, https://84000.co/translation/toh157.

[21] Fabio Rambelli, 'The Dharma of Music: Gagaku and Buddhist Salvation in Medieval Japan', *Japanese Journal of Religious Studies* 48, no. 1: 59, https://doi.org/10.18874/jjrs.48.1.2021.45-71.

[22] Ibid.

This sūtra is highly unusual in that music – and the arts in general – were often considered detrimental distractions from the Buddhist Way, so much so that mediaeval Japanese scholars developed a discourse to counter the dismissive Chinese phrase *kyōgen kigo* (狂言綺語; wild words, fancy phrases)[23] to justify, from a Buddhist point of view, the composition of *waka* poetry (I will return to this in Chapter 3). As King Druma does when he applies the early Buddhist understanding of language as empty signifiers with no inherent substance to the concept of sounds more generally, then, in this section I will look at how Ueda's concept of hollow words – principally explained by Ueda himself through examples from poetry[24] – can be applied to sounds and music, further enhancing the Buddhist and soteriological potential of sound as first expounded in King Druma's sūtra.

Firstly we must consider how sounds can be signs and symbols in something like Ueda's sense.[25] Musical signs are perhaps easiest to define, as they are, like the denotative words of Ueda's signs, objectively real. The sound of a trumpet is the sound of a trumpet, the sound of a violin is the sound of a violin. Likewise, the sound of a minor chord, a major chord, a {0,1,5} set, an A_5 on a piano are all signs which are unmistakably themselves. Slightly more contentiously, we might add that the sound of ensembles can also function as signs – the sound of a string quartet, an orchestra, a jazz trio, a consort of recorders – all signify themselves. To acknowledge that the Bill Evans Trio and the Bad Plus, or the Orchestre symphonique de Montréal and the Berliner

[23] LaFleur discusses the concept of *kyōgen kigo* in the first and fourth chapters of his seminal book *The Karma of Words*. William LaFleur, *The Karma of Words: Buddhism and the Literary Arts in Medieval Japan* (1983. Repr. Berkeley: University of California Press, 2023).

[24] Notably, the primary poetic example Ueda chooses is a contemporary poem by a child rather than a well-known poem from the poetic or religious canon. We will return in later chapters to the importance of finding the hollowness of everyday activities, not just in 'great art'. Ueda, *Kotoba*, 20; Ueda, 'Language in a Twofold World', 772.

[25] The remainder of this section is based on Daryl Jamieson, 'Hollow Sounds: Toward a Zen-Derived Aesthetics of Contemporary Music', *The Journal of Aesthetics and Art Criticism* 76, no. 3 (2018): 331–40.

Philharmoniker sound different from each other does not take away from the fact that the first two both signify jazz trios and the latter two both signify symphony orchestras, in the same way that the word ocean has a denotative meaning (it points to a particular class of objects in the world) despite also having a constellation of connotative, symbolic meanings as well. As any given word can be interpreted as sign, symbol or hollow depending on the context (indeed, the *basho*) of the listener (and speaker), any given sound can be interpreted as a sign, a symbol or hollow.

A further example of a musical sign is what Erik F. Clarke calls musical 'invariants' in his 2005 *Ways of Listening*, which applies James and Eleanor Gibson's ecological approach to perception to the field of musicology.[26] These invariants are identifiable features of music which simply manifest themselves when they are heard. In *Ways of Listening*, Clarke analyses several pieces from multiple genres, but to borrow one example, in his discussion of the first eight bars of Beethoven's String Quartet Op. 132, he identifies 'minor mode', 'motet-like homophony', 'registral expansion' and 'uncadenced ending' as invariants[27] – all signs that are objectively themselves.

It should be noted that I am not suggesting that an 'uncadenced ending' is an objectively real thing that any person could identify without prior knowledge of Western classical music theory and history. But that objection is surely moot as it applies to all languages as well. A unilingual English speaker might just be able to comprehend the word *Mond* in German or *måne* in Norwegian as 'moon', but they'd have no hope with the Icelandic *tungl* or Japanese *tsuki*. And a bilingual English-French speaker could possibly lose the sense of *Mond* as moon given its closeness to the French *monde* (world). That is just to say that linguistic signs are no less reliant on being learned culturally than musical ones – to identify an 'uncadenced ending' as a musical sign

[26] Erik F. Clarke, *Ways of Listening* (Oxford: Oxford University Press, 2005), 35*ff*.

[27] Ibid., 164*ff*.

relies on being familiar with (having learned) the grammar of Western classical music, as the surety that *Mond* signifies moon requires having learned German. The fact that 'their signifieds are not inherent in those sounds and have no substantial reality'[28] doesn't make either one not a sign in Ueda's sense.

Continuing on, a sonic symbol is a sound which transcends its denotative meaning and suggests connotations to the listener. These are subjective and personal, but can also be shared at the level of a subculture (genre) or culture. In Japan, the tiny stone or metal wind chimes called *fūrin* (風鈴) are ubiquitous in the densely humid summer heat, because the high-pitched sound (particularly the heterophony of several, or several tens, of *fūrin* sounding simultaneously) suggests coolness and many Japanese people will insist that the sound manifests as a 'real' sensation of coolness in the listener. Food scientists have found ways of emphasizing different culinary textures (such as crispiness, salinity, creaminess) or dining experiences with music or sound,[29] and innovative chefs like Heston Blumenthal have used their findings to create dishes with musical or sonic elements which are designed to enhance the flavours and textures of food.[30] Musical sounds also have symbolic meanings: If a trumpet's sound is the sign of a trumpet, the association of a trumpet with stridency or militarism is a symbolic one. The minor mode, homophony, registral expansion and uncadenced ending invariants identified by Clarke in the opening bars of Beethoven's Op. 132 are objective signs, but the sense of a 'tragic' minor, 'spiritual[,] calm and patient' homophony, 'seeking/exploring'

[28] Rambelli, 'The Dharma of Music', 59.

[29] Charles Spence, 'Sound: The Forgotten Flavor Sense', in *Multisensory Flavor Perception: From Fundamental Neuroscience Through to the Marketplace*, ed. Betina Piqueras-Fiszman and Charles Spence (Amsterdam: Woodhead, 2016), 81–105.

[30] This example surely invites its opposite, a musical or sound art piece which uses food to enhance the sonic experience. Though Schafer has pointed out that, seen from a certain angle, the Catholic mass has for more than a millennium already been a five-sensory integrated music-theatre (food, drink, incense, architecture) work. R. Murray Schafer, *The Thinking Ear: Complete Writings on Music Education* (Toronto: Arcana Editions, 1985), 286.

expansion and 'unended quest' in the uncadenced ending are all symbolic interpretations. Furthermore, these four invariants can be read together (as words and phrases are read together to produce more complex and rich statements in sentences and paragraphs) to suggest a 'questing and tragic spirituality'.[31]

An understanding of these musical symbols – the grouping of relatively objective (within the semiotic system of the genre in question) invariants into complexes of sound with symbolic meaning(s) – can be shared, and often are. As per McLuhan above, we are usually not even aware of how constructed our symbolic understandings are. How many songs do we hear a few seconds of, process the invariant signs symbolically, categorize it as something we don't like, and turn it off – without actually ever listening to the song itself? Even the classification – the division – of music into genres, subgenres and further sub-subgenres and so on is a symptom of symbolic listening that we absorb as if it were signal. We mistake the subjective for objective and tradition for authority, taking the interpretations of critics, performers, composers, songwriters as if their (objectively subjective) interpretations – their symbolic semiotics of music – were more objective than the impressions of our own ears.

Finally, what are hollow sounds? As with words, any sound affords being perceived as hollow. To become hollow, a sound must appear in a context which jolts the listener into a sense that the bounds of reality itself have expanded thanks to this sound, and/or the sound is so outside the bounds of conventional reality that it functions as a glimpse of the hollow expanse – 'a crack' through which 'the light gets in' in the words of Zen Buddhist-Jewish poet, novelist and songwriter Leonard Cohen.[32]

[31] Clarke, *Ways of Listening*, 175–6.

[32] The chorus of the song 'Anthem' reads:
Ring the bells that still can ring
Forget your perfect offering
There is a crack in everything
That's how the light gets in

The conventional world is Nishida's *basho* of relative emptiness (i.e. the subjective world). What sounds can function as unexpected or hollow within a given *basho* is therefore subjective. The examples I give – here and throughout the book – are therefore inevitably subjective. Some examples of sounds which afford being heard as hollow:

- a sound (timbre) which has never been heard before, thus literally expanding the possibilities of musical sounds in reality (this can be achieved electronically, or by combining instruments in new ways, but what counts as 'new' is too subjective to provide examples here – an encounter with gamelan was perhaps hollow for Claude Debussy in 1889,[33] but would have been commonplace for a resident of Java);
- a harmonic (simultaneously sounding) combination of tones which have never been heard before;
- a melodic (consecutively sounding) combination of tones which have never been heard before;
- a musical form which presents strong and memorable musical material that, over the course of the piece, gradually disintegrates, dissolves into emptiness (esoteric Buddhist practitioner Jonathan Harvey (1939–2012) composed in this way – 'The joy of composing lies in the dissolving of strong ideas; one must have both form and emptiness.'[34]);
- within a piece which otherwise conforms to the conventions of a particular musical genre, something which subverts or

Leonard Cohen, The Future (Columbia Records, 1992)

If we gloss Cohen's 'crack' as an opening or gate into Ueda's 'hollow', then they are in agreement that all words/all phenomena have the potential to awaken – enlighten – anyone. Not incidentally, the composer Cassandra Miller – to whom we will return at the end of this chapter – has written a piece called Perfect Offering (2021) referring to this same Cohen verse.

[33] see Kiyoshi Tamagawa, *Echoes from the East: The Javanese Gamelan and Its Influence on the Music of Claude Debussy* (London: Bloomsbury, 2019).

[34] Jonathan Harvey, 'Spiritual Music: "Positive" Negative Theology?', in *Contemporary Music and Spirituality*, ed. Robert Sholl and Sander Van Maas (London: Routledge, 2017), 322.

undermines those conventions (e.g. introducing a different set of genre conventions or introducing sounds/harmonies/melodies which have never been heard before in that generic context – Edgar Varèse' (1883–1965) use of two sirens in his percussion piece *Ionisation* (1929/1931) is an example of this);

- in a piece with a long run-time, a relatively predictable sonic world is set up (i.e. new generic conventions are created) and thence something that subverts or undermines those newly established conventions is introduced (Morton Feldman's 1–6 hour long late-period pieces are prime examples of this kind of hollowness);
- repetition of musical material so many times or for such a length of time that – like a mantra in meditation – the sonic material which begins as symbolic gradually becomes hollow through overfamiliarity; they have become strange (classical minimalism – La Monte Young (b. 1935), Terry Riley (b. 1935), very early Philip Glass (b. 1937) and Steve Reich (b. 1936), Julius Eastman (1940–90), etc. – are examples of this);
- a situation in which sounds which are familiar and everyday are heard in a new way or in a new aspect as a result of being 'framed' by musical sounds and/or the event of a concert and/or concentrated listening experience (e.g. John Cage's *4'33"*, many Wandelweiser pieces, soundwalks, among others).

There could be endless other examples.

2.4 *Yūgen*

It is important to underline the significance of the unknown in a sound affording being heard as hollow. Equally so, it is important not to make obscurity a prime virtue; the ambiguous interplay of sign/symbol/hollow – or clarity/obscurity – is necessary for a true gasping of the potential hollowness. As Jonathan Harvey said, regarding his conceptual approach to composition via the dissolving of striking musical ideas, 'there must be something worth dissolving. If everything is dissolving, nothing is dissolving'.[35] For example, one reason why some people find listening to postwar European avant-garde music so unrewarding is that, for them, unable to grasp the structure or meaning of anything in the work, all they hear is an unending succession of signs (a viola makes a sound, then a marimba makes a sound, then a harp makes some sounds and on and on, with no sense of how to connect these signal sounds into a symbolic structure or pattern). By aiming to separate themselves from the history of music, the possibilities of intertextuality and generic expectations, by aiming for a pure succession of 'hollowness', those composers held a radical Idealist conception of music's place as completely separate from society and history, and – from the perspective of a great many listeners – in the end closed off the hollow world rather than opened it up. This is not to say that the post-war avant-garde music was ill-judged; learning the conventions of each composer or group of similar composers, being able to hear symbols in the signs, can of course be done through repeated exposure and is often very much worth the effort. The potential for a glimpse of the hollow world is certainly there in much of this repertoire, and much of it is sublime. Listeners, however, can be forgiven for not being able to hear the potential for hollow sounds on their first exposure.[36] On the other hand, music which is too conventional also strongly resists any affordance of being heard as hollow, simply because of its familiarity.

One of the key concepts of mediaeval Japanese aesthetics is *yūgen*, a multivalent concept which nonetheless tends to have something to do with the beauty of darkness, silence, profound mystery and/or obscurity. Fujiwara no Shunzei held that *yūgen* was the most profound poetic state, which could be found in a state of calm and contemplative meditation (*shikan* 止観). In his only major poetic treatise he writes that 'things that otherwise are incapable of being

[35] Ibid., 317.

[36] Jamieson, 'Hollow Sounds', 338–9.

expressed in words will be understood precisely when they are likened to calm-and-contemplation [*shikan*]'.[37] His use of Tendai Buddhist terminology such as *shikan* in this treatise shows that for Shunzei, *yūgen* is an aesthetic which arises only in a state of non-duality between subject and object.

Shunzei's younger contemporary, poet and theorist Kamo no Chōmei says of *yūgen* in his *Mumyōshō* (The Nameless Treatise, 1211–16) that:

> if you look at the autumn hills through a rift in the mist, you catch only a glimpse, and, unsatisfied, try to figure out freely in your imagination how pleasing it might be to see the whole of those scarlet leaves—this is almost better than seeing it clearly. Completely to display your feelings in words by saying of the moon that it is bright, or by praising the cherry blossoms, declaring that they are pretty, how can that be difficult? Where would there be the virtue of the *uta* [歌 En. lyric], which is to be more than an ordinary statement? Only when many ideas [*kotowari* 理] are compressed in one word, when without expressing it you exhaust your mind in all its depth and you imagine phenomena [*koto* 事] of an unseen world, when commonplace things are used to display beauty and in a style of naiveté an idea [*kotowari* 理] is developed to the limit, only then, when both thought and words are inadequate, should you write them down in a short poem which will have the capacity to move heaven and earth and the power to appease both gods and demons.[38]

For Chōmei, then, *yūgen* is impossible to capture in words, that what is directly sayable is not poetry, that the struggle to conceptualize that which is obscured (which, as with the above example of extremely difficult music, is not completely obscured – the initial glimpse through a rift in the mist is necessary for the process to begin, for the viewer/

[37] LaFleur, *Karma of Words*, 90. See Section 3.1 for a more detailed discussion of this treatise.

[38] Kamo no Chōmei, 'Mumyōshō', in *Kabunshū Nōgakuronshū*, ed. Hisamatsu Sen'ichi (1961; repr. Tokyo: Iwanami Shoten, 1974), 35–98; translation Hilda Katō, 'The Mumyosho', *Monumenta Nipponica* 23, no. 3–4 (1968): 409; translation modified

listener not to be lost in the fog), is more pleasurable than a clear, beautiful vision. 'Many ideas . . . compressed in one word' is akin to Ueda's symbolic understanding of linguistic meaning, whereas *yūgen* having 'the capacity to move heaven and earth and the power to appease both gods and demons' can be read as pointing to the moment when that rift in meaning opens and a glimpse of the hollow expanse is, at least momentarily, perceivable.

Yūgen is perhaps best known from Zeami's use of the term in his treatises on nō. Zeami's *yūgen* can be a quality possessed by an actor, a performance, or a nō text itself: in all cases, as for Shunzei and Chōmei, it is a quality of the ineffable and hence indescribable. However, Zeami has practical advice for actors on how to cultivate yūgen (his treatises are, after all, secret documents written only for the eyes of his acting troupe and family members on how to succeed in the business of *sarugaku* nō). In the undated treatise 'An Effective Vision of Learning the Vocation of Fine Play in Performance' (*Yūgaku shudōfū ken* 遊楽習道風見), 1420's 'A Course to Attain the Flower' (*Shikadō* 至花道), and 'Figure Drawings of the Two Arts and the Three Modes' (*Nikyoku santai ningyōzu* 二曲三体人形図), Zeami focusses his definition of *yūgen* on the figure of the male youth whose appearance, natural charm and unbroken voice naturally has *yūgen*.[39] By carefully cultivating the arts of singing and dancing at this stage (but not acting or wearing a mask, which would obscure the youth's charm), some aspect of this naive and ephemeral *yūgen* can be solidified into a more mature form of mastery later in life. As Tom Hare has put it '[s]ome have gone so far as to say that the boyish "prettiness" (i.e. yūgen) Zeami speaks of . . . is the basis for all yūgen in the noh.'[40]

The word *yūgen* is typically written with the characters 幽玄, where the first character connotes depth, darkness, seclusion, transience and even the spirit world; and the second character blackness, distance

39 Matsuoka, *Embodied Performance*, 207*ff*.

40 Thomas Blenman Hare, *Zeami's Style: The Noh Plays of Zeami Motokiyo* (Stanford: Stanford University Press, 1986), 19.

and depth. However, Zenchiku – whose lifetime comes near the end of *yūgen*'s heyday as the principal aesthetic paradigm in Japan[41] – will at times write the word in phonetic *kana* rather than using Chinese characters. Mark Nearman reads this orthographic choice as implying a double meaning, both the above 幽玄 (darkness, profundity, obscurity) but also 幽現. This compound has the same first character but a different second one, meaning reality, especially a return to reality (e.g. after dreaming), being alive (as opposed to dead) or to manifest. In other words, the secondary meaning is, in Nearman's words 'the hidden made manifest',[42] or to recast it in the terms we have been using so far throughout this book, the hollow made tangible.

Zenchiku's *yūgen*, in contrast with Zeami's, is more about the actor's interior state rather than the beauty of the performance (though the latter flows from the former). As is typical of Zenchiku's focus on the spiritual and soteriological aspects of art, he claims that the borders of *yūgen* are transcended as and when any person exhibits buddha nature (*busshō* 仏性), and conversely, anyone who does not exhibit buddha nature cannot achieve the highest level of performance (i.e. *yūgen*).[43] As all beings – even non-sentient beings such as trees, grasses, waters and the land itself – have buddha nature,[44] it is the expression or the realization of one's buddha nature that matters with regard to *yūgen*. In his late treatise 'Notes on the Essentials of Attaining the Way' (*Shidōyōshō* 至道要抄), Zenchiku elaborates the most complex conception of *yūgen*. Without going into every detail, Zenchiku emphasizes that *yūgen* is deeply tied to Buddhism and the *kami*, and that it is not only deep, distant and

41 Matsuoka Shinpei, '*Yūgen ga enjakusuru toki: Ikkyū Zenchiku no sekai*', *Bungaku* 7, no. 2 (1996): 40.

42 Mark J. Nearman, 'The Visions of a Creative Artist: Zenchiku's *Rokurin Ichiro* Treatises Part 2', *Monumenta Nipponica* 50, no. 3 (1995): 286.

43 *Zeami Zenchiku*, 376.

44 This is according to the doctrine of the Buddhahood of Non-Sentients (*sōmokukokudo shikkaijōbutsu* 草木国土悉皆成仏) which was held by most mediaeval Buddhist sects in Japan. See Fabio Rambelli, *Vegetal Buddhas* (Kyoto: Italian School of East Asian Studies, 2001).

profound, but also strong and gentle. Most importantly, *yūgen* is not superficial: 'When only the surface is beautiful and intriguing, it is no different from being a ghost [*bakemono* 化物]. Therefore, one cannot call "*yūgen*" something that does not reflect knowledge of True Nature [*shōri* 性理].'[45] In other words, without a full understanding of Buddhist ontology, an artist or a work cannot express *yūgen*, and any attempt to do so will result in a superficial imitation of the real thing. It will be obscurity without profundity. Conversely, a work possessing *yūgen* is necessarily a true manifestation of buddha nature and something like the two truths (Ueda's twofold nature of reality).

Yūgen, then, is a dialectic between light and dark, youthful beauty (whether that be fleeting flowers or boyish charm) and its inevitably quick decay. It is an expression of the Kegon Buddhist concept of the unimpeded interpenetration of principle (emptiness, *ri* 理, a character which is read in Chōmei's text as *kotowari* and expresses the insubstantial concept of 'ideas') and phenomena (things, *ji*, *koto* 事).[46] It is not a mere preference for an aesthetic of dark over light,[47] but 'a dynamic process by which one is propelled into obscurity, potentially entering a realm that transcends light and darkness.'[48] As Izutsu Toyoko (井筒豊子) writes, *yūgen* – regardless of the particulars of the word's use in different time periods and by different artists and theorists – is a product of the contemplative perception of the artist, born of meditative observation

[45] Arthur H. Thornhill III, *Six Circles, One Dewdrop: The Religio-Aesthetic World of Komparu Zenchiku* (Princeton: Princeton University Press, 1997), 50.

[46] Arthur H. Thornhill III, '*Yūgen* after Zeami', in *Nō and Kyōgen in the Contemporary World*, ed. James R. Brandon (Honolulu: University of Hawai'i Press, 1997), 40.

[47] As, arguably, it degenerated into among aesthetes of the Modern era, for example the narrator of Tanizaki Jun'ichirō's famous 1933 essay 'In Praise of Shadows' (*In'ei Raisan* 陰翳礼讃). The unorthodox but persuasive idea that this text is a satirical essay mocking the ideas presented rather than advocating for them has been argued by Ryan Morrison. Ryan Morrison, 'Study Guide: Tanizaki Jun'ichirō "In Praise of Shadows" (In'ei raisan; 1933)', 『*Behold My Swarthy Face*。』 (2014)

[48] Ibid., 58–9.

of phenomena.[49] *Yūgen* manifests in a place where the perceiving subject and the perceived object meet and dissolve into each other.

As a listener, then, *yūgen* can be that obscure, distant, difficult-to-comprehend sound that compels you to dive into, exploring its depth to a point where you are unsure if you will resurface, or if you even need to resurface. But when you resurface – penetrating beyond the sound to the *principle* (*ri*) of sound, being penetrated by the *principle* of sound – you *may* (nothing is guaranteed) experience something of Ueda's hollow expanse.

2.5 Ten ox pictures

How do we get to the stage of understanding that allows us to listen to the hollowness of sounds, to be able to play in the hollow expanse? There are of course many paths – as many paths as there are people, one supposes. Zeami and Zenchiku both offer models of training for nō, guides for bringing up the next generation of actors. Zeami's *Fūshikaden*, arguably his most practical training manual, details the training necessary for a nō actor starting at the age of seven and continuing to beyond the age of fifty. Zenchiku's (admittedly somewhat less practical) treatise *Six Circles, One Dewdrop* is a collection of six circles containing images that can be interpreted as a guide to training.[50]

49 Izutsu Toyoko, 'Preliminary Essays', in *The Theory of Beauty in the Classical Aesthetics of Japan*, by Izutsu Toshihiko and Izutsu Toyo (The Hague: Martinus Nijhoff Publishers, 1981), 27.

'Contemplative experience, first of all, implies a negative attitude toward, or rather a total negation of, the cognitive focus unilaterally directed from the subject to the object, which further implies that the subject has to relinquish the logico-linguistic thinking whose most conspicuous characteristic consists in being causal, successive and linear'. Ibid., 32.

50 It also can be read as the structure of a nō play, an outline of the arising, flourishing and eventual extinguishing of a vocal sound in nō (and all things in this world of impermanence), among others.

The form of *Rokurin ichiro*'s six circles with images – revealed to Zenchiku in a vision by the god of poetry Sumiyoshi Daimyōjin (住吉大明神)[51] – was almost certainly influenced by an older set of images (each linked to short poems) used to explicate the Zen concept of 'forgetting the self'. These are the Ten Ox Pictures (*Jūgyūzu* 十牛図) by Línjì zōng Chán (Rinzai-school Zen 臨済宗禅) master Kuòān Shīyuǎn's (廓庵師遠 Jp. Kakuan Shion, *fl.* twelfth century). These pictures have been used as guides in zen meditation practice for a millennium, inspiring not just meditators but also acting as triggers for philosophical reflection and musical composition. As we shall see in the next section, Cassandra Miller (b. 1976) has found them useful,[52] and John Cage – an artist and writer as well as a composer – has made his own series of ten drawings and poems on the theme: *Zen OX—Herding Pictures* III (1988).[53]

The Ox in these drawings is a symbol that has meant different things to different commentators over the centuries. One common interpretation is that the ox symbolizes the mind; in this reading, the ten pictures depict the process of taming the mind through the practice of meditation. For Ueda, however, the Ox is the 'original self', that aspect of the self which is lacking in the practitioner in Picture 1 ('Seeking the Ox').[54] In Pictures 2–4 ('Seeing the Traces', 'Seeing the Ox' and 'Catching the Ox'), the practitioner is gradually getting closer to their original self, while in Pictures 5–6 ('Domesticating the Ox' and 'Riding the Ox Home') they have begun to understand it. In Picture 7 ('Forgetting

[51] Susan Blakeley Klein, *Dancing the Dharma: Religious and Political Allegory in Japanese Noh Theater* (Cambridge, MA: Harvard University Press, 2021), 87*ff*.

[52] Luke Nickel, 'Scores in Bloom: Some Recent Orally Transmitted Experimental Music', *TEMPO* 74, no. 293 (2020): 55.

[53] Sugimoto Hiroshi, *Honkadori Azumakudari* (Yokohama: Kuma Publishing, 2023), 178–85.

[54] Ueda Shizuteru, *Jūgyūzu*, ed. Ueda Shizuteru and Yanagida Seizan (Tokyo: Chikuma Shobō, 1992), 33. An English exegesis is in Gereon Kopf, '"The Self That Is Not a Self": Ueda and Kuoan's Ten Ox Pictures', in *Tetsugaku Companion to Ueda Shizuteru: Language, Experience, and Zen*, ed. Ralf Müller, Raquel Bouso, and Adam Loughnane (Cham: Springer, 2022), 317–36.

the Ox While the Person Remains'), the Ox is 'forgotten' per Kuòān's title, but Ueda interprets this picture as showing the unification of the original self and the practitioner, not as a return to the original self. If for Zeami the essence of *yūgen* in a mature performer is the unification of the naivety of early youth with the experience of age, then we might also say that this seventh picture represents a performer on the cusp of achieving *yūgen*.

Pictures 1–7 all take place in the *basho* of relative nothingness, that is, the space of meaning or the conventional world (the pictures are all very much literal renderings of the titles in these seven pictures). Once the practitioner has unified with their original self as the 'true self', then they may be able to awaken to the hollow expanse. This is represented in Pictures 8–10. Picture 8 ('Forgetting the Ox and the Person') is the most striking in that it is completely blank (the self as empty). Picture 9 ('Return to the Origin') has no sentient figures, but shows a tree blossoming (the self as radically unified with – interpenetrated by – all phenomena). Picture 10 ('Entering the Marketplace with Full Hands') shows the self as an older man in the marketplace talking to a younger man: This represents the dependent, relational nature of the self, the dialectic of speaker and listener (and also sharing one's experience with those who are inexperienced). It's an image of returning to the conventional world, what in nō theory – in a modified phrase originally derived from Zen – is called *kōko kyakurai* (向去却来).

While the first seven pictures are linear (like conventional time), the final three are cyclical, constantly in rotation (mystical, non-teleological, non-Modern time). Rein Raud describes achieving enlightenment (i.e. awakening) as like riding a bicycle: Once you have ridden a bike once, you never forget how to do it, and yet, you wouldn't want to be on your bike all the time. Likewise, one cannot live in the hollow expanse permanently – there is no meaning there. You go there to cleanse your mind (Picture 8), and then you come back, to be with and among the phenomenal (Picture 9), to communicate with – to teach and learn from – other beings (Picture 10). This cycle of delusion in the conventional world—awakening (hollow expanse)—return to the conventional world is commonly recounted in Zen teaching with the following saying (this version is John Cage's retelling from the piece *Indeterminacy*):

> Before studying Zen, men are men and mountains are mountains. While studying Zen, things become confused. After studying Zen, men are men and mountains are mountains. After telling this, Dr. Suzuki [Suzuki Daisetsu 鈴木大拙] was asked, 'What is the difference between before and after?' He said, 'No difference, only the feet are a little bit off the ground.'[55]

Ueda emphasizes the dangers of spending too much time in the hollow expanse – it's not mentally healthy to be so divorced from conventional reality (the world of the hollow is not benignly mystical but fictional – in the sense of both creative invention but also lies, fraud and hypernormalization). But equally, it's not advisable to avoid this mystical world either. What Ueda suggests is living in the conventional world while playing in the hollow expanse – the latter chiefly through art (poetry is his usual example, but surely any truly creative practice would offer access to glimpses of the hollow expanse).

2.5.1 Cassandra Miller's *Duet*

This chapter has touched on various aspects of Japanese and East Asian philosophy more than sound *per se*, but I want to finish this exploration of ontology by applying these concepts directly to an interpretation of a piece of music: *Duet for Cello and Orchestra* (2015) by the previously-mentioned Cassandra Miller.

Like much of Miller's work, *Duet*'s surface-level musical material is derived from meticulously detailed transcriptions of a found sonic object. In this case, that found object is Sardinian folk singer Maria

[55] Cage, *Silence*, 88. A more scholarly translation of the original parable – which is from the *Addition to the Records of the Transmission of the Lamp* – can be found in Kopf, '"The Self"', 326.

Carta's (1934–94) performance of 'Trallallera', in a live performance found on the album *Nottes de incantu 1974–1992* (2005). Carta's performance consists of two verses of four phrases each. All four phrases finish with a long-held note, with a final scoop upwards (first and fourth phrases) or downwards (second and third phrases). In this performance, Carta is accompanied solely by a guitar.

Miller's piece was written for (and commissioned by) the American cellist Charles Curtis, a performer known for his work with a variety of experimental composers. Curtis's performance style is relatively introspective, contemplative – especially compared to what Miller herself, in the piece's programme notes, calls the 'extraverted, romantic character of an orchestra'[56] – and as such poses an interesting question for the composer of a piece for soloist with orchestra. How will the 'self' that is the character of the individual 'cellist' be relationally defined *vis-à-vis* the mass of instruments behind them?

Rather unusually for a concerto-like work – though, notably, the piece is not called a concerto – for the first two-thirds of the piece, the soloist is accompanying the orchestra. Mimicking the uncomplicated harmonies of 'Trallallera''s guitar accompaniment over the first twenty minutes of the piece, the cello plays only two pitches (double-stopped unison G_2 and D_3), at an unchanging, relaxed pace and moderate volume (*mezzo-piano*). This texture, which I call the 'ground', is accompanied only by extremely quiet tubular bell (D_4 and F_4) and bass drum rolls. The transcription of Carta's vocal melody appears in the orchestra.

During the first two-thirds of the piece the orchestra plays twelve phrases (three 'verses') while the solo cello 'ground' continues unchangingly. The first four phrases – transcribed from a single, four-phrase verse of Carta's 'Trallallera' in G minor – are played by trumpets

[56] Cassandra Miller, 'Duet for Cello and Orchestra', on *Faber Music* website, https://www.fabermusic.com/music/e3017d0d-f43e-4015-9b67-892fa1b210cf.

instructed to play 'as a mariachi band'. This four-phrase pattern, each phrase ending with a long note and flourishes matching Carta's performance (upward, downward, downward, upward), is largely maintained throughout the next two 'verses' as well. This first section – the 'ground' accompanying brass instruments playing the melody – lasts for four minutes, giving listeners time to become accustomed to the virtual world Miller is creating.

Having very firmly established this virtual sonic world, Miller begins to expand it by adding more instruments. In the second 'verse' the bassoons and most of the strings enter. These instruments echo the 'ground' and the brass from the first 'verse' (both of which also continue to play), but they are slightly behind the beat and in a different key: C minor. Despite the echoes being displaced in time, the final flourishes of each phrase are simultaneous across all the instruments who play them.

In the third 'verse', each phrase tends to be longer and more texturally complex than the previous one. In its first phrase, all of the previous instruments continue in the keys they were playing previously, but with the addition of flutes (echoing the brass) and clarinets (echoing the bassoons) in B♭ minor and rhythmically displaced. Phrase two sees cor anglais and French horns added at different rhythmic displacements and in E♭ minor, and violins I & II also in E♭ minor echoing the trumpets. In phrase three, the horns take up the melody in A♭ minor, with the trombones shifting into that key as well. This is the most complex and polytonal texture in the piece, with the melody being played heterophonically in seven different keys simultaneously. In the fourth phrase almost all the instruments gradually shift from the melody to the 'ground' except the piccolo, which blasts out the melody over the pulsing polytonal ground, though ending this final phrase without the expected upward flourish.

In the following five or so minutes, the solo cello, tubular bells and piccolo drop out, but all other players continue playing the 'ground' without change, in seven different keys, and in seven different rhythmic positions. The same four measures repeat again and again, and though this is perhaps a kind of minimalism, the context, the polytonal harmonic richness and the absolute lack of either harmonic or rhythmic progression mean that it does not sound, from this listener's perspective, in the way minimalism sounds. Despite about ten pages of the score being written out with identical four-bar phrases, the experience of listening to this feels complex and messy, like something magical and alive rather than a mathematically precise rhythmic repetition. As this section comes to an end, parts gradually begin to fade out over two minutes, one at a time until finally only two orchestral cellos are left, playing the 'ground' in C minor.

In the final four minutes the two orchestral cellists continue their 'ground' while the solo cello returns with a solo passage (a kind of cadenza) entirely on natural harmonics. The soloist plays in an improvisatory manner, free from the rock-steady pulse of the orchestral celli. There are four phrases, with only short rests between each phrase.

Why is this piece meaningful? How might this succession of sounds organized in time be interpreted as saying something to or about us and our world?

The first twenty-minute section presents a portrait of the conventional world. There might be a Self which is, unusually for a concerto, represented by the orchestra, whose musical material is derived from the inflections and performance practice of an individual human in conventional reality: Maria Carta. Then there is the 'ground' (i.e. the solo cello and percussion) which is, perhaps, that which is lacking – what is needed to complete – the Self: the Original Self.

Though the musical narrative does not mirror the Ten Ox Pictures precisely, the general progression is similar. At first, the picture is relatively simple: a reflection of a defined self in search of a seemingly independent Original Self. But gradually, both the self and the 'ground' become increasingly complex, encompassing alternative ways of being in and perceiving reality. If the orchestra is understood as a questing Self – searching out and practicing these alternate ways, both enriching and confusing them, bringing them to a point where they question 'conventional reality' – things are not as simple as they seemed at first.

As in Picture 7 in the Ten Ox Pictures (in which the Original Self and Self merge but only within conventional reality), until the final phrase of the opening section, however, there is always a point of convergence: the heterophonic alternative ways of being come together for the long-held notes and flourish at the end of each phrase (a holding onto the Self as Self). Simultaneously, the Self is becoming aware that their understanding of reality, the so-called outside world (i.e. the 'ground') is also becoming more complex.

In the second section, the Self has been forgotten, and the seven alternative ways of perceiving and being in the world that the Self had splintered into before dissolving now are in and of reality itself. The selves and the worlds are no longer different things; they are one thing and no thing at all (Picture 8: 'Forgetting the Ox and the Person'). The protagonist is at play in the hollow expanse, if only for a moment (only four bars) that seems to last so much longer (more than five minutes). This is a climax, a place of spiritual ecstasy where the experience of the listener – as a being – can mirror that of the musical narrative, hearing the minute differences as the musicians on stage repeat (though exact repetition is impossible) the same two chords over and over from seven different perspectives (all nature is manifesting as One, as in Picture 9), affording a sense of timelessness that could be an instant suspended forever, or forever metonymically compressed into a magical instant. These notes – unchanged, but never the same – repeat for five minutes, followed by two more minutes of afterglow as it fades away.

The final section returns us to the opening gesture. We perceive it as being the same – two regularly alternating notes, at the interval of a perfect fifth – but everything about it is actually different. The protagonist of the narrative has been changed by the experiences of spiritual and mental disintegration and ecstasy in the previous sections. They are returned to the world, and yet encountering two other cellists still at the beginning of their journey (Picture 10). And by moving away, in the solo cello part, from precise rhythms and pulsation, allowing more of a note of freedom, Miller also introduces a greater experimental affect – that is, an in-the-moment-ness – into these final minutes of the piece.

In summary, at the beginning, the 'ground' is the 'ground' and the Self is the Self (a sonic image of the conventional world); in the middle section, the self has dissolved into the 'ground' (the hollow expanse); at the end, the 'ground' has become the self, and the self has become the 'ground' – interconnected, interpenetrating, but also, in their way, distinguishable. This is a return to the conventional world with the knowledge of the hollow expanse – a knowledge of reality's twofoldedness – an experience which changes one's perception of everything, allowing one to live more in the moment, to be in this world rather than the fiction that is conventional reality. Read this way, *Duet* affords being heard as a narrative of an individual discovering the hollowness of reality and thence returning to the phenomenal world (*kōko kyakurai*). But also, because of its clever use and subversion of multiple generic expectations (of concerti, of tonality, of repetition, of minimalism) it not only affords being heard as a depiction of that journey, it can also be heard as hollow in itself, and thus affords guiding listeners along a similar journey towards the limitless possibilities for play in the hollow expanse.

3

Culture and nature

3.1 Poetic palimpsests

Exiting the hollow emptiness of *śūnyatā*, and Nishida's standpoint of pure experience in the *basho* of absolute nothingness, Ueda claims our every experience in the conventional world is conditioned by language. But what is language, and whose language is it? Though Japanese philosophy has in general focussed on these questions via the medium of poetry, I contend that 'poetry' can be interpreted as a metonym for culture in general.

Fujiwara Shunzei, in his 1197 treatise *Poetic styles from the past* (Korai fūteishō 古来風体抄), advanced the idea that poetry shapes the world. Though there may be objective things in 'reality', without poetry (i.e. culture) we would not be cognisant of them. 'Whether we seek out the cherry blossoms of spring, or view the tinted leaves of autumn, if we did not have what is called poetry, no one would know the color or the scent.'[1] Though we might be able to have a pure experience of the beautiful autumn colours or delicate scents of spring, without a poet at one point in the past having named those things, given expression to those experiences in language that was – at least at the time of its initial conception – hollow, we would not have given our attention to these phenomena. Like the uncountable phenomena that pass us by every

[1] Haruo Shirane, ed., *Traditional Japanese Literature: An Anthology, Beginnings to 1600* (New York: Columbia University Press, 2007), 588. '春のはなをたずね 、秋の紅葉をみても、歌といふものなからましかば、色をも香をもしる人もなく' Fujiwara no Shunzei, 'Korai fūteishō', in *Zokugun Shoruijū*, vol. 16-b, 3rd edn, ed. Hanawa Hokiichi, rev. Ōta Tōshirō (Tokyo: Zokugun Shoruijū Kanzeikai, 1989), 678. Modified.

day, these things that we valorize for their beauty would be invisible, insensible to us had poets (culture) not taught us they were worth noticing.

Shunzei's poetics were rooted in Tendai Buddhist thought, and its founder Zhìyǐ's (智顗; Jp. Chigi; 538–597) major treatise, *Larger Treatise on Cessation and Contemplation* (Móhē Zhǐguān 摩訶止観; Jp. Makashikan) is an important point of reference in the *Poetic styles from the past*. Shunzei's model of how the poetic canon – in other words, your cultural context – influences how you interpret objective phenomena is borrowed from Zhìyǐ. In turning your attention to an objective phenomenon in the world, you focus on it and in doing so 'cease' (*shi* 止) the regular flow of conventional time, allowing you to 'contemplate' (*kan* 観) the phenomenon. The first step here (the 'cessation') might be likened to Nishida's pre-linguistic pure experience, and the latter step (the 'contemplation') likened to interpretation (or relative nothingness). When we notice the drifting scent of fragrant blossoms in the air, we attend to this sensation ('cessation'), and we recall the poems, stories, songs and our own subjective memories relating to this phenomenon ('contemplation').[2]

Shunzei's wider Tendai Buddhist argument is that if you stopped the process at mere attention ('cessation'), your experience would reveal something to you about the conventional world. But in order to understand the ultimate truth that conventional phenomena are grounded in the Uedan hollow expanse, you need the hollow words of poetry – you need to interpret ('contemplate') the phenomenon that you have been attending to. This is because the interpretation of any 'real' phenomena through culture and memory will cause dissonance – the cherry blossoms of the poems, the cherry blossoms of paintings, the cherry blossoms of your memory will not be identical to the ones in front of your eyes. The autumn leaves are not as brilliantly red as the

2 Michael F. Marra, *Essays on Japan: Between Aesthetics and Literature* (Leiden: Brill, 2010), 65.

poems say, or as they are in the (heavily processed and edited) pictures from last year on your phone.

One aspect of what Shunzei is saying is simply that – in general – we do not perceive that which we are not aware of. Shunzei calls this naming of phenomena 'poetry', and it accounts to a certain extent for the differences in patterns of thought and behaviour between speakers of different languages. Interpreted in this way, Shunzei's idea is not particularly radical, or unique to Japanese aesthetic thought. Oscar Wilde, for instance, notes in his essay 'The Decay of Lying – An Observation' that:

> At present, people see fogs, not because there are fogs, but because poets and painters have taught them the mysterious loveliness of such effects. There may have been fogs for centuries in London. I dare say there were. But no one saw them, and so we do not know anything about them. They did not exist till Art had invented them.[3]

A similar phenomenon has been often noted in the Romantic European reconceptualization of mountains as beautiful.[4] Audre Lorde also echoes this sense, saying that 'Poetry is the way we help give name to the nameless so it can be thought. The farthest horizons of our hopes and fears are cobbled by our poems, carved from the rock experiences of our daily lives.'[5]

The most radical interpretation of Shunzei's concept here is that what you sense with your eyes when you focus your attention on (have a pure experience of) a particular phenomenon is only provisionally true. The ultimate truth is in the poetry, the cultural remembrance that the pure experience evokes. This radical interpretation can

3 Oscar Wilde, *The Critical Writings of Oscar Wilde: An Annotated Selection*, ed. Nicholas Frankel (Cambridge, MA: Harvard University Press, 2022), 229.

4 Robert Macfarlane, *Mountains of the Mind* (London: Granta, 2003), 72*ff*.

5 Audre Lorde, 'Poetry is Not a Luxury' (1977), in *Teaching Black: The Craft of Teaching on Black Life and Literature*, ed. Ana-Maurine Lara and drea brown (Pittsburgh: University of Pittsburgh Press, 2021), 126.

be experienced, for example, on the nō stage – always already an empty, hollow place[6] – for example in Zenchiku's play *Kakitsubata* (杜若).[7] The main character is an iris flower who is attached to the unsurpassed beauty of her purple hue. This attachment to her own beauty is actually also a result of poetry, since it was Ariwara no Narihira's (在原業平; 825–80) praise of the *kakitsubata* iris that gave her her self-confidence. During the final scene of Zenchiku's play, the iris becomes awakened and recognizes that all things are interconnected and all flowers and all colours have their own beauty. The *shite* (lead actor) is still wearing the fancy purple *karakoromo* (唐衣) cloak while the chorus celebrates the character's enlightenment, saying that the sleeves of the cloak have faded to white. The audience – looking directly at the brilliant, flashy purple – are told by to ignore our conventional, provisional, faulty senses and understand the poetic truth – the ultimate truth – is that the cloak has become white. A simple example, as all theatre requires suspension of disbelief, but nonetheless Ṣhunzei's thought can be read in such an Idealist way as overriding any sensed phenomena in favour of linguistic expression.

But there is also a middle way interpretation, which is that both of the previous interpretations embody a kind of truth. The two truths coexist as a palimpsest: the pure physical phenomenon is mentally overlaid with the intellectual, linguistic interpretation of it. The pure phenomenon is a truth, and the poetic/cultural interpretation is also a truth. Becoming aware, via the process of 'cessation and contemplation', of the dissonance between the two – or perhaps it is more apt to say the polyphonic relationship between the two – affords awareness of the ultimate truth. This is a way into awareness of the hollow expanse via art.

6 See Ueda Shizuteru, 'The Place of Man in the Noh Play', *The Eastern Buddhist NEW SERIES* 25, no. 2 (1992): 77.

7 Koyama Hiroshi, Satō Kikuo, and Satō Ken'ichirō, eds, *Yōkyokushū* vol. 1 (Tokyo: Shōgakukan, 1973), 331–40.

When describing in a poem a scene from nature – say, falling cherry blossoms – a poet like Shunzei would not draw on the illusory, ever-changing phenomena that he could perceive with his own sensory faculties. Instead, he would draw on the words and phrases that already exist (such as the common allegory of cherry blossoms falling like snow) in the canon to express a more timeless, ultimate truth. Shunzei's ideal of poetry was to express new ideas with old words. These new ideas conjure up virtual mental images that had not previously been expressed linguistically (not in writing, at least), and as such, created out of emptiness new ways of experiencing phenomena. These new ways of perceiving gave all those who heard or read the poem a new set of interpretive resources for describing the world. As Michael Marra states,

> The poem's form (*sugata* 姿) produces, justifies, and treasures the paradoxes of a decentered truth that refuses to accept the idea that flowers cannot dissolve into snow, or that snow cannot solidify into flowers. Rather than represent 'beautiful flowers' as poets had done in the past, Shunzei creates a reality in which 'beautiful flowers' speak the impossibility of representation.[8]

This building of an artistic corpus of allegorical imagery related to places and concepts which informs interpretation is something most artists have done throughout history.[9] But in Japanese literature, painting and music, concepts of intertextuality, distributed authorship and ambiguous layers of interpretation have been theorized for more than a millennium, yielding hermeneutic traditions and methods which are far richer than the still-young traditions of Western postmodernism can offer.

[8] Marra, *Essays on Japan*, 66–7.

[9] The opposite approach – attempting to ignore tradition and culture and understand the thing as itself, an approach which can be likened to Husserl's phenomenological *epoché* – has certainly yielded fascinating and obsessive art projects, a notable example being Paul Cézanne's (1839–1906) late series of more than eighty oil and watercolour paintings of Mont Sainte-Victoire – though, being notable, one cannot now easily observe Mont Sainte-Victoire without thinking of Cézanne's interpretations.

3.2 utamakura: from place to hollow play

If phenomena as they are in pure experience could be classified as 'nature'[10] – in other words, that which is untouched by human culture – then, as we have seen with both Ueda and Shunzei, human culture (the conventional world) is layered like a palimpsest atop this ground of physical reality. A prime example of how human culture – poetry and the arts – is layered onto 'nature' is the landscape. Though, of course, human cultures alter the landscape physically through living in it, hunting through it, building on it, farming in it, we will concern ourselves here solely with the concept of the landscape.

As far as we can tell, the *kami* (神 spirits, gods) of the pre-literate ages of Japan seem to have been spirits of great power who were to be appeased, rather than benevolent deities living in harmony with humankind. Take, for example, *Hitachi no kuni fudoki* (常陸国風土記), one of the earliest of the five extant early eighth-century reports (*fudoki*) produced for the central government about the features, customs, myths and histories of local provinces (likely compiled between 713–28). The province of Hitachi (*Hitachi no kuni*) largely overlaps the contemporary prefecture of Ibaraki (茨城県), which is, at its closest, a little less than 17 km northeast of Tokyo on Japan's Pacific coast. The *fudoki* describes the founding of a new rice-farming area in the early sixth century by a man called Matachi (麻多智) of the Yahazu (箭括) clan. The settlers were continually harassed by *kami* in the form of horned snakes called *yatsu* (also pronounced *yato*) *no kami* (夜刀の神, En. *kami* of the valley) who could curse and end one's lineage with a glance. Matachi, angered by the reaction of 'nature' – the *kami* representing in the most reductive reading just snakes, or more broadly, the valley, or metonymically 'nature' as a whole – to the intrusion of farmers, kills several of these *kami* and pushes them back from the rice paddies. He declares that the tops of the

[10] The quotation marks around the word 'nature' are indicative of the evident impossibility of discussing anything untouched by human culture; by discussing it, or even simply viewing it or thinking about it, human culture has irrevocably changed it.

mountains will be for the *kami* and the bottom of the valley for farming, and having pacified the *kami*, sets up a shrine (*yashiro* 社) to make offerings to appease the *kami* into the future, a shrine which his family retains the priesthood of at the time of writing some two centuries later.[11] The relationship between humans and 'nature' described here, then, is adversarial and hostile, ending in an uneasy truce mediated by religious specialists (Matachi's Yahazu family).

Aside from the initial declaration of a border between the *kami* and the farmers, and the establishment of a *yashiro* to mark that border and be the site of offerings to the *kami* from the farmers via the priests, we are not told what language is used by Matachi or his descendants to communicate with the *kami*. Almost definitionally, though, the language the Yahazu priests would have used would have been hollow – otherwise it would not afford an opening up to the world of the *kami* – and likely it would have been poetic. Poet Takahashi Mutsuo (高橋睦郎; b. 1937) says that place names were the foundation of Japanese poetry.[12] These place names were, for example, sites of battles among humans (the spirits of the fallen heroes of which could become *kami*), or sites of encounters with *kami* deities of nature. By invoking the names of places where *kami* of heroes died, or where *kami* of nonhumans were known to dwell or manifest, the poets would appease the *kami* spirits, protecting the living from the *kami*'s wrath, but also remembering fallen heroes and marking out the places where wrathful, vengeful or powerfully indifferent nonhuman spirits might be encountered. These words shaped humans' relationship with the land and 'nature', land and memory. Containing words that shaped the landscape and acted as a gate between humans and *kami*, living and dead, these poems were *spells*.

[11] Akimoto Kichiro, ed., *Fudoki*, Nihon Koten Bungaku Taikei, vol. 2 (Tokyo: Iwanami Shoten, 1958), 55. See also Michiko Y. Aoki, *Records of Wind and Earth: A Translation of Fudoki with Introduction and Commentaries* (Ann Arbor: Association for Asian Studies, 1997), 50.

[12] Takahashi Mutsuo, *Shishin nisennen: Susanoo kara 3/11 e* (Tokyo: Iwanami Shoten, 2011), 123.

These spells-as-poems or poems-as-spells – the earliest extant Japanese poetry written down, collected in the late eighth-century anthology *Man'yōshū* (万葉集; literally meaning Collection of Myriad Leaves) – shaped how humans interacted with and understood the landscape then and continue to shape it now. But the understanding of the landscape as being filled with powerful spirits to be appeased gave way, over the following century (in Takahashi's account), to a more abstract understanding of the forces of 'nature'. Many of the poems in the *Man'yōshū* are by emperors and courtiers, but there are also many poems by commoners, soldiers and travellers. However, in the subsequent imperial anthologies – starting with the early tenth-century *Kokin wakashū* (古今和歌集) – most if not all the poems were written solely by the aristocratic classes. In these twenty-one anthologies, compiled over more than 500 years, place names began to be increasingly associated not with historical human events or the dwelling-places of *kami*, but with seasons and particular seasonal phenomena. Thus, whereas in earlier poetry of the seventh and eighth centuries place names stood – as signs – for themselves, and the poetry described the actual events which happened or actual *kami* who dwell there, by the early tenth century place names stood – as symbols – for seasons. These later poems were no longer spells which placated *kami*, they were metonyms for cherry blossoms or autumn leaves. A long process of abstraction from the material reality of land in which the effects of the palimpsestic layer(s) of culture can be physically understood – in a word, disenchantment[13] – had begun.

[13] I bring in the narrative of disenchantment with some caution and not uncritically. Richard Seymour points out that disenchantment is 'a tale that modernity has created about itself, its origins, and its telos, but . . . is both analytically and ethically suspect'. Richard Seymour, *The Disenchanted Earth: Reflections on Ecosocialism & Barbarism* (London: Indigo Press, 2022), 60. See also Jason Ā. Josephson-Storm, *The Myth of Disenchantment: Magic, Modernity, and the Birth of the Human Sciences* (Chicago: University of Chicago Press, 2017).

During these six centuries, poetry went from being an enchantment that facilitated communication between humans and 'nature', to being an aristocratic pastime used to show off one's knowledge of the canon (e.g. matching place names with the 'correct' seasonal image) during drinking parties. This is not to denigrate the more abstract and intellectual poets of these years, such as Shunzei and his even more avant-garde son Fujiwara no Teika. With an incredibly rich intertextual aesthetic which confounds interpretation, their poems are so far removed from grounding in conventional reality that their ground in ultimate reality is hard to miss: they approach hollowness and enchantment from the side of abstract intellectualism rather than material reality, avoiding the pitfalls of poetasters and dilettantes.

By the end of this era, in the late mediaeval period some 200 years after Shunzei and Teika, the great poet Shōtetsu – a teacher of Zenchiku – said that the famous place names in poetry had no relation to the physical places they once were signs of:

> If someone should ask me what province Mount Yoshino is in, I would reply that with cherry blossoms I associate Mount Yoshino, and with autumn leaves, Mount Tatsuta, and that I write my poems accordingly, not caring whether these places are in the province of Ise or the province of Hyuga or wherever. It is of no practical value to learn and remember in which provinces these places are located. But though I make no effort to memorize such things, they become known to me in the course of time, so I have learned that Yoshino is in Yamato Province.[14]

The place names have been completely hollowed out of their signal content, and are now purely empty placeholders for symbolic concepts. For Shunzei, when a viewer went to a place famous in poetry and noticed that the material reality of the place did not always match the poetic depiction of the place, that viewer's perceptions of the

[14] Shōtetsu, *Conversations with Shōtetsu*, trans. Robert H. Brower (Ann Arbor, Center for Japanese Studies, 1992), 77–8.

landscape were reshaped by the poetic-cultural universe as much as, if not more, than the material one. In contrast, for Shōtetsu, material reality is no longer even relevant.[15]

The name for these places (place names) which have been used in poetry as signs, symbols and hollow words for at least as long as poetry has been recorded is *utamakura* – *uta* meaning 'poem' or 'song', *makura* meaning 'pillow'.[16] The etymology of this word is unknown, though one theory relates back to those more humble travellers of the early *Man'yōshū* collection who would sleep on the hard earth with pillows of grass, associating travel to distant places with dreams, and thence with the creativity of poetry. In Takahashi's 2005 collection of *utamakura*-based poems called *utamakura awase* (歌枕合) – his practical attempt as a poet to recover some of the spiritual power (*reiryoku* 霊力) of *utamakura* place names in poetry – he posits an alternative reading of the word *makura*.[17] Read as 真•座 (*ma-kura*), it means 'seat of truth'; read as 間•座 (also *ma-kura*), it means 'place between' or 'void' – or 'hollow place'. Dropping the meaning-giving Chinese characters and allowing the word *utamakura* to exist as sound only – an exegetical technique also used by Zenchiku himself (see Section 2.4) – all these meanings can be manifest at once. In this reading then, *utamakura* is a poem or song as place in-between, an empty, hollow place, wherein there is truth – poetry as ultimate, hollow truth. *Utamakura* poetry are poems which afford us a temporary seat (place, *basho*) in the hollow expanse.

15 In the early modern period, the Zen monk Hakuin Ekaku wrote in his *Ten virtues of nō chanting* (utai no juttoku 謡之十徳; n.d.) that the first reason to practice nō chanting is to be able to see places without having to physically go to them Harada Kaori, 'Hakuin zenji to nōgaku', *Kokusai zen kenkyū* 3 (2019): 105.

16 For a detailed discussion of *utamakura*, see Edward Kamens, *Utamakura, Allusion, and Intertextuality in Traditional Japanese Poetry* (New Haven: Yale University Press, 1997).

17 Takahashi Mutsuo, *Utamakura Awase* (Tokyo: Shoshi Yamada 2005), 156–7.

3.2.1 Sugimoto Taku's *May (Tama)*

The Tamagawa (多摩川; En. Tama River), part of which forms the easternmost border between Tokyo and Kanagawa Prefecture (神奈川県), is an *utamakura* place name which has been part of the poetic canon since the *Man'yōshū*. This anonymous poem appears in book 14:

> たま川に晒す手づくりさらさらに何そこの子のここだかなしき
> *tamagawa ni sarasu tezukuri sarasara ni naniso konokono koko da kanashiki*
> Why is this girl dearer and dearer to me, like the handmade cloth washed in the Tama River bleaching in the sun[18]

This poem contains three ideas which become associated with the *utamakura* Tamagawa in future centuries: cloth (*nuno* 布), making by hand (*tezukuri* 手づくり) and exposure (*sarasu* 晒す; exposure to the elements, but also by analogy to danger or shame). These spawn other related associations: the sound of fabric being beaten to soften it, the season of autumn and the sound of wind (these latter two also suggesting loneliness, which might also be implied by the Musashino (武蔵野) area's distance from the capital).[19]

Guitarist Sugimoto Taku is a composer and guitarist from Tokyo, known for his sparse compositions and improvisations. In a 2018 book *Gakufu to kaisetsu* (楽譜と解説; Scores and Notes), he quotes approvingly the essayist Inagaki Taruho (稲垣足穂; 1900–77) saying that 'Art is an exploration of a childlike mind'.[20] Such an art is one which rejects the conscious influence of the weight of history: approaching the composition of music with a childlike mind might

[18] Translation mine, with reference to Alexander Vovin, *Man'yoshu: A New English Translation Containing the Original Text, Kana Transliteration, Romanization, Glossing and Commentary*, vol. 14 (Leiden: Brill, 2012), 63.

[19] Katagiri Yōichi, *Utamakura Utakotoba Jiten Zōteiban* (1999. Rev Tokyo: Kasamashoin, 2001), 262–4.

[20] '芸術とは幼心の探求である。' Sugimoto Taku, *Gakufu to kaisetsu* (Tokyo: Saboten Shobō, 2018), 5.

be likened to creation through Nishidian pure experience, or as close to it as is possible to get. It also echoes Zeami's injunction to perform nō with a beginner's mind (*shoshin* 初心),[21] a sentiment which is also found in Zenchiku's treatises.[22] Whatever originality Sugimoto claims for his works comes from the stripping away of the artist's individuality and anything like a system of composition or interpretation.[23] The interpreter, however, is under no obligation to listen in the manner in which it was composed.

On 23 May 2021, Sugimoto released *May (Tama)* on YouTube, a 23'48" solo performance on the banks of the Tama River, underneath the railway bridge which spans the river at Futakotamagawa Station.[24] A few weeks previous to that, on 7 May 2021, he released a CD and digital recording on Bandcamp called *May* (without any parenthetical location information), which he had recorded and edited over the two previous days, 6 and 7 May 2021.[25] It is 34'41" long, almost 11 minutes longer than the Tama River version of the piece.

Simply put, *May (Tama)* is a palimpsestic layer of guitar sounds – largely open strings activated and held for long durations with e-bows and clear, plucked high notes and harmonics (these are also audible for a long time, though they fade out naturally) – heard over the sounds of the riverbank. Notably, we do not hear the sounds of the Tama River itself, which is very wide and relatively shallow at this point, and likely a few tens of metres away from the microphones (in the video we do not see the river either). Instead, what we hear as the sounds of the riverbank are the wind, the young men just behind Sugimoto practicing rugby tackles, the trains overhead, a passing airplane. The

21 '初心不可忘', Do not forget your beginner's mind (or heart-mind), in *Kakyō* (1424). *Zeami Zenchiku*, 108–9. Zeami, *Performance Notes*, 139.

22 *Zeami Zenchiku*, 389, 391.

23 Sugimoto, *Gakufu*, 6.

24 Sugimoto Taku, *May (Tama)* (YouTube, 2021), https://youtu.be/R8V3uecqZBA.

25 Sugimoto Taku, *May* (Bandcamp, 2021), https://takusugimoto.bandcamp.com/album/may.

YouTube performance is clearly a single take, a document of a live performance: the running time includes setting up as well as the applause of an unseen audience behind the camera. In contrast, the officially released version is clearly edited together, with at least three audible cuts.

It is very likely that Sugimoto chose the Tama riverbank location for its convenience, its size and it being outdoors (May 2021 was still a time when indoor performances were difficult to organize because of COVID-19 restrictions), and unlikely that he chose it because of its 1400-year-old history as an *utamakura*. And yet, as Marra wrote about Shunzei's poetics – 'each viewer [becomes] a poet when confronted by the "actual" scene, inasmuch as his perception [is] immediately modified by textual knowledge'[26] – in listening to and viewing Sugimoto's *May (Tama)* I become a co-composer, modifying the pure experience of sound with my cultural knowledge of the river. The wind of the poems is very audibly present in the YouTube recording, and visually present via the camera shaking in its stronger gusts. The season is different from the poetic autumn and the sun is behind clouds. No-one is hand-making cloth, but Sugimoto is hand-making music and the practicing athletes calling to each other surely echo the communication of workers weaving. The regular rhythms of the occasional passing train too echo those rhythms of fulling cloth. Each echo of the past – of the tradition – reinforces the accumulated cultural associations of the river, while adding their own dimensions. And where there are differences, both in the riverbank scene itself (the concrete, the graffiti) and the artistic atmosphere (the spring season, the cloudy weather, the rugby players instead of cloth-makers), these differences highlight the gaps between past and present, physical reality interpreted conventionally and cultural preconceptions. In these gaps, there is a gate which can be entered, a crack through which the hollow expanse can be sensed, if that's a path the interpreter wants to take.

[26] Marra, *Essays on Japan*, 66.

3.3 Spirits of place

Not all places can be *utamakura*, places which are 'permeated with memory' in the words of nō scholar Matsuoka Shinpei.[27] Just as meanings accrue around places and place names, they also fade away. In Buddhist terminology, they arise and they are extinguished. One may, like poet David Jones in his modernist masterpiece *The Anathema* (a Greek word meaning 'things set apart'), acknowledge and regret the loss of meaning:

> If the poet writes 'wood' what are the chances that the Wood of the Cross will be evoked? Should the answer be 'None', then it would seem that an impoverishment of some sort would have to be admitted. It would mean that that particular word could no longer be used with confidence to implement, to call up or to set in motion a whole world of content belonging in a special sense to the mythos of a particular culture and of concepts and realities belonging to mankind as such. This would . . . remain true even if we were of the opinion that it was high time that the word 'wood' should be dissociated from the mythus and concepts indicated. The arts abhor any toppings off of meanings or emptyings out . . . [28]

While 'the arts' might abhor such loss, all things are impermanent as all things are grounded in hollow emptiness. Nevertheless, while even one artist has these old meanings and associations in mind, they are not in fact lost – just more obscure (and potentially more expressive of *yūgen*).

Nō, at least the *mugen* nō (nō of dreams and illusions) of Zeami and Zenchiku, thematizes this sense of loss and impermanence. The plot of an archetypical *mugen nō* is that a learned man (a Buddhist monk, or *kami* worshipping priest; this secondary role is known as the

[27] Matsuoka Shinpei, 'Managing the Poetic *topos*: The Aesthetics and Methods of *waka* and Zeami's noh Plays', *Nō and Kyōgen* 12 (2014): 64.

[28] David Jones, *The Anathemata* (1952; repr. London: Faber & Faber, 2010), 23–4.

waki) comes to an *utamakura* location. Recognizing that the place he is in is a place of cultural memory preserved in poetry, he thinks about the poems (quoting several of them) – exactly as Shunzei suggests a visitor could. A local person (the main character, or *shite*) appears and discusses the location and the poems and people associated with it. The *shite* is then revealed as the spirit of one of the people (sometimes a nonhuman person, as in *Kakitsubata*) associated with the location. Why is that spirit still there? Typically (though not always), it is because that spirit has a continuing attachment to the place – an attachment being a Buddhist 'sin' which would prevent rebirth. Letting go of the attachment to that location – whether the attachment is a grudge or a love – is necessary to continue the cycle of birth and death.

The *shite* is, then, a spirit of the *utamakura* place, manifested – brought into being – by the power of the poetry (which is already music – it is sung on stage; the word '*uta*' is inclusive of both the English words poem and song). The spirit – which, in some cases, has been apparently waiting around half a millennium for some learned figure to come and engage with them – is rooted, grounded, in the place, but obsessively so (e.g. the iris flower in *Kakitsubata* attached to her own beautiful purple colour). *Mugen* nō is usually in two halves, with the first seemingly taking place in the conventional world, and the second in the hollow world. This second half is generally considered to be the dream of the sleeping *waki*. There, the *shite* appears as they had done in their glorious past, erasing time and allowing the dead to commune with the living – and in most cases, be absolved (saved) by the *waki* monk or priest.

However, I would argue that the *shite* in the first half too can be read as a construction of the *waki*'s mind. At the very least, if the conventionally real setting of the first half implies that the *waki* character does meet a local person in the conventional reality of the staged scene, the fact that the *shite* he meets happens to be the spirit of the place's cultural-historic memory itself seems less likely to mean that the spirit was always there than that we (as the audience) are seeing the scene through the *waki*'s eyes. It is the *waki* who, through his knowledge of both religious texts and poetry, manifests the spirit of the poetry of this *utamakura* place. As Japanese literary scholar Donald Keene says, '[t]he reason for traveling to [*utamakura*] places . . . was to steep oneself in their atmosphere, savoring both what remained from the past and had changed'.[29] The *waki*, savouring the memory-spirit permeating the place, allows his knowledge of cultural history and poetry to change his perception of physical reality – because he knows that his sensory organs are fallible, but poetry (i.e. art) reveals ultimate truth. The local person he imagines he meets – or the regular person he does meet – is conceived of by him (and us as audience) through this mythopoetic, palimpsestic lens.

Mugen nō, then, starts from these basic premises: that the world is twofolded (conventional and hollow), that the curtainless nō stage is a perfect metaphor for the ultimate limitless freedom we have while still being bounded by conventional reality (i.e. the physically bounded stage), and that culture manifests our perceptions and understandings of conventional reality. What we view on the nō stage, from start to finish, is the *waki*'s perceptions of events, mediated by poetry and focussed on place.

3.4 Ecological perception

All understanding and interpretation of objective phenomena is mediated by memory, cultural and personal. Nō – especially *mugen* nō – is an illustration of this through a Buddhist worldview, which has been wrestling with these ideas for millennia. In Western psychology as well, the idea that each individual holds a different sense of conventional reality and will interpret the same sensory input more or less differently

[29] Donald Keene, *Travelers of a Hundred Ages* (New York: Henry Holt and Company, 1989), 220.

from another has gained traction in the last half-century, initially through the work of James and Eleanor Gibson.

The Gibsons' theory of ecological perception emphasized the mutuality of subject and object, seer and seen.[30] They recognized that each perceiver was also being perceived by the myriad things in their environment. They also recognized that a single phenomenon in an environment can be perceived, interpreted and understood in many different ways, which collectively they call its affordances. For example, a river affords quenching thirst for most animals, affords being a home for fish, affords a place for *satoyama* (里山) villagers to wash their vegetables and affords being classified as an 'externality' for capitalists who want to dump liquid waste at no cost. As Dōgen similarly wrote in his *Shōbōgenzō* fascicle '*Sansuikyō*' (山水経, Landscape as Sutra[31]):

> Some beings see water as wondrous blossoms, but they do not use blossoms as water. Hungry ghosts see water as raging fire or pus and blood. Dragons and fish see water as a palace or a pavilion. Some beings see water as the seven treasures or a wish-granting jewel. Some beings see water as a forest or a wall. Some see it as the dharma nature of pure liberation, the true human body, or the form of the body and the essence of mind. Human beings see water as water. Water is seen as dead or alive depending on [the seer's] causes and conditions.
> Thus, the views of all beings are not the same.[32]

Dōgen further emphasizes later in this sutra how important it is to detach your understanding of the world from an anthropocentric perspective.

As we saw in Section 2.3, Eric F. Clarke applied the Gibsons' ecological perception model to musicology in his book *Ways of Listening*. Clarke examines several aspects of the theory, one of which is

[30] James Gibson, *The Ecological Approach to Visual Perception* (Boston: Houghton Mifflin, 1979).

[31] Title translation: Raud, et al., *Forgetting the Self*.

[32] Dōgen, *Shōbōgenzō*, 192–3. Dōgen, *Treasury*, 158–9; translation modified.

the idea of virtual worlds. A virtual world, in audio terms, is the sound source(s) from which you might imagine the sounds you are hearing through speakers or headphones originated. If you are listening to a recording of a symphony orchestra, for instance, you might conceive that the sound emanates from a virtual world such as a concert hall. You would probably imagine one that you had been to, or seen pictures of, regardless of where the recording had actually been made. It might have been made in a recording studio, and be made up not of a single performance, but dozens of takes edited together to produce a version of the piece almost unachievable on stage. If the audio engineer has done their job well, however, most people won't notice those edits, and will imagine a virtual world in which they are hearing an orchestra on stage in a concert hall – the place most people encounter orchestras.

3.4.1 Michael Pisaro-Liu's *fields have ears (1)*

Michael Pisaro-Liu's *fields have ears* is a series of ten pieces composed between 2008 and 2016, written for vastly different ensembles from 1 to 80 musicians (including electronics or field recordings in five of the pieces), and lasting anywhere from 10 minutes to over an hour.[33] The title is a reworking of a German proverb – and the title of a well-known Hieronymus Bosch drawing – 'Das Feld hat Augen, der Wald hat Ohren' (The Field Has Eyes, The Wood Has Ears).[34] Collectively, the ten works constitute a series of musical experiments, exploring how variables of space and location affect the perceptual experience of audience members. As such, it is fruitful to listen to and think about these pieces through the lens of ecological perception theory, in addition to a Shunzei-style *utamakura* approach which considers

[33] This section draws heavily on Daryl Jamieson, 'Uncanny Movement through Virtual Spaces: Michael Pisaro's Fields have Ears', *MUSICultures* 45, no. 1–2 (2018): 238–54.

[34] Michael Pisaro-Liu, 'Some Thoughts on the "Fields have Ears" Series (and a Few Remarks on the Current Gravity Wave release)' (Gravity Wave Blogspot, 2012), http://michaelpisaro.blogspot.jp/2012/03/some-thoughts-on-fields-have-ears.html.

cultural products (songs and poems) as palimpsests which overlay and shape our understanding of 'nature' and place.

Fields have ears (1) (2008) is written for piano and four-channel playback (field recordings plus noise and sine tones). What follows is an edited, highly subjective description of the experience of listening to the piece on Philip Thomas' recording on the Another Timbre label (and also informed by a live performance by Nishioka Reina I produced in 2022[35]), emphasizing how Pisaro-Liu seems to be deliberately playing in the hollow crack he opens up in conventional reality through his juxtaposition of 'natural' and 'artificial' sounds.

The piece begins with a quiet hiss, some unidentifiable white noise. This could be wind or an ocean, but suggests microphone noise to me. My perception of the sound as mechanical immediately lends a rough authenticity to the piece: I feel I can trust the virtual world I'm imagining behind the speakers as a true – not heavily edited or manipulated – documentation of the 'real' (conventional) one. Seven seconds into the piece, bird calls ring from both stereo tracks (they are clear and distinct, and sound to my ears like small songbirds mixed with the croaking sound of a larger bird – perhaps a crow). The initial feeling of trust doesn't fade. I believe in this virtual world now; it affords being interpreted as a documentation of a 'real' place.

The piano enters at 0:18, with a quiet, moderately low single note, towards the bottom of a typical male human's singing range. The piano's second intervention in the soundscape is at 0:32, a softer dyad repeating the previous note and adding a note a minor third above it. The birds and white noise obliviously continue around these piano notes, which, though quiet, are undeniably not a part of the virtual field I've constructed in my head. They are an unexpected sound; if I didn't know any more about the piece, listening to the recording on headphones might tempt me to imagine a virtual world which includes a piano in a

[35] Michael Pisaro-Liu, *Fields have Ears (1)* (Kyushu University Design YouTube, 2022), https://youtu.be/_4ZxdFXMj7w (accessed 15 September 2025).

meadow. However, in a concert hall, I can still hear the field recording as a 'natural' document and the live piano as a separate, complementary element, a human commentary on the 'natural'.

Over the next four minutes, a low-pitched, very quiet sine tone (which rises in pitch every minute) becomes apparent, fading in and out of my attention. There are more varieties of bird calls – some insistently repetitive, and therefore memorable – and buzzing insect noises, as well as distant noises of what might be traffic or perhaps a helicopter. The 'field' becomes a more complex environment, touched with the human and occasionally inflected by delicate piano sounds which span the full range of the instrument and a variety of intervals. The sine tones sound alien, intrusive and unnaturally stationary.[36] This is the virtual world set up, in my hearing at least, by the first five minutes. This virtual world might be all I ever hear, if I continued as a casual listener, not attending to the details of the piece: a field, distant human sounds, a rising sine tone fading in and out, and a piano in the auditory foreground. In this reading, the piano and the sine tones seem like musical elements imposed on a documentation of a natural soundscape, the eponymous 'field'.

However, deep, attentive listening out reveals the extent to which the initial impression is a manipulation, reflecting the essential hollowness of the apparently solid virtual world. Presaged by thirty seconds of pink noise, there is a momentous but almost undetectable change at the five-minute mark. What happens is extremely subtle, but happens again at precisely ten and fifteen minutes: the field recordings playing on the four speakers repeat from the beginning, but rotate to a different speaker. Different listeners will catch on to what is happening at different points over the four rotations – the four repetitions – and some may not consciously figure it out at all. For me, the repetitive bird calls were what first made me realize that I was hearing the same material presented again from a different direction. The reuse of the same fragments of sound rotates the listener in the imaginary/hollow field without themselves 'really'

[36] Sine tones are sounds with the most regular possible sound waves.

moving. It also shifts them back in time, to an alternate, slightly different version of the same past. Without moving, the virtual sonic world we thought we were in is suddenly shifting each listener in four dimensions. The 'repetitions' of the five-minute field recordings, however, are not exact; they fade in and out and are otherwise manipulated differently each time. There are, for instance, times when the field sounds – the wildlife, the wind, even the distant helicopter and airplane sounds which are now a part of nature in the modern world – are edited away, leaving only sine tones, piano and isolated bird calls (around 7:25 is the first time this happens). This again reveals the hollowness and the artificiality of the virtual 'field'.

Pisaro-Liu has written that the pianist in this piece is meant to be an ear.[37] The pianist, then, is explicitly also a listener. Like the *waki* in a *mugen* nō, they are both a perceiver and a creator of the virtual world they and we (the audience) also perceive. A piece which begins with a seemingly documentary-style aural portrait of a virtual world intruded on by human (piano) and mechanical (sine tone) presences ends with the human perceiver as the unmoving axis around which the virtual world uncannily rotates, while the mechanical sine tones shift from menacing to reassuringly predictable. Expectations I had as the piece started were overturned as it enacted a subtle opening of its seeming conventional virtual world into a hollow one.

Fields have ears (1) invites us to imagine a richly textured, highly detailed image of its virtual source, and then gently, slowly shows how this is a hollow fiction. The piano, however sympathetic its tones are to the pre-recorded soundworld (accordant – or not – with the sine tones, accompanying the bird calls), is not a natural part of the scene; it reveals its artificiality from the start. But as the work progresses, from its first tape hiss, to the four-fold variation and rotation of the virtual space, through the dropping out of most naturalistic sounds in favour of isolated birdcalls over droning sine tones, and finally to the increasing prominence of the very artificial-sounding sine tones (gradually rising

[37] Pisaro-Liu, 'Some Thoughts'.

out of the background into the foreground), the environment's virtual source is increasingly made to seem hollow, unreal or not possibly within what we call the 'real' world. It's a sophisticated aural paradox, which, like a zen kōan, points at a deeper truth about the limits of human perceptual capacities by exposing how our minds construct virtual spaces which we believe in as if they were objectively true.

3.5 Onmyōdō geomancy

Although over the eighth–tenth centuries place names in *waka* ceased to signal actual places and instead became symbolic of seasons and emotional states, there was one way in which poems maintained an allegorical connection to the land. This was through *onmyōdō* (陰陽道; En. Yin-Yang) practices and the esoteric connections between place, directions, seasons, musical modes, musical instruments and poetry (songs) that this system of correspondences entailed.

Onmyōdō encompasses geomancy (and is thus related to *fūsui* 風水 Ch. *fēng shuǐ*), astrology, calendar making and time keeping. As with Pythagorean musical theory and the music of the spheres in European thought,[38] in the Confucian Chinese music theory which was inherited by the Japanese beginning in the late sixth century music was both a barometer of the health of the nation and society, as well as a way of manifesting and reproducing the nation and society. The *Kangen ongi* (管絃音義 The Meaning of Instrumental Music, *c.*1185) opens with the statement that 'Instrumental music is the foundation of the myriad things',[39] and musical instruments such as the *koto* (箏) and *biwa* (琵琶) had the magical power to affect individuals and society, according to

[38] Daniel K. L. Chua, *Absolute Music and the Construction of Meaning* (Cambridge: Cambridge University Press), especially Chapter 3.

[39] '管絃者萬物之祖也' David T. Bialock, 'From *Heike* to *Nomori no kagami*: *Onmyōdō* and the Soundscapes of Medieval Japan', *Cahiers d'Extrême-Asie* vol. 21, *The Way of Yin and Yang: Divinatory Techniques and Religious Practices* (2012): 176.

this system of correspondences. In Yin-Yang five phases theory (*in'yo gogyō setsu* 陰陽五行説), each of the phases of matter – wood, fire, metal, water and earth – corresponded to one of the five cardinal (or relative) directions – respectively east (left), south (front), west (right), centre and north (behind). These in turn related to the seasons – respectively (now excluding 'centre') spring, summer, autumn, winter – and guardian animal deities (*shijin* 四神) – Azure Dragon (*seiryū* 青龍), Vermilion Bird (*suzaku* 朱雀), White Tiger (*byakko* 白虎), Black Turtle-Snake (*genbu* 玄武).[40] The four strings of the *biwa*, the five notes of the scale and the five modes (scales) themselves are also mapped onto this system of correspondences, as were the five poetic lines of *waka* (the Japanese word for poetic lines is the same as the one used for the elemental phases, *gyō* 行). Poetry and music were thus vital to cosmological order, and musicians of the mediaeval period therefore were not only entertainers. They were also *onmyōji* (陰陽師; En. Yin-Yang practitioners) who practiced divination, rituals of appeasement for the earth gods (*jijinkyō* 地神經), and 'spirit pacification (*chinkon* 鎮魂), including the placation of "vengeful spirits" (*onryō* 怨靈) and communication with the dead, the purification of defilements (*haraikiyomeru* 祓い清める), and border rites (*kyōkai girei* 境界儀禮) aimed at expelling malign influences'.[41] It is thus not surprising perhaps that many of the nō stories, especially in the early fifteenth century, also feature pacification of vengeful spirits, communication with the dead and purification of defilements. What we see in nō is a theatrical abstraction from what lower-class (i.e. illiterate) musicians and entertainers had been doing in reality for hundreds of years prior.

Nō plays are intended to be performed in particular months or seasons, sometimes because of the dramatic content or the seasonal associations with the *utamakura* location, but sometimes for

[40] Ellen Van Goethem, 'The Four Directional Animals in East Asia: A Comparative Analysis', in *Feng Shui (Kan Yu) and Architecture*, ed. Florian Reiter (Berlin: Humboldt-Universität zu Berlin, 2011), 201.

[41] Bialock, 'From *Heike*', 167–8.

particular ritual functions. *Okina* (翁) – the oldest play, which isn't really a nō play at all but more of a ritual performance – is usually the first performance of each year on each stage, but is also enacted on other auspicious occasions. Frank Denyer draws our attention to the Chinese zither (*gǔqín* 古琴) tradition, in which the notation (called *qínpǔ* 琴譜) specifies not only the sequence of sounds and how to play them, but also the 'performance location, season and time of day, as well as suggestions about dress'.[42] What music is varies according to the 'conventional reality' of each society. There are often unwritten assumptions about how and when music is to be performed: in the case of mediaeval and Renaissance Western European church music, for example, these are routinely ignored, since the 'disenchanted' conventional world of Modernity does not pay heed to the pre-Enlightenment, Catholic cosmology, with its ecclesiastical calendar and myriad saints days. *Messiah* was written for Easter, not Advent, the season when it is almost exclusively performed.

But, as site-specific art and music have become more prevalent over the past decades,[43] and everything old (such as specifying when and where a piece can be performed) is new again,[44] is it time to reconsider the artificially limited and sound-proofed concert hall, and once again situate music in particular times and places within wider society, the five directions, the four seasons and the cosmos at large? Could music today still purify spiritual (or mental) defilements?

[42] Denyer, *In the Margins*, 35.

[43] Scholar of site-specific performance Nick Kaye pinpoints the start of this concern in contemporary art practices within 1960s minimalism. Nick Kaye, *Site-specific Art: Performance, Place and Documentation* (London: Routledge, 2000), 2.

[44] DeWoskin points out that the timbral focus of the *gǔqín* (which he romanizes as *ch'in*) surpasses in complexity anything in the Western tradition, and also makes special mention of the 'highly developed choreography of hand movements . . . expressed in the traditional *ch'in* notation system'. Kenneth J. DeWoskin, *A Song for One or Two: Music and the Concept of Art in Early China* (Ann Arbor: Center for Chinese Studies at the University of Michigan, 1982), 122–3. Many in the West seem to think that the idea of specifying and notating these aspects of musicking was invented by Anglo-European postwar avant-garde composers.

3.6 Hollow landscapes

In his previously mentioned essay 'Language' (Section 2.2), Ueda does address one example of the twofold nature of the world being expressed outside of language. He analyses a passage written by his teacher Nishitani Keiji reminiscing about his seaside hometown in Ishikawa Prefecture in an essay called 'The Luminous Scenery of Okunōtō' (Okunōtō no fūkō 奥能登の風光).[45] In it, Nishitani recalls picking shellfish with 'transparently thin and pink' shells on a seashore that 'had a clarified purity about it that made it, too, seem somehow not of this earth.'[46] He recalls it as if it were a mythical vision from Chinese or Greek legend, allowing those ancient stories to filter through and colour his memories. His own childhood recollections were inevitably also filtered and coloured by time; he was over seventy years old when he wrote the essay. With the concrete place itself as a base, his subjective memory and the cosmologies of multiple civilizations layered atop reality to create a sense of otherworldliness.

From Nishitani's essay, Ueda posits a distinction between a 'scenic view' (*fūkei* 風景) and 'luminous scenery' (*fūkō* 風光). The former, he suggests, is when a human perceives the natural scene as picturesque: landscape as artwork. In other words, they mentally frame it, imposing anthropocentric values on it, perhaps pull out their camera and take a picture as if the picture made the experience more true rather than less. The latter, on the other hand, is 'untouched by human hands', which I take to mean not so much that humans have never touched it (neither scientific Modernity nor Kegon/Zen interpenetrative ontology would suggest that anywhere on earth was literally untouched by humans) but that the human viewer doesn't impose their own values or 'artistic' standards on it. The dichotomy of scenic view:luminous scenery is about whether the viewer perceives the place or accepts the occurrence of perception

45 Nishitani Keiji, *Nishitani Keiji Chosakushū*, vol. 21 (Tokyo: Sōbunsha, 1990).

46 Ueda, 'Language in a Twofold World', 779–80; Ueda, *Kotoba*, 37.

in a dynamic exchange, and thence what cultural or personal memories the place brings to the viewer's mind and palimpsestically layers atop the scene. Whether one is viewing a scene in 'nature', reading poetry or listening to music, because all phenomena are grounded in the hollow expanse, 'everything has the potential' to 'disclose the originally invisible twofoldness of the world/hollow-expanse as a visible twofoldness within the world'.[47]

[47] Ueda, 'Language in a Twofold World', 780; Ueda, *Kotoba*, 38.

4

Non-fiction

4.1 Living sound and experimental/non-fictional music

Nishida said that 'Concrete reality that is directly given to us is fluid, developmental, does not halt for an instant, that is to say, it is something that is alive'.[1] Similarly, one of the corollaries of the Kegon Buddhist ontology of unimpeded interpenetration of phenomena and phenomena (*jiji muge hokkai*; see Section 1.1.1) is that if all phenomena are interpenetrating all other phenomena, and if we humans are what we call conscious and sentient, then all phenomena are – to some degree – conscious and sentient. This includes not just animals – which most people would have no problem considering conscious – but also plants,[2] waves, mountains, moons. But the implications don't stop at solid phenomena; they also apply to waves of energy[3] and, especially notable for this discussion, waves of sound.

1 Nishida Kitarō, 'Bergson's Philosophical Method', in *Nishida Kitarō zenshū* 1, ed. Fujita Masakatsu and Kosaka Kunitsugu (Tokyo: Iwanami), quoted in Fujita Masakatsu, 'The Development of Nishida Kitarō's Philosophy: Pure Experience, Place, Action-Intuition', in *The Oxford Handbook of Japanese Philosophy*, ed. Bret W. Davis (Oxford: Oxford University Press, 2017), 395.

2 Chapter 6 will address plant consciousness more deeply in relation to nō theatre, but see also Stephan V. Beyer on plants and shamanism in the Amazon and Monica Gagliano on the nascent science of plant consciousness. Stephan V. Beyer, *Singing to the Plants: A Guide to Mestizo Shamanism in the Upper Amazon* (Albuquerque: University of New Mexico Press, 2009); Monica Gagliano, *Thus Spoke the Plant* (Berkeley: North Atlantic Books, 2018).

3 David Graeber notes that the uncanny unpredictability of the behaviour of electrons at the quantum level of reality – what he calls 'free' and Karen Barad calls 'queer' – means 'that at the very foundations of physical reality, we encounter freedom for its own sake – which also means we encounter the most rudimentary form of play'. David Graeber, 'What's the Point If We Can't Have Fun?', *The Baffler* 24 (2014), https://thebaffler.com

Jo Kondo has said that he 'regard[s] each sound in music as having an independent life', an idea which he takes directly from the Kegon Sutra.[4] From this, he develops an ethical standpoint towards what he calls 'listening composition' in contrast to 'speaking composition'.[5] In listening composition, the composer primarily listens to the sounds themselves, attending to the sounds in a concentrated – one could say meditative – manner, approaching them as beings with some level of sentience, consciousness and life of their own, not trying to straitjacket them into an abstract mathematical system or manipulate them with anthropic so-called 'expressive' intent. Morton Feldman's compositional approach mirrored this ('I don't push the sounds around'[6]), though without the Buddhist ontological or ethical foundation. The contrasting, modernist avant-garde position – which we could call 'continuity Romanticism' – is that the composer's job is to control, corral and deploy sounds in order to serve human ends. Igor Stravinsky (1882–1971) says that 'The phenomenon of music is given to us with the sole purpose of establishing an order in things, including, and particularly, the co-ordination between *man* and *time*.'[7] On the other hand, Feldman – like Kondo, Cage, Linda Catlin Smith (b. 1957) and other experimental composers (not to mention uncountable numbers of musicians in traditions outside of Western art music) – adopts the 'listening composition' approach of letting the sounds, as living beings, simply be themselves, and to the extent that a composer writes the sounds down, these composers are – almost like anthropologists of

/salvos/whats-the-point-if-we-cant-have-fun (accessed 16 September 2025). Karen Barad, 'Nature's Queer Performativity', *Kvinder, Køn & Forskning* 1-2 (2012): 25–53.

4 Daryl Jamieson, 'Varje ljud har sitt eget liv', *Nutida Musik* 291 (2023): 24. See also Daryl Jamieson, 'Does a Sound have Buddha-Nature? Kegon Thought and the Aesthetics of Sound', *The Journal of East Asian Philosophy* (2024), https://doi.org/10.1007/s43493-024-00042-x.

5 Kondo, *Homo audiens*, 67.

6 Feldman, *Give My Regards*, 143.

7 Igor Stravinsky, *Chronicle of My Life* (London: Victor Gollancz, 1936), 92. Emphasis in original.

sound – recording what the sounds themselves seem to want. Smith, for example, describes her method of composition as

> primarily a method of listening. I spend time finding or creating a fragment of music – a beginning maybe? – that interests me . . . . I listen to it, and wait to hear what it seems to require. This is difficult to describe because it seems so simple. But it is a complex activity . . . . This compositional approach is a kind of extreme awareness, . . . requir[ing] a kind of active reflection . . . . It is similar to how I imagine *ikebana* [生け花] . . . . A sense of balance or rightness; an attention to the detail of these flowers or musical fragments; a sense of space, or phrasing – this is what I bring to the process. I compose this way because I want to stay aware of the experience of listening to the piece, because the experience of listening to it is the piece.[8]

In her description of her own compositional process, Smith invokes *ikebana*, a method of flower arranging related to the way of tea (*sadō* 茶道) and which literally means living flower. In a 1953 essay on *ikebana*, Nishitani wrote that its 'beauty is ephemeral and yet it is as if its transience had been transformed into a beauty of a higher order . . . . Through it [the cutting of the living plant] the emptiness that lies hidden in the depths of the plant is unveiled.'[9] Listening composition as a method – and Kondo's Kegon Sutra-derived stance that each sound has an 'independent life' – recalls the eleventh-century treatise on landscape gardening called the *Sakuteiki* (作庭記, Records of Garden Making), attributed to Tachibana Toshitsuna (1028–94). In it, he advises gardeners to 'follow the requests' of the principal stone of the garden,[10] attributing both a life, as well as a will, to non-sentient rock. Listening composition combines both of these stances: by allowing sounds to

8 Linda Catlin Smith, 'On Listening: A Lecture', *Linda Catlin Smith: Composer* (1992), http://www.catlinsmith.com/writings/on-listening-a-lecture.

9 Nishitani Keiji, 'Ikebana', in *Japanese Philosophy: A Sourcebook*, trans. Jeff Shore, ed. James Heisig, Thomas Kasulis, and John Maraldo (Honolulu: University of Hawai'i Press, 2011), 1200.

10 Jiro Takei and Marc P. Keane, *Sakuteiki: Visions of the Japanese Garden* (Tokyo: Tuttle Publishing, 2001), 4.

sound as themselves, it respects the life and will of the sounds; and in capturing sounds as living beings – as opposed to lifeless, manipulable objects – on the page or on a recording device, it affords the possibility of the hollow expanse being heard ('unveiled') through the practice of listening to them.

Ueda says that the 'true actuality of human being is that of "playing in hollowness while abiding in actuality"', rather than the reality-lite or -free zone of existence of one who (through self-delusion or in attempting to delude others) 'toys with actuality while abiding in hollowness'.[11] He calls out the media for its 'dismantling of reality', which he notes 'is progressing at an accelerated rate' (this essay was originally published in 1997, and so the 'media' Ueda is referring to is presumably largely TV and movies, the present-day [2025] world of social media and smartphones having not yet come into existence). Nevertheless, for Ueda, abiding entirely in conventional reality would also be an untruth; a balance of actuality and hollowness is necessary for human flourishing (even, perhaps, for human *being*).

Adam Loughnane, in an article on the 'risks' for poets (for which we can read 'artists') of abiding in the hollow expanse, points out that for artists 'abiding in hollowness' does not mean not a free flowering of creativity, but merely an affirmation of 'the self, the subject or "consciousness". It is a type of freedom tied to the myth of "originality" and the root of naïve ideas of creative freedom and individual creative genius.'[12] In other words, abiding in the hollow while generally ignoring the 'real' leads to the kind of abstract structuralist, formalist or self-aggrandizingly Romantic conceptions of art and the artist which can lead people into ignorance of the true nature of reality – not least, the artist themself.

[11] Ueda, 'Language in a Twofold World', 783–4; Ueda, *Kotoba*, 42–3.

[12] Adam Loughnane, 'Ueda and Heidegger: Playing in Hollowness, Abiding in Actuality and the Risk of Poetic Language', in *Tetsugaku Companion to Ueda Shizuteru: Language, Experience, and Zen*, ed. Ralf Müller, Raquel Bouso, and Adam Loughnane (Cham: Springer, 2022), 259.

Kondo insists that listening composition is 'purposeless'.[13] It is an activity engaged in for the sake of itself, a listening out of the self in non-hierarchical communion with other life forms – the sounds themselves, but also other sound-making objects, animals, landscapes and people (a term not limited to humans). Conversely, composition for the purposes of communication from a composer to a listener via a performer (a hierarchical series of relationships) is 'speaking composition'. Like all binaries, such as the binary of conventionally real and hollow, a composer should aim to balance these two approaches rather than focus on one or the other. Surely some structuralists have at some points in their lives been carried away, 'forgetting themselves' (per Dōgen) in the pure hollow magic and mystery of the sounds themselves. Likewise, many listening composers will have occasionally made use of a tried-and-true compositional technique or formula to solve a problem.

There are other ways of framing this binary of listening *v.* speaking composition (which, like all binaries, is in practice a continuum). One of these, useful within the context of recent Western art music history, is experimental *v.* avant garde. Experimental music can be and has been defined in many ways. Cage's 'hard' definition[14] is that an experimental action is 'an action the outcome of which is not foreseen', and more specifically that experimental composition 'is composing in such a way that what one does is indeterminate of its performance'.[15] James Tenney (1934–2006) had a somewhat different definition of experimental practice. For him, it was 'more literally an experiment, like a scientific experiment, and in science, in scientific work, one experiment always does lead to another one'.[16] Experimental

[13] Kondo, *Homo audiens*, 71*ff*.

[14] Bob Gilmore, 'Five Maps of the Experimental World', in *Artistic Experimentation in Music: An Anthology*, ed. Darla Crispin and Bob Gilmore (Leuven: Leuven University Press, 2014), 25.

[15] Cage, *Silence*, 69.

[16] quoted in Gilmore, 'Five Maps', 26.

composition – encompassing both Cage's and Tenney's definitions – might then be defined as a kind of listening composition, or at least is abiding in the listening while perhaps playing in the 'speaking' (as perhaps when one is designing an initial 'experiment' – though the results of that initial experiment would then lead to the next experiment via 'listening').[17]

Another complementary binary to consider is composer and writer Jennie Gottschalk's (b.1978) proposition of experimental music as non-fictional. She contrasts the feeling she had while listening to a 'beautiful and well crafted' piece of music – noting that 'it was about a world that didn't exist' (i.e. it was fictional in the way a beautifully written fantasy novel is fictional) – to listening to music by experimental composers such as Alvin Lucier and Michael Pisaro-Liu, 'music that is about the time and place in which it occurs'. She continues:

> When experimental music is effectively made and presented, it speaks to our interaction with the world. It goes from the center – what we already know – to the margin – what we don't know – and back again, so that new realities are present along with, or sometimes even in place of, our previous perceptions of our own lives. This work does not suggest 'other' worlds, but instead strengthens relations with this world.[18]

I read Gottschalk as writing about the same distinction as Ueda. A hollow work – a piece which readily affords being heard as hollow – is one in which, through attentive listening, you learn more about the time and place (*basho*) of the composition, or of the performance, or of the listening (and perhaps all of these). A 'hollow' listening experience necessarily brings to your attention something that you had never noticed or known before; it manifests something new to

[17] The idea of compositions as 'series' of related works, each exploration of the consequences of earlier pieces in the series, is widely used by Wandelweiser composers. See James Saunders, 'Testing the Consequences: Multipart Series in the Work of the Wandelweiser Composers', *Contemporary Music Review* 30, no. 6 (2011): 497–524.

[18] Gottschalk, *Experimental Music*, 4.

your consciousness, but not something fictional. That learning about – that 'strengthening of relations between' – yourself and the world could be learning about the conventional world or could be understanding something about the interpenetration of the conventional and the hollow. But it cannot be a pure sense of the hollow expanse only, because that is fictional, a 'dismantling of reality'. As composer Ichiyanagi Toshi (一柳慧; 1933–2022) said:

> When a composer puts meaning into sound and invents fixed forms he objectifies himself through his own ego. Through his attitude one is removed from his own time quality. The Self is there without inventing it. And that entity of Self includes everything. It is not necessary to build fictitious reality.[19]

Formalist music, truly abstract musics: these are conceived of as purely hollow fictions, about the 'self' (ego) of the composer, not about the world. Abiding in the fictional in this way has a reactionary political aspect. Matthew Holt has noted,

> in the *Communist Manifesto* Marx and Engels in effect argue that capitalism – the epoch of the bourgeoisie – *fictionalises* the world, turns all relations, material and social, spiritual and temporal, into fictional relations. More specifically, that fictionalisation is understood under – or rather *as* – the comic genre (as opposed to the tragic, the epic, or the lyric). With one vital difference: for Marx and Engels capital isn't humorous.[20]

Which, again, is not to say that fictionalization is bad: per Ueda, it is to say that abiding in a fictional world (the world of capitalist Modernity, artificially supposing oneself cut off from 'nature', which is just another word for 'reality') while on occasion 'toying with' reality results in one's

[19] Quoted in Takemitsu Tōru, *Confronting Silence*, trans. and ed. Yoshiko Kakudo and Glenn Glasow (Berkley: Fallen Leaf Press, 1995), 12.

[20] Matthew Holt, 'Capital as Fiction: The Communist Manifesto', in *Literature and Politics: Pushing the World in Certain Directions*, ed. Peter Marks (Newcastle upon Tyne: Cambridge Scholars Publishing, 2012), 19.

alienation from society and the communion of all things. Fictional music – most common practice Western art music and most music produced in Modern societies – can be engaged with, played and enjoyed. But one's life overall needs a balance of fictional and non-fictional, hollow and real, with the balance in favour of the latter of each of those binaries.[21]

The more regular, predictable in form a music is, the less real ('natural') and more fictional it is, and the more restrictive its affordances. For commercial reasons, pop music is definitionally predictable and easy to listen to, and thus provides an example from the extremity of fictional musics. Like realist painting, fictional music (pop or otherwise), however effective it is at conjuring up a specific virtual world, is essentially – necessarily – restricted in its hermeneutic affordances. Experimental, non-fictional music, by contrast, is characterized by its radical openness to interpretation – it can mean whatever each listener wants or needs it to mean for them, at that time, in that place. Like the *Zhōuyì* hexagrams beloved of John Cage, the interpretation is much more about the perceiver than the work itself; as the 'Great Commentary' (*Xìcí* 繫辭) on the *Zhōuyì* says, any instruction received from the oracle is 'like an echo'[22] of the question put by the questioner – in other words, the instruction essentially reframes the questioner's query, but does not provide any answer. As the *Zhōuyì* translator Richard Rutt says of the *Changes* – in words equally applicable to the open interpretive field of experimental

[21] Composer Gérard Grisey (1946–1998) had his own similar dichotomy, between composers whose music is 'discursive' – Arnold Schoenberg (1874–1951), Alban Berg (1885–1935), Luciano Berio (1925–2003) and Pierre Boulez (1925–2016) were his examples – and those whose music reflects the 'state of the world' – like Johannes Ockeghem (*c.*1410–97). He put himself in the latter category, but recognized that, in his case, he was not purely reflective of reality but his music included some discursiveness. Gérard Grisey, *Écrits ou l'invention de la musique spectrale*, ed. Guy Lelong and Anne-Marie Réby (Paris: Musica Falsa, 2008), 273.

[22] Richard Rutt, *Zhouyi: A New Translation with Commentary of the Book of Changes* (London: RoutledgeCurzon, 2002), 54.

music – 'all good oracles [are] ambiguous. Their ambiguity is . . . a stimulus to the mind'.[23]

In some sense the fictional:non-fictional dichotomy is itself false – as it is in literature – because, regardless of the composer's intentions, a live performance is always being created in the time and place it is being performed and a listener always brings their own perspectives, experiences and biases to bear on any piece they hear, composing a unique sonic event that is to some extent different from the experience being had by the person next to them. In this way, every sound is non-fictional to some extent. In another sense – because we construct or, perhaps, compose virtual sonic worlds in our brains out of the sense data we gather through the imperfect sensors our bodies possess – every musical work we perceive is a fiction, a virtual sonic world that we individually create. However, as a shorthand way of acknowledging that a greater amount of leeway given to performers in a score (meaning any set of instructions for making music) makes it more responsive to and potentially enlightening about the time and place in which it was made than a score in which the composer controls as many parameters as they can, non-fictional and fictional are useful designations. They are endpoints of a continuum, not a binary.

As each visitor to an *utamakura* landscape 'became a poet when confronted by the "actual" scene, inasmuch as his perception was immediately modified by textual knowledge',[24] each listener is a composer, and all listening is composition. When you listen to any collection of sounds, you are consciously or unconsciously filtering what sounds you direct your attention towards and which you ignore, and which 'noise' you cannot ignore but wish you could. As a listener, which is to say, as a composer of your own soundscape, you can choose to be a listening composer. You can listen to the monumental abstract sonic constructions of Stravinsky or Stockhausen as a

[23] Ibid.

[24] Marra, *Essays on Japan*, 66.

listening composer – turning off the noise-cancelling function on your headphones, throwing open your windows, focussing your ears as much on the coughs and sweetie wrappers being unwrapped with painful slowness as the sounds of the performers and letting the sounds of here and now be with the sounds of the fictional. As all conventional phenomena are rooted in the hollow, all fiction is rooted in and interpenetrated by the real – the composer or artist cannot help but be a part of society, of reality, no matter how much they cling on to the myth of their individual genius.

4.2 Space v. place

Modern musicians and artists often talk about 'space'. They want to create an 'acoustic space' with their compositions, 'fill a space' with sound or light, creating illusions of 'sonic space', 'architectural space' or 'infinity space'.

Space (Jp. *kūkan* 空間) itself is an illusion. As Tim Ingold says in his aptly named essay 'Against space', space 'is the most abstract, the most empty, the most detached' term we use to describe our environment.[25] A space is essentially a fictional construction, something modern artists conceive of in order to maintain the illusion that they are creating something *ex nihilo*. It flatters the ego of the artist and allows for the audience to conceive of the artist as the sole creative genius behind the work. In other words, it is a convenient fiction that affords the individualism of capitalist Modernism manifesting in the arts, ignoring the network of relations which shape every one of our lives, every action we take, every work *we* produce. Gordon White underlines the wider political violence inherent in this concept: 'The construction of space is explicitly imperial. It forcefully replaces a web

[25] Tim Ingold, *Being Alive: Essays on Movement, Knowledge and Description* (2011; repr. London: Routledge, 2022), 177.

of contexts and relations with a nothingness, waiting to be filled with a new power narrative that uses this nothingness as a large part of its justification: *terra nullius*.'[26]

Place (*basho*) on the other hand, is real. You can touch a place, dwell in a place, travel through a place. What any given place is – a kitchen, a home, a city – is defined by and manifested through language in the conventional world. For Ingold, all places are manifested through and interlinked by lines of 'wayfaring', creating what he calls a *meshwork*.[27] This, as a metaphor, is similar to the Vedic image of Indra's net. Indra's net is an infinitely large net with a jewel at each node, and every one of the infinite number of jewels in the net reflects every other jewel. This image was widely used in Kegon (and other Mahāyāna) Buddhism to illustrate the concept of unimpeded interpenetration of phenomena and phenomena: Each phenomenon in conventional reality (i.e. jewel in Indra's net) reflects to some degree every other phenomenon in conventional reality, and these infinite phenomena are all grounded (em*place*d) in emptiness or the hollow expanse (i.e. the net which holds the jewels in *place*).

For artists, exchanging space for place can be a process of throwing off the expectations of Modernist thought and artistic practice, the quest for individuality, originality and conceptual control over all aspects of one's work. One example of this process is the photographer Yamagami Shimpei (山上新平; b. 1984), whose earlier series focus, Cézanne-like, on photographing a single location over a period of time, as if obsessively searching for the elusive perfection of a single shot which will define this place. His series *Spectrum* and *The Disintegration Loops*, published together in 2022 as *helix*, both take the same patch of scruffy woodland in Kamakura (a seaside area south of Tokyo, and the administrative capital of Japan from the late twelfth–early fourteenth centuries) as their subject, the former series in black and white, the

[26] Gordon White, *Ani.mystic: Encounters with a Living Cosmos* (London: Scarlet Imprint, 2022), 164.

[27] Ingold, *Being Alive*, 181.

latter in colour.[28] Similarly, *liminal (eyes) YAMAGAMI* (2022)[29] consists solely of black and white photographs of sunlight reflecting off waves in the Sagami Bay, off the coast of Kamakura. However, in the preface to his third published book, *Epiphany* (2023), he notes a change in his approach, writing, 'I started with a thoroughly challenging point of view, now I focus on the plain and undramatic'.[30] Unlike the landscapes and seascapes of the previous series, *Epiphany* focuses on small details of human and nonhuman animals, plants and trees, books and water. Rather than affording the impression of an obsessive investigation of a conceptual space applied to a real-world place, this series feels like a photographer moving ('wayfaring') through the world, noticing overlooked, small phenomena and directing his attention – and camera – there. It affords being read as photography as a practice of living – the interpenetration of practice and life – rather than an art practice separated from living.

The concert hall and the recording studio are spaces separated from living. Cut off from the world by thick soundproofed walls and accessed through heavy doors, these spaces are the epitome of acoustic *terrae nullius*. Everything that happens inside a concert hall or recording studio is controlled by the space and those present within it; nothing from outside – from the world, from reality – is able to enter. In a concert hall, of course, the audience – other people – do enter,[31] and they can bring some element of indeterminacy to the sound world inside the hall. But Modern listeners are trained to ignore those unintended sounds of humans simply being, and if they persist, surrounding audience members or ushers might even request that the 'noisy' patron leave. To the extent possible, nothing should be allowed to sully the pristine magnificence of the artists' work. In

[28] Yamagami Shimpei, *Helix* (Tokyo: minä perhonen, 2022).

[29] Yamagami Shimpei, *Liminal (Eyes) YAMAGAMI* (Tokyo: bookshop M, 2022).

[30] Yamagami Shimpei, *Epiphany* (Tokyo: bookshop M, 2023), n.p.

[31] One hopes! Audiences showing up is not something that 'contemporary music' musicians can take for granted . . .

a recording – whether made in a studio or at a live performance in a hall – any such extraneous 'noise' can and usually will be edited out. Noise here can include any sound not notated or wanted by the composer or performing artists, such as audience members sneezing or turning the pages of the programme, but can extend to removing the sound of musicians' breathing or the mechanical sounds of the instruments themselves. This essential artificially seeks to sever not only the interpenetrative relationship between the musical sound and the outside world, but between the sound and the human and instrumental bodies required in order to produce this sound. The most extreme example of this disembodiment of sound is electronic music created entirely inside a computer, allowing a composer to control literally every aspect of a piece virtually.

4.2.1 Toshiya Tsunoda's *Field Recording Archive*

Though music created entirely inside a computer might be the most fictionally disconnected from reality, for most of the twentieth century, most electronic music made from recordings of reality too were at pains to put some distance between the place of recording and the virtual acoustic space of the composition. Works in genres such as *musique concrète* and *musique acousmatique* were based in whole or in part on recordings of sounds in nature (broadly interpreted as including human and nonhuman sound sources). Lindsay Vickery *et al.* have pointed to this insistence on abstracting sound from its source as an 'ideological impediment' that had to be overcome in order to allow sounds to be presented in sound art as signifying themselves.[32] It is an act of appropriation, an enclosure from which, over the past few decades with the rise of field recording as a genre in its own right, sound art has been slowly breaking out of.

[32] Lindsay Vickery, et al., 'Between the Real and the Imaginary: Ecostructural Approaches to Composing with Field Recordings and Acoustic Instruments', *Proceedings of the 2016 Annual Conference of the Australasian Computer Music Association* (2016): 82.

Tsunoda Toshiya, almost inarguably Japan's most well-known field recording artist, first trained as a landscape painter. His recordings have always been tied to a sense of place, almost all of them having been made around the Miura Peninsula. This protrusion of land just an hour southeast of Tokyo, separating Tokyo Bay from Sagami Bay, is the place where, in 1853, Commodore Perry landed his black ships, which began the process of forcing Japan to open its borders to 'free' trade and capitalist Modernity.

In the liner notes to his five-disc collection *Extract From Field Recording Archive*, Tsunoda writes about the differences between 'space' and 'place' from his point of view as a field recording and sound installation artist.[33] He says that, while 'place' points to a concrete location, 'space' is used abstractly and conceptually to point to something subjective; 'space' is virtual, and 'place' is physically real. He says that, until 2013, 'I ha[d] always thought that the most important thing was the "space" rather than the "place". . . . I thought, in order to make a recording to be considered "art" work, it was required to be a recording of a certain space'.[34]

Tsunoda began to question the 'ideological impediment' (in Vickery *et al.*'s words) of abstraction in 2007. Prior to that, his works were based on the idea of capturing the unique vibrations of a particular place, and then by categorizing the vibrations of different places, juxtaposing them on albums or in installations, he could transform a recording of a place into a virtual sonic space. On the first three discs of *Extract From Field Recording Archive*, Tsunoda arranges the recordings – all of which are vibrations recorded by contact microphones and small microphones between 1993–99 – in this recontextualized manner, one which deemphasizes the place of the recording and draws attention instead to the commonalities among the virtual sonic spaces of the recordings on each respective album. The first album, originally

[33] Tsunoda Toshiya, *Extract From Field Recording Archive*, liner notes trans. Yuko Zama (Erstwhile Records, ErstPast 001-5, 2019).

[34] Tsunoda, *Extract*, 4, 29.

released in 1997, collects stationary waves (largely unchanging drone-like recordings of a place's characteristic vibrations); the second, from 1999, collects vibrations which pass through and are transformed by a hollow object (such as a bottle or pipe); the third, from 2001, focusses on solid vibrations which are inaudible to humans and can only be recorded with piezoelectric contact microphones (e.g. vibrations moving through metal fences or asphalt road surfaces). All of the recordings on these three disks afford being heard as recordings of 'places', but the framework of the original releases deemphasized this, encouraging abstract, conceptual listening instead.

Tsunoda states that during the recording, researching and creating the installation (and eventual CD release) of *Low Frequency Observed at Maguchi Bay* (間口湾の底周波, 2007) that he began to rethink his ideas of 'space' and 'place'.[35] The CD release of *Maguchi Bay* consists of eight tracks. The odd-numbered tracks are between 2'11" and 13'05" in length and are recordings of the vibrations of the currents and the tides constantly churning around a very rough seafloor and breaking against an old breakwater to which the contact microphone is attached. The even-numbered tracks are each the same as their preceding odd-numbered tracks but have had a low-pass filter at 20Hz applied to them. 20Hz is the threshold of human hearing, so the even-numbered tracks are inaudible to human listeners. In the installation version of the piece (2005), a large speaker sits exposed on the floor, 'a moving sculpture'.[36] Visibly vibrating, the speaker tries vainly to communicate these powerful, very-low frequency sounds to an audience who can see but not hear them. The spirits of 'place' are mutely trying to speak to a people who do not have the ears to listen.

Tsunoda says that the field work for *Maguchi Bay* was conducted over nine years, 1996–2005, because the source of the unusually turbulent low-frequency sounds was not initially obvious. Makuchi

[35] Ibid.

[36] Will Montgomery, 'Quiet storms: Toshiya Tsunoda', *The Wire* (2011), https://www.thewire.co.uk/in-writing/essays/p=9937.

Bay[37] was a place he had known from childhood, but the contact microphone allowed him to connect with the place in a completely different way, one that triggered curiosity and eventually a deepening of his understanding and even love of the place.[38] It is this attentiveness not only to his senses, but also to that what is not audible or visible to human perception, which led him to reevaluate the relative importance of concrete and abstract, place and space, in his work.

Returning to the *Extract From Field Recording Archive*, disc 4 consists of recordings made in 1994 and 1995. This time period is contemporary with the first three discs, but on this disc (which had not been released prior to 2019), the organizing principle is place rather than space: all the recordings were made at Nagaura Port. Notably, as Nagaura Port had become exclusively for military use from 2014, this place is now – for civilians – a place of memory. Like an *utamakura*-based poem, Tsunoda's recordings both trigger and create memories of a place that is now off-limits to close observation. Nagaura, as a place, exists less in phenomenological reality, and more in memory and culture.

The fifth and final disc of the set contains recordings from after 2007, and, aside from the first two tracks, all of the tracks are from after 2013, the year when Tsunoda says he consciously changed his working methods towards a focus on 'place'.[39] He says at the end of the notes that his narrow focus on vibration phenomena has come to an end, and that he would adopt a more open approach to recording in future, allowing for much more contingency and indeterminacy.[40] Through the experience at Makuchi Bay and subsequent work, he

[37] Tsunoda notes that the title of the artwork contains a misspelling, since the bay is actually named 'Makuchi', not 'Maguchi'. Tsunoda, *Extract*, 5, 29.

[38] Montgomery, 'Quiet Storms'.

[39] Tsunoda, *Extract*, 5, 29.

[40] An early example of this new way of interacting with place is his 2016 double-album Somashikiba ソマシキバ, on which see: Daryl Jamieson, 'Field Recording and the Re-enchantment of the World: An Intercultural and Interdisciplinary Approach', *The Journal of Aesthetics and Art Criticism* 79, no. 2 (2021): 213–26.

realized that '[i]f I tried to find something particular, I would only be able to find what I was searching for'.[41] In other words, focussing on the conceptual creation of virtual sonic space – a kind of Modernist 'speaking composition' – precludes the possibility of actually listening to what the nonhuman place is saying. Opening one's ears, forgetting the cultivated artistic self, opens the artist up to far greater possibilities. As Michael Pisaro-Liu has written on the process of editing a field recording:

> Whenever I make [a field recording], I'm excited for the moment of playback, away from the site. The question is always the same: What didn't I hear? And, by extension: If I cut something out, do I run the risk of not really hearing a crucial fact of the environment? Is there an ethics of this situation? It may depend on whether one arrives with a preconceived notion of what should be recorded, or whether a part of the process is to learn what sounds.[42]

Tsunoda's reasons for his shift of focus from 'space' to 'place' echo Pisaro-Liu's final sentence here: it's a difference between arriving in the field with an artistic-concept driven preconceived notion of what should be recorded, versus an openness 'to learn what sounds'.

The final track of *Extract*, Disc 5 Track 13, is titled 'On the edge of the shore' (*Namiuchigiwa* 波打ち際). Translated literally, the title means 'the liminal place where waves lap'. This marks an opening up of the virtual sonic space from steady-state or cyclical vibrations recorded largely with contact microphones to the shore of a cove on the Western side of the Miura Peninsula recorded with omnidirectional microphones (standard microphones which don't shepherd the ear towards a particular focal point). However, Tsunoda avoids this becoming a completely non-fictional documentary recording through his unusual

[41] Ibid., 27, 41.

[42] Michael Pisaro-Liu, 'Ten Framing Considerations of the Field', in *The Experimental Music Yearbook*, ed. Sara Roberts (2010): 3, https://www.experimentalmusicyearbook.com/ten-framing-considerations-of-the-field.

spacing of the microphones – seven metres apart. When listening to the recording – especially on headphones – the constant slow lapping of the waves against the shore of the cove sounds ever so slightly unnatural. As the waves roll from right to left, there is a slight yet perceptible delay in the progress from one ear to the other. In addition, some gurgling sounds are audibly much louder in one ear. Concentrated, deep listening to these details affords a stretching of the ears seven metres wide. What lies between the ears, then, is an emptiness, a hollowness. This sensation of sound not quite behaving as one expects it to in conventional reality summons up an auditory equivalent of Nishitani's 'luminous scenery' – a scene, a place, permeated by personal, cultural and historic memory, a place that uncannily discloses its own hollow ground.

4.3 The *waki*'s mind

A wayfaring visitor, passing through, is captured by the pure experience of a scenic view. Recalling the history of the place – subjective memories of, or cultural artefacts associated with, it – the visitor's perception is modified. The scenic view acquires an aura, a luminosity. Within the mind of the viewer, something is triggered by this combination of objective physical reality overlayed by a palimpsest of cultural reality. Images from memory, figures from the past who are associated with this place are brought to life in the visitor's mind. The visitor imagines speaking with these ghosts and memories, communicating with them, witnessing the past events which bring meaning to the place. Time seems to collapse, as childhood happenings and figures, historical or mythical events replay in the mind as if they were happening in the present. As words and sensations manifest things, people (human and nonhuman) and occurrences, the triggering phenomena retreat and overlap with the glow of emptiness.

The preceding paragraph could describe a *waki* in a *mugen* nō play, arriving at an *utamakura* location and, through his knowledge of poetry, encountering the spirit of the place, which could be a *kami*, a warrior, a wronged woman or a beautiful flower. Though the story of such nō plays is often that the spirit attached to the place is in need of salvation (e.g. prayers from the wayfaring monk), if we interpret the entirety of the nō playing out in the mind of the *waki*, it is in fact the monk who has the uncanny experience of the hollow expanse; the *shite* is merely a manifestation of the hollow expanse in the suggestible mind of the *waki*. It is not that a spirit (be it god or daemon, ghost or nonhuman metamorphosed into a human form) appears in reality; the drama of nō is the powerful affordance of culture (poetry and music) to disclose to the *waki* the hidden ground of the hollow expanse within conventionally real phenomena. The *waki*, who exists in the contemporary timeline of the playwrights, stands in for us, the audience. By portraying this uncanny encounter with place, the play becomes a further layer of culture which affords triggering a soteriological response in the audience. We are also wayfarers, having stopped at the place of the nō theatre, and this place too affords (like all phenomena) being experienced as hollow.

That paragraph, though, also and equally describes the elderly Nishitani recollecting his childhood in Okunōtō. For the luminosity of the hollow expanse to shine through reality, one need not use poetry or theatre: recalling the place itself (beaches are always liminal, thin places, at the border between land and sea), the transparent pink shellfish and his own youth was enough for the scenery to glow. We could frame Nishitani's essay as if it were a nō play, where the *waki* (elderly Nishitani) returns to the beach where he played as a child, and encounters the *shite* (the spirit of the boy Nishitani) hunting for shells. But we could also reverse this interpretation, and say that every *waki* in a *mugen* nō is just an ordinary person moving through the world with an open-enough mind to be enchanted by what they find there, and whose experience of the world is enriched – further opened up – by engaging with cultural and personal memories and histories in relation to the place they are in.

The work of Tsunoda, and many other field recording artists, affords being interpreted in this way too. The artist goes to a place. Why do they choose that place? If they seek out or create a 'space', the journey towards awakening may end there.[43] If a place is chosen for its historical, cultural, political or personal significance, and if the artist is open to hearing differently – if the purpose of the recording is, in Pisaro-Liu's words, 'to learn what sounds' – then it is more likely that something uncanny, something suggestive of the hollow might be experienced. The field recording artist is also a *waki* figure, bringing the audience to a place where something uncanny may be experienced (for the audience, whether in a nō theatre or listening to a recording, the travel is virtual). Whether any given audience member also experiences that uncanniness is partly down to the artist's skill in drawing attention to the hollow – the 'crack' – in everything, and partly down to the mental state of the listener themself.

The fictional field recording artist often has a preconceived notion of what they want to record before they go into the field, with the intent of using – manipulating – that sound in a particular way in a 'speaking' style of composition. One well-known example of such a speaking style of fictional field recording artist is Chris Watson (b. 1953). Watson's Bandcamp site explicitly says that he uses his recordings as material for artistic manipulation, editing 'his field recordings into a filmic narrative', a kind of fictionalization.[44] His album *In St Cuthbert's Time* aims to imaginatively recreate 'a 7th Century Soundscape of Lindisfarne' and 'to reflect upon the daily and seasonal aspects of the evolving variety of ambient sounds that accompanied life and work during that period'; in doing so

[43] But it may not: Every phenomenon has the potential to disclose hollowness, though it is less likely to do so when perceived with intention, rather than attention. Per the Tsunoda quotation earlier, '[i]f I tried to find something particular, I would only be able to find what I was searching for'.

[44] Chris Watson, *Chris Watson* (Bandcamp), https://chriswatsonreleases.bandcamp.com.

it collapses time and space, editing out anachronistic sounds: it is historical fiction.[45]

This kind of work, which seeks to recreate and reinhabit an imagined past, is an example of what Svetlana Boym has called restorative nostalgia. Restorative nostalgia 'proposes to rebuild the lost home and patch up the memory gaps',[46] in contrast to reflective nostalgia, which is 'more concerned . . . with the irrevocability of the past and human finitude . . . . is more about individual and cultural memory'.[47] Tim Rutherford-Johnson borrows these categories to discuss how tonality has been used in postmodern contemporary music, categorizing 'the neo-tonality of John Adams or David Del Tredici [as] restorative, whereas that of Laurence Crane or Peter Garland, which uses tonality against the background of modernity, [as] not'[48]: restorative as a reactionary return, reflective as a cherishing of the past within the present.

In this framework, an album like *In St Cuthbert's Time* can be read as restorative – a desire not just to go to and record in a sacred, thin place, but to manipulate those recordings to create a virtual sonic world in which there are no petroleum-powered fishing boats off the coast or aircraft overhead. *Mugen* nō, as well as Nishitani's 'The Luminous Scenery of Okunōtō', are both reflective, in that the present-day (the conventional world of the *waki* and the elderly Nishitani) coexist with the cultural and personal memories evoked by the place: '[R]eflective nostalgia cherishes shattered fragments of memory.'[49] Or, as Ueda notes

[45] This is not to say I don't love it this album (I do), nor that Watson is not an excellent composer (he is) – it is a categorization, not a value judgement. As noted previously, works composed with fictional intent can still be listened to non-fictionally, and some fictional works so listened to can be as or more revelatory to audiences than non-fictional ones.

[46] Svetlana Boym, *The Future of Nostalgia* (New York: Basic Books, 2001), 41.

[47] Ibid., 49.

[48] Rutherford-Johnson, *Music After the Fall*, 238.

[49] Boym, *Nostalgia*, 49.

of *mugen* nō, 'the past is brought into the present by way of death' (i.e. the spirit played by the *shite*). To the extent that Tsunoda's field recordings can be said to be nostalgic or concerned with the past – perhaps the prime example is *Somashikiba*, a 2106 work built around exploring two burial grounds in the Miura Peninsula where farm animals were interred in the early Modern period – his recordings are, unsurprisingly, filled with tractors, cars and other motorized vehicles. *Somashikiba* is a work about a place which is open to the past, the luminous hollow, but also to the present.

4.3.1 Sam Dunscombe's *Two Forests / Oceanic*

As noted in Section 1.3, Zeami writes in *Fūshikaden* that plays set in *utamakura* locations should quote the poems which made that location famous at key climactic points in the play (*tsumedokoro*). However, some place names refer to more than one location, either by accident or deliberate borrowing. The riverside garden at Kawara-no-in (河原院) in Kyoto created by Minamoto no Tōru (源融; 822–895) is one of the latter. Designed to imitate the still-famous and 800 km-distant seascape of Matsushima (松島) in present-day Miyagi Prefecture (宮城県), this garden is named Shiogama (塩釜) – literally meaning 'salt kiln', indicating a place where sea salt is harvested – after the town of the same name on Matsushima Bay; Shiogama is also the *utamakura* place name symbolic of that famously beautiful seascape.

In his play *Tōru* (融), Zeami plays on the ambiguity of place and the idea that the garden designer was deliberately evoking a far-off *utamakura* location to deepen the uncanny, *yūgen* atmosphere of the play.[50] The conventional time of the play (the *waki*'s time) is, as always, in Zeami's 'present' (the fifteenth century), some six centuries after the garden was made and thence fell into ruin. The old man the *waki* meets

[50] I have written in detail about *Tōru*: Jamieson, 'Spirit of Place'. There is a full translation of the play in Royall Tyler, *Joy, Despair, Illusion, Dreams: Twenty Plays from the Nō Tradition* (New York: Columbia University Press, 2024), 244–58.

in the abandoned (and purportedly haunted[51]) ruin of Tōru's Kawara-no-in pleasure palace repeatedly speaks as if he is in the Shiogama on the Pacific coast rather than the Shiogama on a Kyoto river bank. In scene 2, the old man says 'I feel the cold salt spray on my sleeves/It's that kind of autumn night on the bayshore', but in scene 4 – an *utamakura tour de force* – he is firmly back in Kyoto, scanning the horizon from East to South to West, and naming (and quoting fragments of poetry about) fourteen *utamakura* sites on the edges of the city.[52] In other words, the virtual world Zeami palimsestically layers over the hollow emptiness of the nō stage is in two places at once.

But these two Shiogamas are not two random places. They are linked allegorically by their shared name, and linked historically by the garden being an imitative homage to the coastal scenery. Thus, though it is not conventionally 'realistic' to be in two places at once, or two time periods at once (the *waki*'s 'present', and the *shite*'s 'past'), *Tōru* has a kind of dream logic which is appropriate for the 'dreams and illusions' (*mugen*) style of nō, the style of nō which is of greatest relevance to this book's argument.

Both of the two tracks on Sam Dunscombe's album *Two Forests / Oceanic* (2023) feature field recordings from multiple places. In the first piece – '2F' – these different places (principally 'a sequoia grove in central California and the Amazon Rainforest outside Manaus, Brazil' – the titular two forests) are presented in sequence, as a kind of virtual wayfaring. 'O', the second track, layers recordings of several oceans. Both pieces have very subtle layers of electronic sounds – functioning in a similar way to the sine waves in Pisaro-Liu's *fields have ears (1)* (see Section 3.4.1). The pitches for these sounds are explicitly not well-tempered but are just-intonation gamuts derived from Dunscombe's

[51] For the most detailed treatment of the historical Tōru and his garden, and the ghost stories which circulated for centuries after Tōru's death, see Furanku Berunāru [Bernard Frank], *Fūryū to oni: Heian no hikari to yami*, trans. Furanko Junko (Tokyo: Heibonsha, 1998), 10–86. In English, Atkins gives a thorough summary: Atkins, 'Depictions of the Kawara-no-in'.

[52] Hare provides a detailed analysis of this key scene. Hare, *Zeami's Style*, 112–16.

analyses of the birdsong (in '2F') and the rhythmic phases of the waves (in 'O'). In other words, the pitches are attuned to the sounds already existing in the recordings,[53] and provide a musical element which is rooted in the contemporary human, conventional world (a function akin to the *waki*'s in nō) to bridge the uncanniness of being sequentially or simultaneously in multiple distant places.

As with Tsunoda's subtle distortions of the virtual sonic world achieved with his choice and placement of microphones, Dunscombe achieves a similar subtlety of temporal distortion of conventional reality via the use of editing tools such as delays, loops and the speeding up or slowing down of sonic material. In the liner notes to '2F', she says that '[m]y hope is to create a sense of place-gone-strange, of space and time simultaneously expanding and contracting in dialogue across octaves, miles, and minutes'.[54] This sentence could equally describe the effect Zeami achieves in *Tōru*'s play with reality between two distant places in two different times. Musically, much of nō's uncanny atmosphere is created by the constant ebbing and flowing of the pulse, making it very difficult to follow the beat (especially for beginners, but this is true even for professionals). The natural variation in the rate of ocean waves striking a beach has a similar uncanny-yet-familiar feeling, not predictable and not regular, but neither is it confrontingly awkward or abstract. Keeping in mind that pitch is a secondary musical characteristic, a mere manifestation of rhythm (as referenced in Section 1.1), it is entirely appropriate that in 'O' Dunscombe bases the just-intonation pitch set for the electronic part on the rhythmic phases of the waves.

As with a listening composition piece notated and performed in a typically art-music fashion, what we hear when we listen to *Two Forests / Oceanic* is the trace of a composer listening intently, using their musical training and skills to analyse what they hear, and present to

[53] See Chua on the historical importance of music being attuned to the cosmos in pre-Modern European tradition. Chua, *Absolute Music*, Part 1.

[54] Dunscombe, *Two Forests*.

the audience a music which is attuned to the lives of the sounds and the places from which those sounds were sourced. The composer's will is attenuated, and the interventions (editing sound files, adding carefully chosen pitches and rhythms, etc.) are subtle but meaningful, enhancing our understanding of the sounds and their world.

Two Forests / Oceanic was written with a purpose, which is to provide an alternative to well-tempered Modern classical music or New Age music in psychedelic-assisted therapy. Having never had access to such therapy, I cannot directly judge its success on this count, but simply as music, it affords the listener an experience of losing a 'normal sense of time' (through the subtle rhythmic variations), 'loss of normal sense of where you [are]' (being transported between the two forests, or simultaneously amidst multiple seascapes), and 'awareness of life and living presence in everything' (the independent life of sounds themselves, as well as the sentient and non-sentient beings in the forest and ocean). The quoted phrases are taken from the 'Mystical Experiences Questionnaire', one of the clinical tools used to evaluate the results of psychedelic-assisted therapy.[55] Further, it affords feelings of 'oneness', in other words, a sense that conventional reality – be it a forest, an ocean or the room in which you listen to the recording – is grounded in the limitless interpenetrative openness of the hollow expanse. Dunscombe's achievement here is to create two field recording pieces which are edited, layered and not 'conventionally real', but which still sound like non-fictional, experimental works about the mind and its perception of the truth of reality rather than fictionalizations and abstractions assembled to meet an artist's ego-focussed desire.

[55] Yonezawa Kengo, et al., 'Development of the Japanese version of the 30-item Mystical Experience Questionnaire', *Neuropsychopharmacol Rep* 44 (2024): 282.

5

Soundwalkings

'solvitur ambulando *(solved by walking)*'

—Latin proverb

Though seemingly first used by artist and composer Max Neuhaus (1939–2009) to describe his early work *Listen* (1966), 'soundwalk' as a term was popularized by and remains closely associated with Hildegard Westerkamp. Westerkamp worked as a researcher at the World Soundscape Project (WSP) at Simon Fraser University in British Columbia with R. Murray Schafer (1933–2021), the head of the WSP. She independently (re)coined the word in the early 1970s. Westerkamp's classic definition, first advanced in 1974, is that a soundwalk is 'any excursion whose main purpose is listening to the environment. It is exposing our ears to every sound around us no matter where we are.'[1] In a 2020 discussion with Jacek Smolicki, Westerkamp affirms her early definition of the genre, but adds that 'it is also about "discovering one's own listening"'.[2]

Half a century on from Westerkamp's popularization of this sound art genre, a myriad of approaches to the practice of soundwalking have been developed. These include scientistic approaches, that is, close observation of sounds from an assumed objective position. There are even International Organization for Standardization guidelines on how

[1] Hildegard Westerkamp, 'Soundwalking', *Sound Heritage* 3, no. 4 (1974): 18.

[2] Jacek Smolicki, 'Introduction', in *Soundwalking: Through Time, Space, and Technologies*, ed. Jacek Smolicki (London: Routledge, 2023), 7.

to conduct soundwalks to gather scientific data.[3] Some take a more artistic approach, treating the soundwalk as a composition and the map as a score. Others treat it more like a meditation, a kind of spiritual experience of communing with the nonhuman. Some use technology to enhance and/or record their experiences; others resolutely reject any technological mediation. Needless to say, many soundwalkers' practices combine aspects of multiple approaches.[4]

5.1 Purposeless listening

In Section 4.2 I used 'wayfaring' – borrowed from Tim Ingold[5] – to describe the linear movements of people (human and nonhuman) which spread out like a net, at the nodes of which places emerge or arise. 'Wayfaring', while being a perfectly fine word to describe being in the world, implies to me a directionality that I do not always feel I possess as I move through this life. Rambling – particularly in its usage as walking 'for pleasure' (*OED*) – or, even more apropos, stravaiging – Scottish for 'to wander about aimlessly' (*OED*) – seem like better words to describe the kind of movement I am often engaged in when I am outside, walking and listening to the sounds in my environment.

What kind of activity is this purposeless – rambling, stravaiging – listening? The aimlessness is not an ambivalence towards the direction my feet are taking me. Rather, I mean that the listening is not undertaken with a specific intent in mind. As Tsunoda writes (quoted

[3] ISO 12913-2. International Organization for Standardization, *Acoustics—Soundscape: Part 2: Data Collection and Reporting Requirements* (Geneva: International Organization for Standardization, 2018), https://www.iso.org/standard/75267.html. For a practical example, see Simona Mancini, et al., 'Soundwalk, Questionnaires and Noise Measurements in a University Campus: A Soundscape Study', *Sustainability* 13, no. 2 (2021): 841.

[4] An excellent overview of the variety of soundwalking practices can be found in the edited volume Smolicki, *Soundwalking*.

[5] Ingold, *Being Alive*, 181.

above in Section 4.2.1), 'If I tried to find something particular, I would only be able to find what I was searching for.'[6] I may go out with the intention to seek out a particular bird's mournful song, for example, or to calm myself down by listening to the rhythm of waves on the beach, or make my way to a concert hall to hear a Beethoven sonata, and while these are fine things to do, they are not aimless or purposeless. To hear the unexpected, you must not presuppose what you will hear. This is especially true if what you hope to encounter are the small, quiet voices which you don't know to expect. These neglected, forgotten sounds are only audible if you are not intent on hearing something else.

Crucially, though, in order to hear the unexpected, to have new worlds arise in your consciousness, you also cannot go out with the intention of hearing the unexpected either. To purposely listen without purpose is oxymoronic and self-defeating. As Dōgen says in the '*Zazengi*' (坐禅儀; Rules for Zazen) fascicle of *Shōbōgenzō*, *zazen* (seated meditation) 'is not conscious endeavor. It is not introspection. Do not desire to become a buddha.'[7] In order to achieve awakening, the one thing you must not do is consciously intend to achieve awakening. Likewise, when we listen with *attention* (as opposed to listening with *intention*), any preconceived notion we have of what we will hear must be abandoned before we can actually hear anything aside from our own thoughts. This is, in other words, a hearing prior to listening, akin to Nishida's pure experience prior to the division of subject (listener) and object (listened-to). In this model, in the unity of listener and listened-to, there is only listening – the momentary arising of the activity of perceiving sound and sound being perceived.[8]

Nishida's colleague Watsuji Tetsurō (和辻哲郎; 1889–1960) defined humanity (*ningen* 人間) via its constituent characters – *nin* (人 also

6 Tsunoda, *Extract*, 27, 41.

7 Dōgen, *Shōbōgenzō*, 223; Dōgen, *Treasury*, 579.

8 Cf Anttoni Kuusela, 'Listening Without a Listener – Understanding the Self and the Activity of Listening to Music Through Nishitani Keiji's Philosophy', *The Journal of East Asian Philosophy* 4 (2025): 123–36. https://doi.org/10.1007/s43493-024-00046-7.

pronounced *hito*, meaning human person) and *gen* (間 also pronounced *aida* or *ma*, meaning the emptiness between) – as the empty space between humans. This concept, called in general '*aidagara*' (間柄; betweenness), is a relational definition: humanity is not some quality that any one person can possess, rather it is something that is enacted in the relationships between human beings. Similarly, no sound has any meaning independently. A sound is only realized as a sound when it is in relationship with another being. This could be between other sound(s) (e.g. even in classical Western music-theoretical terms, any single pitch is meaningless on its own; it requires at least one other pitch to create an interval, a dyad or a sense of movement or stasis, consonance or dissonance) or between listener(s). Listening, as a concrete instance of being, arises out of the hollow emptiness between the listened-to and the listener.

If sounds have independent lives, that implies that we have an ethical obligation to sounds as we have towards other living beings – human or nonhuman, sentient or non-sentient. When we listen to a sound, we enter into a relationship with another living being. Entering into that relationship with the intent to manipulate it is a Modernist, instrumentalizing approach which establishes a hierarchy of dominance – the listener as a master who forces the sound (I hesitate to describe the sound as a 'listened-to' in this instance of domination) to be what the listener wants. In contrast, in a pure experience of listening, the listened-to and the listener are in a relationship of mutual openness such that there is no difference between the listener and listened-to, as both (all) parties mutually listening.[9] This pure experience of listening from the standpoint of the hollow expanse cannot be a permanent one. It is something that one enters into and returns from, back to conventional reality.[10] But, following such an experience, conventional reality is

[9] For an in-depth discussion of the ethics of dialogue, and the interpenetrating roles of host and guest, in Ueda, see Ishihara Yuko, 'Dialogue as Human Existence: Ueda Shizuteru's Zen Buddhist Philosophy and a Care Ethics of Play', in *Care Ethics and Beyond: Moral, Epistemological, and Cross-Cultural Perspectives*, ed. Seisuke Hayakawa and Michael Slote, 73–92 (Cham: Palgrave Macmillan, 2026).

[10] This is the *kōko kyakurai* mentioned in Section 2.5.

more 'luminous' in the way Nishitani's scenery is in his essay about his childhood home, and the hollow expanse seems more present than it had been. Furthermore, such a listening practice engenders further practice, as Tenney's musical experiments engender further experiments.

Under capitalist Modernity, purposeless listening has further political resonances beyond the ethical treatment of non-sentient sounds as living beings. Kondo writes that, for composers of listening compositions, 'composing becomes a free activity once it has been emancipated from purpose'.[11] Under a socio-economic system which is dedicated to squeezing the maximum amount of surplus value from every worker, where some companies expect employees to be on call – at the very least, available by email – at all times, composing (i.e. listening) without purpose (without creating economic value for yourself or anyone else) is a quiet rebellion against the system. Even if we all must eat, must all take part to some extent in society (conventional reality), we can still dive into the wider possibilities of freedom from coercion and wage labour when listening. 'People's freedom to live their own lives – in other words, freedom of mind – is best cultivated through purposeless activity.'[12] Listening composition (i.e. experimental music) eliminates the hierarchy of composer–performer–audience in favour of what Kondo calls 'a shared object of listening'.[13] Furthermore, when listening with openness from the standpoint of the hollow expanse, both the 'object' of listening (the sound, that listened-to) and the listening subject are themselves dissolved into the endlessly arising present of listening *now*.

Writing about urban walking in the tradition of Charles Baudelaire and Walter Benjamin's flâneur, Frédéric Gros points out three subversive aspects to the practice of aimless rambling amidst a sea of people who

[11] Kondo, *Homo audiens*, 78.

[12] Ibid., 80.

[13] Ibid.

are rushing about with purpose.[14] Firstly, by rejecting the purposeful directionality of the moving crowd, 'the stroller is *out of synch*' (it is notable that Gros chooses a rhythmic – i.e. musical – analogy), and thus is 'abstracted' from the masses without being excluded or distanced. This detachment allows for heterodox perception: the ability to see, hear and think differently. Secondly, the flâneur subverts the speed of the urban walker (the rush to get things done, almost always to the profit of someone other than oneself): 'The flâneur's body moves slowly, but his eyes dart about and his mind is gripped by a thousand things at once.'[15] Of course, the soundwalking flâneur's ears also probe the urban environment at a speed and distance that neither the legs nor the eyes can match. Thirdly, the flâneur notices things that would otherwise go unnoticed, and, more subversively, things that others would prefer to go unnoticed. Fourthly, 'the stroller does not consume and is not consumed' – they reject the capitalist imperative to promote at all times the circulation of money – but they also collect, 'capture', a 'drizzle of images stolen in the improbable instant of the encounter'.[16] Soundwalking, or any kind of aimless stravaiging, is in this way extremely democratic – there is no requirement for any equipment at all.

In the act of listening with attention in awareness of the contingent relational definition of all conventional phenomena, you can become aware of overlooked, quiet, oppressed sounds and voices – voices that some would prefer to go unnoticed. Beauty appears where you might not expect to find it, and, conversely, familiar sounds become defamiliarized, enchanted. Noise – 'random fluctuations that obscure or do not contain meaningful data or other information' (*OED*) – cannot exist in such a listening practice, since there is no meaningful (purposeful, communicative) data to be obscured. Consequently,

14 Frédéric Gros, *A Philosophy of Walking*, trans. John Howe (2009; London: Verso, 2014), 178*ff*.

15 Ibid., 179.

16 Ibid., 180.

conventionally 'noisy' sounds may well disclose themselves as fascinating, complex and polyphonic.

A listening practice devoid of intention is limitless in scope. As such, the unexpected sounds listened-to might include the voices and cries of the oppressed, nonhuman *and* human. Crossing back into the conventional world of communicative speech (while retaining the embodied knowledge of sound as limitlessly ambiguous, hollow, *yūgen*) – abiding in conventional reality while playing in the hollow – this kind of listening practice affords becoming a kind of anarchist-inflected politics of care. This could be care for the Other, a refusal to see people as categories, and dissolving of borders of all kinds – between human beings, between humans and nonhumans, sentient and non-sentient beings, between countries, races, religions and so on.[17] As David Graeber wrote, 'If artistic avant gardes and social revolutionaries have felt a particular affinity for one another's language and ideas, it appears to have been insofar as both have remained committed to the idea that the ultimate, hidden truth of the world is that it is something that we make, and could just as easily make differently.'[18] The linguistically defined conventional worlds that we all abide in are essentially hollow: as such, they are also infinitely malleable.

5.1.1 Pauline Oliveros's 'Native'

Pauline Oliveros (1932–2016) was a composer whose later work, from the late 1980s, centred around the idea of 'deep listening'. Earlier, for example in her collection of text scores *Sonic Meditations* (1971), she wanted her music to 'erase the subject/object or performer/audience relationship' and promote sonic communication 'among all forms

[17] On the ethical implications of what he calls 'minor acoustics', see Brandon LaBelle, 'Minor Acoustics: Sound Art, Relationality, and Poetic Listening', in *The Oxford Handbook of Sound Art*, ed. Jane Grant, John Matthias, and David Prior (Oxford: Oxford University Press, 2021), 453–70.

[18] David Graeber, *Revolutions in Reverse: Essays on Politics, Violence, Art, and Imagination* (London: Minor Compositions, 2011), 47.

of life'. She was 'especially interested in the healing power of Sonic Energy'.[19] Though there is a healing purpose to the *Meditations*, that comes from the process of sonic (and sometimes linguistic) communication within the community of meditators and among the wider human and nonhuman environment, leading to identifying as a part of something bigger than oneself. Similar to the practice of *suizen* (吹禅; literally breathing zen) – a practice of meditation while breathing through a shakuhachi – these *Sonic Meditations* are explicitly not music, although 'a kind of music occurs naturally' through the process of the meditations. In addition to filling the hollow between subject and object, performer and audience (there is no audience), these pieces also blur the border between spiritual – or healing – practice and music/sound work. Oliveros is a composer (and accordionist), but, as she herself says, the music which results from these text scores is only a 'welcome by-product'.[20]

Most of the *Sonic Meditations* require at least a few other people – they are 'intended for group work over a long period of time with regular meetings'[21] – and they were written for, dedicated to and first performed by the ♀ Ensemble. However, some of the text scores can be performed alone, and one of them can be interpreted as a soundwalk (though Oliveros does not use that then-recently coined word). That meditation (number V) is called 'Native'.

The score of 'Native' reads as follows: 'Take a walk at night. Walk so silently that the bottoms of your feet become ears.'[22] Most soundwalks which have grown out of the WSP and Westerkamp's conception of the genre centre on the *place* of the soundwalk. This is doubtlessly a result of the acoustic-ecological focus of the WSP: Soundwalking, as described by Schafer, originated as a tool to analyse the amount of sound (and

19 Pauline Oliveros, *Sonic Meditations* (Sharon, VT: Smith Publications, 1971), Introduction II.

20 Ibid., Introduction I.

21 Ibid.

22 Ibid., V.

noise pollution) in a particular, usually urban, built environment. 'Native', however, does not specify place in any way, but rather specifies the time: it must be performed at night. One presumes that this is a practical instruction to cultivate the sharpening of ears over the eyes. But it also affords having the effect of increasing the sense of *yūgen*, of the uncanny beauty that can arise in darkness and obscurity.

The ears, however, are not just the ears on your head, but 'the bottoms of your feet become ears' as well. Sound is, after all, vibration – waves of energy moving through the atmosphere, striking your eardrum and causing it to resonate sympathetically. Vibrations can move through other media than just air, and those that propagate via solid earth can be heard by contact microphones, as with Tsunoda's recordings of vibrations. They can also be felt as touch – hearing being merely a specific subset of touch. One possible interpretation, then, of Oliveros' soundwalk instruction is to be aware that all vibrations are sonic, and every part of your body, from the head to the toes, can hear – and in this soundwalk, you should attend to what you can hear with the whole body. Coupled with the imperative to 'walk so silently', this could also be an oblique reference to the famous John Cage story of the anechoic chamber, a place so quiet that Cage could only hear the sound of – perceive the vibrations within – his own body.

Another, Zen interpretation of this instruction is possible. In Dōgen's '*Keisei Sanshoku*' (渓声山色; Voices of the Valleys, Colours of the Mountains) fascicle, he says

> When you encounter a true teacher, you . . . hear with the body, you hear with the mind. To hear with the ear is commonplace, but to hear with the eye is not necessarily so. . . . See large and small buddhas as the voices of the valleys and colours of the mountains; this is liberation.[23]

To hear with the body, mind and eye, is to hear as a buddha, to hear from a place of liberation. Not only are all the sonic phenomena preaching

[23] Dōgen, *Shōbōgenzō*, 123–4; Dōgen, *Treasury*, 93. Translation modified.

the dharma, you are the sounds, and the sounds are you. In this hollow place, subject and object, listener and listened-to are undifferentiated. Ueda says that 'in passing through the linguistic world that is layered over the world, or in interrupting its worldly references, language reflects the limitless openness' of the hollow expanse.[24] Paradoxical language, such as that frequently used in Zen, but also in poetry, and in this specific instance, in Oliveros' soundwalk instruction that 'the bottoms of your feet become ears' is a concrete instance of hollow words, language which affords triggering a revelation of the truth of the hollow expanse grounding conventional reality.

5.2 Nature in Japanese philosophy and aesthetics

Nature, as a concept meaning all the physical phenomena of the world in total, is currently called *shizen* (自然) in Japanese. This is how the European concept of 'nature' (Ltn. *natura*) is translated. Although the word *shizen* (along with *jinen*, the same characters with a different, but related, meaning and pronunciation) pre-existed contact with European thought, this meaning (and pronunciation) of the word has been standard Japanese only since the late nineteenth century. Prior to that time, there were multiple different words which covered similar but not identical concepts. As words, sounds and other perceptions manifest things in conventional reality, what words we use – how we classify and categorize and signify phenomena of any quality – greatly affects how we are in the world. In considering how to think about 'nature' differently than its sense in capitalist-Modern societies, it is useful to first think about how what we call 'nature' was named (manifested) by different societies in the past.

The earliest recorded Japanese word for the abstract idea of nature is not a noun but the adverbial and adjectival *onozukara* (おのづから

[24] Ueda, 'Language in a Twofold World', 778.

or 自ら), a word which means 'of itself'. The same Chinese character can also be read as *mizukara*, meaning 'by myself' or 'from myself'.[25] As Hubertus Tellenbach and Kimura Bin point out, that these two concepts – that which exists of itself without human mediation and that which is by or from a human self – can be written with the same characters 'points towards a deeper insight by which [Japanese people] apprehend *Onozukara* and *Mizukara*, *nature* and *self*, as originating from the same common ground'.[26]

Shintō, an anachronistic name I will use for convenience to describe the worship of *kami* across the Japanese archipelago in and prior to the mediaeval period, is often characterized as a nature religion. To the extent that this is true (and almost every claim about 'Shintō', especially prior to the state Shintō which began to be consolidated in the early modern period, is both true and false, since it is an umbrella term covering diverse local practices across a vast geographical area) it is with regard to the *kami* themselves (Shintō 神道 literally translates as 'the way of the *kami*' 神の道). The word *kami* seems to have originally meant shadow (now *kage* 陰, 影, 蔭, 翳), and it, along with the related word in the language of the indigenous Ainu people of northern Japan *kamui*, are closely related with the word *kuma* (隈), meaning a hidden place.[27] *Kami* were thus originally spirits of the deep, dark, hidden places – beings which inhabited the forests, mountains and distant islands. In other words, *kami* were manifestations of the nonhuman world, and Shintō was a way for humans to appease these forces – indifferent at best, hostile at worst (recall the *kami* in Hitachi discussed in Section 3.2)

[25] These two words have the same suffix in older orthography, though in modern orthography *onozukara* is written 自ずから to distinguish the two words. Hayashi Ōki and Andō Chizuko, eds, *Kogorin* (Tokyo: Taishūkan, 1997).

[26] Hubertus Tellenbach and Kimura Bin, 'The Japanese Concept of "Nature"', in *Nature in Asian Traditions of Thought: Essays in Environmental Philosophy*, ed. J. Baird Callicott and Roger T. Ames (Albany: State University of New York Press, 1989), 154–5.

[27] Tadashi Ogawa, *Phenomenology of Wind and Atmosphere*, trans. Lorenzo Marinucci (Sesto San Giovanni: Mimesis International, 2021), 29–30.

– through offerings, song and dance. *Kagura* (神楽), ritualized music and dance still performed at shrines all over Japan, literally means entertainment for the *kami*, and is hypothesized to be one of the antecedents of nō.[28]

In lieu of a noun for nature as a whole, there were words in mediaeval Japan which used aspects of 'nature' as metonyms for all phenomena. These include grasses-trees-land-soil (*sōmokukokudo* 草木国土), '"mountains-rivers-grasses-trees" (*sansensōmoku* 山川草木) and "the interwoven variety [literally the 'forest web'] of the myriad phenomena" (*shinrabanshō* 森羅万象)'.[29] This latter image of a forest web is particularly interesting in relation to the metaphor of Indra's net, commonly used in Kegon Buddhism to concretely explain the idea of the universe as unimpeded interpenetration of phenomena and phenomena (*jiji muge hokkai*). All phenomena, each alive, each enacting buddha nature, each existing in its own positionality, nevertheless reflect all other phenomena, in a universe-wide web of interpenetrating reflections. As all phenomena are also impermanent (*mujō* 無常), this web is also constantly, dynamically in flux as different nodes of the web incessantly arise and are extinguished. The phenomenal universe, then, is an endlessly undulating, vibrating, resonating web of energies, all endowed with buddha nature. In the philosophy expounded by the Kegon sutra, if not by all Buddhist sects, the forest web of myriad phenomena would surely include living sound as well as the plants, animals and non-sentient phenomena such as rocks and waters.

Dōgen's Sōtō Zen also holds that all phenomena have buddha nature. For Dōgen, the landscape is of particular importance, with

[28] Benito Ortolani, *The Japanese Theatre: From Shamanistic Ritual to Contemporary Pluralism* (1990; rev. Princeton: Princeton University Press, 1995), 89*ff*. The etymology of *kagura* is believed to be *kam*(*u*) + *kura* (seat); Ibid., 13–14. This is the same *kura* which Takahashi Mutsuo speculates is the root of the final two syllables of *utamakura* (see Section 3.2).

[29] Bret W. Davis, 'Natural Freedom: Human/Nature Nondualism in Zen and Japanese Thought', in *The Oxford Handbook of Japanese Philosophy*, ed. Bret W. Davis, (Oxford: Oxford University Press, 2018), 705.

two of the most poetic and often quoted fascicles of his *Shōbōgenzō* concerning how humans interact with the non-sentient landscape. These are the '*Sansuikyō*' and the '*Keisei sanshoku*'. *Sansui*, comprised of two characters literally meaning mountain and water, means landscape in the sense of landscape painting. Already in the title (En. Landscape as Scripture) Dōgen is both referring to viewing nature through the lens of human art (conventional, anthropocentric view) and reading nature as a holy sutra (ultimate truth). It begins with the strong statement that 'In this very moment, the landscape actualizes the ancient Buddhist path', before proceeding to the discussion of the narrowness of anthropocentric perception, and thus the necessity of non-anthropocentric perception.[30]

In '*Keisei sanshoku*', whose title metonymically takes the sounds of the valley as the voice of Buddha and the colours (which can be understood as form) of mountains as his body, Dōgen discusses three cases of Chinese Zen practitioners who have had breakthroughs in their Buddhist practice while in nature. In the first case, lay practitioner and writer Sū Shì (蘇軾; Jp. So Shoku; 1037–1101), also known by his pen name Dōngpō (東坡; Jp. Tōba), became awakened when he heard the sound of a stream in the valley, hearing in a new and radically open manner. Dōgen comments that 'During past springs and autumns, Dōngpō had not seen or heard the mountains and waters. He saw and heard them for the first time that night.'[31] The second example concerns the scholar Xiāngyán Zhìxián (香嚴智閑; Jp. Kyōgen Chikan; d. 898) whose extensive book-learning was not sufficient to trigger awakening. Having burned his books and become a recluse, he is awakened while sweeping the path of his hut by the sound of a stone flying from his broom and striking a bamboo plant. Dōgen, also a poet, wrote a *waka* which makes a similar point, with the echoes of monkeys being the key aural image of awakening:

[30] See also Section 3.4.

[31] Dōgen, *Treasury*, 86. Translation modified.

> 谷のひびき峰になく猿たえだえにただこの経をとくとこそきけ[32]
> *tani no hibiki mine ni naku saru taedae ni tada kono kyō wo toku to koso kike*
> Valley ceaselessly echoing monkey cries from the mountaintops:
> listening only to this sutra.

Like the reflection of the moon in water, an echo of a sound is doubly empty; it is an empty mirroring of something empty to begin with. As Miranda Shaw points out, in interpreting this poem, 'to listen to an echo is to be reminded of the dependent co-arising of all phenomena. Therefore, metaphorically and literally, the monkey is delivering a profound discourse on impermanence and dependent origination.'[33] This is just one example of how, for Dōgen, nature is constantly espousing Buddhist truths, if only we are open enough to perceive them.

Dōgen's third example in '*Keisei Sanshoku*' is of the Zen Master Língyún Zhìqín (霊雲志勤; Jp. Reiun Shigon; n.d.), who was awakened by seeing peach blossoms in full bloom. Dōgen wants to emphasize that, for all three examples, while the trigger for each awakening was a natural sound, vision or possibly scent, it is only because each person was already practicing open perception that they could be so affected. When, and only when, 'you have true practice, then valley sounds and colours, mountain colours and sounds, all disclose the eighty-four thousand teachings of the Buddha.'[34] Perceiving nature with attention, and without intention, affords the possibility of a transformative experience. Emphasizing perceiving with openness and without restricting yourself to perceiving only what you already expect – what you have been taught to expect – in the fascicle '*Gyōbutsu igi*' (行仏威儀; The Behaviour of Practicing Buddhas) Dōgen recommends

32 Dōgen, 'Wakashū', 153.

33 Miranda Shaw, 'Nature in Dogen's Philosophy and Poetry', *The Journal Of The International Association Of Buddhist Studies* 8, no. 2 (1985): 124.

34 Dōgen, *Treasury*, 94. Translation modified.

going beyond conventional capacities to 'hear sounds with your entire eye and see colours with your entire ear'.[35]

Zenchiku, borrowing a phrase from Wèi Qìngzhī's (魏慶之; d.1272) *Shīrén yùxiè* (詩人玉屑; Jade Splinters of the Poets), encapsulates the relationship between the artist's intention and nature itself with Wèi's phrase 'images in the intent, intent in the images'.[36] In his late treatise *Rokurin kanjō hiki*, Zenchiku relates the 'images' to Buddhist forms (phenomena) and the conventional world, and the 'intent' to emptiness (hollowness) and absolute truth. In the highest level of artwork, then, the artist's intention and nature mutually interpenetrate, manifesting an artwork which expresses the twofold reality of the world.[37]

5.3 Soundwalking as practice

Soundwalking can be conceived of as a form of practice (*shugyō* 修行), or even perhaps Confucian ritual (Ch. *lǐ* 禮).[38] *Shugyō* can, in a Zen context, mean religious practices such as *zazen* (or *suizen*) meditation

[35] 満眼聞声、満耳見色 (*mangen monshō, manni kenshiki*). Dōgen, *Shōbōgenzō*, vol. 1, 167; Dōgen, *Treasury*, 269.

[36] 意中之景、景中之意 (*ichū no kei, keichū no i*). In Wèi's original meaning, the phrase refers to the subtle depth of poetic meaning which emotional expression imbues in a description of landscape, and reciprocally that a description of landscape imbues into the poem's emotional expression. *Zeami Zenchiku*, 171.

[37] Paul S. Atkins, *Revealed Identity: The Noh Plays of Komparu Zenchiku* (Ann Arbor: University of Michigan Center for Japanese Studies, 2006), 51–2.

[38] For an overview of Confucian ideas of self-cultivation of ethical and social skills through embodied, aesthetic, ritual practices such as martial arts, calligraphy and music, see: Geir Sigurðsson, 'Making More Sense: A Confucian-Hermeneutic Path to Aesthetics', *Journal East Asian Philosophy* (2024), especially §4.

Confucianism undoubtedly had an influence on early Chán (Jp. Zen) Buddhism, despite also having many philosophical disagreements. On Confucianism and Chán approaches to education see: Cheng Hsueh-Li, 'Confucianism and Zen (Ch'an): Philosophy of Education', Journal of Chinese Philosophy 12 (1985): 197–215.

For a comparative discussion of the role of silence in Confucianism, Daoism and Chán philosophies of education and cultivation see Li Lin, 'Teaching Beyond Words: "Silence" and its Pedagogical Implications Discoursed in the Early Classical Texts of Confucianism, Daoism and Zen Buddhism', Educational Philosophy and Theory 52, no. 7 (2020): 759–68.

or contemplating sutras, but can also refer to daily activities which are undertaken with regularity and follow a set pattern. These include all the daily activities needed to maintain the temple (e.g. cleaning the floors, tending to the garden), eating and cleaning oneself. In the *Shōbōgenzō*, in addition to philosophical reflections on Buddhist teaching, not only are there instructions for *zazen*, but also fascicles which Dōgen solely devotes to instructing the monks on how to 'Wash the Face' (*Senmen* 洗面) and 'Clean [Purify] the Body' (*Senjō* 洗浄). Furthermore, the first section of Dōgen's *Regulations for Eiheiji Temple* (*Eihei Shingi* 永平清規) called 'Instructions for the Monastery Cook' (*Tenzo Kyōkun* 典座教訓) is devoted to the importance of the cook and of the practice of cooking as an expression of ultimate reality (the hollow expanse).[39] Cooking, polishing floors, washing and going to the toilet all afford being conceived of as 'practice' in the sense of a regular activity which, if consistently practiced, will become absorbed into the 'self' and can be done unconsciously. The ability to consciously construct the so-called 'self' in this way is an illustration of the contingent emptiness of the 'self'.

Soundwalking – 'exposing our ears to every sound around us no matter where we are'[40] – can be such a practice. John Cage 'listen[ed] to [*4'33"*] every day', but not by sitting down and meditating on silence. Rather, he says, 'I turn[ed] my attention toward it. I realize that it's going on continuously. So, more and more, my attention, as now, is on it.'[41] Soundwalking is a specific form of realizing *4'33"*, but it is, perhaps more importantly, a ritual practice of opening the ears 'to every sound around us' while consciously limiting the amount of sound we ourselves make. If *4'33"* is a kind of meditation focussed on listening, then

[39] Kōshō Uchiyama Rōshi has written an entire book of commentary on this text: Dōgen and Kōshō Uchiyama Rōshi, *How to Cook Your Life*, trans. Thomas Wright (1983; Eng. trans. Boulder: Shambhala, 2005).

[40] Westerkamp, 'Soundwalking', 18.

[41] William Duckworth, 'Anything I Say Will Be Misunderstood: An Interview with John Cage', in *John Cage at Seventy-Five* (Lewisburg: Bucknell University Press, 1989), 21–2.

soundwalking is a kind of walking meditation (*kinhin* 経行) focussed on listening.[42] In the '*Zazen shin*' (坐禅箴; The Point of Zazen) fascicle of *Shōbōgenzō*, Dōgen says that *zazen* 'is not limited to sitting or lying down', and, quoting Dàhuì Zōnggǎo (大慧宗杲, Jp. Daie Sōkō; 1089–1163), that one should not become 'identified with [confined by] the sitting form'.[43] The forms of a soundwalk, then, can be similarly multifarious – of fluid motion, of nodes of stillness along a path of wayfaring, or of simply sitting. The important element in any given soundwalk is listening with attention, without intention. But for soundwalking to become a practice – a ritual – which can open up new versions of the 'self' – to discover 'one's own listening', in Westerkamp's words – and afford disclosing glimpses of ultimate reality, one indispensable element is regular repetition.

If a soundwalk is a music or sound composition, what is the score? A score for a soundwalk needs only to be some words, concepts and or images (on paper or, more likely, merely in the mind) which enable the work/walk to be re-performed and reinterpreted again and again. A map of the route, the meandering line which the rambler stravaigs, the set time of day the soundwalker departs, the set length of time they soundwalk, the pace or rhythm of their stride, are all conceivable as possible scores in this sense. Most mornings before I sit down to write or compose, provided it is neither too rainy or too hot, I soundwalk along the beach near my home for twenty minutes or so, following one of two routes. Already, this is quite a lot of detail for a text score, giving a relative time of departure (which is usually realized at about 7:15 in the morning), a duration, and a choice of two possible paths. Of course, before this very moment, I had not written this down as a 'work', since it has purely been my personal practice. Each practitioner or group of

[42] Bruce has proposed 'soundsitting' as a complementary practice to soundwalking, and this too could be included in the broader category of practices of listening meditation. Neil Spencer Bruce, 'Extending Soundwalking Practice: Soundsitting as an Inclusive and Complementary Method to Soundwalking', *Acoustics* 5, no. 3 (2023): 788–97.

[43] Dōgen, *Shōbōgenzō*, 236, 238; Dōgen, *Treasury*, 307–8.

practitioners – not being identified with/confined by any received or dictated form – can decide their own soundwalking methodology.

Cage turned his *attention* to the continuous sounds of the 'world worlding'.[44] All sound is life, and all sounds are alive; each sound – like each listener – is a golden phenomenal wave on the sea of ultimate hollow emptiness, and each sound – also like each listener – enacts buddha nature. In a soundwalk, the listener turns their attention to the continuously arising and extinguishing living sounds and sounds of life which surround us at all times and are generally ignored. It can be humbling, walking along a familiar path, to suddenly become aware of a small sound that you had never before noticed, or to register a previously unheard aspect or resonance or rhythm of a familiar sound, to encounter the ignored or oppressed as an equal – to viscerally know that that sound, in addition to whatever combination of factors set that sound in motion, is of no lesser value than the listener. In the first instance of pure experience there is neither listener to listened to, only listening. In the pure moment, when past and future (meaning time, which means rhythm) drops away, leaving only the radical now – the pure, unmediated experience – of listening and sounding, each sound is heard in a relation of equality with every other sound.

Like a *waki* in *mugen* nō, the soundwalker-*cum*-listener is a wayfarer who radically opens themself to a place and thence can be changed by that place. As in Zenchiku's highest level of nō, this awakening and humbling experience of interpenetration through attentive listening and landscape sounding can only be achieved with regular practice (though meditating with a purposeful goal is a sure way to not achieve it – it happens as it happens, through practice, but not because of practice).

[44] Carl Mika, Vanessa Andreotti, Garrick Cooper, Cash Ahenakew, and Denise Silva, 'The Ontological Differences Between Wording and Worlding the World', *Language, Discourse & Society* 8, no. 1(15) (2020): 17–32.

5.4 All sound is *yūgen*

The regular practice of opening yourself up to sound – listening with attention – through soundwalking or sound meditation will by definition result in hearing unexpected and surprising sounds, and in listening to the familiar in unexpected and surprising ways. It is because of the everyday familiarity of walking – especially, but not exclusively, a *practice* of walking – that the irruption of the sonic unfamiliar into your consciousness affords being perceived as hollow. If a sound suggestive of the hollow expanse can be 'listened out'[45] of this road which I walk down every, so might the hollow be lingering everywhere, in the silence of the world worlding, in music (both experimental and fictional), in poetry, in washing the face, in preparing vegetables for a salad,[46] and in everyday interactions between persons (human and nonhuman).

What makes a sound suggestive of the hollow expanse? This is, in some ways, a personal question, so a subjective answer, rooted in embodied experience, is all I can offer. But it would not do to avoid the question: pure experience – the dissolving of the subject-object relation into an interpenetration of pure sounding and pure listening – is necessarily pre-linguistic, since the categorization of phenomena into nameable things is an action of reflection that impinges on the hollow purity of the experience with conventional reality. But aesthetics is a form of communication and interpretation and cannot be pure experience; though rooted in embodied pure experience, it also must be put into the imperfect vessel of language in order to be shared with others.

One of the most memorable sonic experiences of my life came as I was soundwalking and field recording on Mount Katsuragi (葛城山, also pronounced Kazuraki) in Nara, on 2 March 2017. An *utamakura*

[45] Kondo, *Homo audiens*, 107*ff*.

[46] Knowles, 'Proposition'.

location associated both with being an origin place of Shugendō (修験道) ascetic mountain practice[47] and with the idea of interruption (interrupted or foreshortened love). This latter association came about because of the story concerning En no Gyōja (役小角; 634–701), the purported founder of Shugendō, who ordered a daemonic *kami* to build a stone bridge between the peaks of Mount Kazuraki and the nearby Mount Mitake, which they began but failed to complete.[48] I was there because of a project related to the poet-priestess Shokushi Naishinnō (式子内親王; 1149–1201), who had written:

> 知るらめや葛城山にゐる雲の立ちゐにかかるわが心とは
> *Shirurame ya Kazuraki-yama ni iru kumo no tachii ni kakaru waga kokoro towa*
> Does he know how like a cloud on Mount Kazuraki I rise and sit, and how I feel every time?[49]

While on the mountain top, I stopped and made a field recording for half an hour, during which I closed my eyes and listened intently to the early spring environs. I was surprised to hear, coming from behind me, the sound of heavy traffic, like one would hear from a not-too-distant highway. Surprised, I opened my eyes and whipped around, attempting to see from where – nearly a kilometre above sea level – the traffic sound could be coming. The thought of En no Gyōja's mythical bridge having been turned into a highway crossed my mind. Of course, I soon realized it was the wind, and my mind had misinterpreted – or, better, creatively interpreted – the white noise into a surreal, hollow experience blending place and mythology,

47 Shugendō is a syncretic religion focussed on ascetic practice in mountains. Founded in the seventh century, it draws on *kami* worship, folk beliefs, esoteric Buddhism and Daoism. In the middle ages, shugendō practitioners were said to be particularly attracted to beautiful young men. Sachi Schmidt-Hori, *Tales of Idolized Boys: Male-Male Love in Medieval Japanese Buddhist Narratives* (Honolulu: University of Hawai'i Press, 2021), 119*ff*.

48 Katagiri, *Utamakura*, 109–10.

49 Princess Shikishi, *String of Beads: Complete Poems of Princess Shikishi*, trans. Hiroaki Sato (Honolulu: University of Hawai'i Press, 1993), 46. Shikishi is an alternate pronunciation of Shokushi's name.

ancient history and current reality (intrusion of the built environment even into alpine locations; I had been somewhat despondent about the ropeway access to the peak and the banality of the nearby touristic mountain lodge). All of this, a palimpsestic layering of hollow, surreal fiction onto sensed reality, was facilitated by the inherent ambiguity of the sense of hearing.

Whether a sound is intended as musical, linguistic/communicative or purposeless, from the point of view of a listener, a sound which affords suggesting the hollow is one that is ambiguous, unexpected, unfamiliar or obscure. Drew Daniel states that 'all sound is queer'.[50] Eve Kosofsky Sedgwick writes that 'one of the things . . . "queer" can refer to [is] the open mesh of possibilities, gaps, overlaps, dissonances and resonances, lapses and excesses of meaning when the constituent elements of anyone's gender, of anyone's sexuality aren't made (or can't be made) to signify monolithically', but also that much queer studies research 'can't be subsumed under gender and sexuality at all'.[51] Daniel writes of a particular 'queer encounter with sound':

> In the night, I am roused from dreams by a collective screaming. The night is torn by cries that pour forth from a permeable darkness. Where do these hidden choruses begin? Who makes up the we in which I am now entangled against my will? Pulling at the curtains to look out into the street I see that the bare tree in front of the hospital suddenly has leaves again. Adjusting, coming back to consciousness, I look again and see that they are not leaves, but gigantic crows, whose croaks and shrieks have stopped me from sleeping, again. Of course, it's only the birds. The sound of the world shrinks back, tamed, relocated within a bestiary, taxonomized, found. . . .
>
> As I see and recognize and know and name the mysterious screaming as 'crow sound', I become a second Adam, asserting dominion over creation through the sorrowful descent into language. But I wish to rewind to the moment of confusion, the primordial chaos in which

[50] Drew Daniel, 'All Sound is Queer', *The Wire* 333 (2011): 42–7.

[51] Eve Kosofsky Sedgwick, *Tendencies* (Durham: Duke University Press, 1993), 8–9.

> the sound is within me and I am ignorant, in the dark, traversed by vibrations I cannot yet place, cannot yet hear as the sound of crows.[52]

The 'primordial chaos' he relates here is the ambiguous and obscure irrupting into his conventional reality. That it can be identified and tamed – and soon is – is not meaningful in the initial chaotic instant of pure experience, 'in which the sound is within' him – has interpenetrated with him – and has, through the obscurity lent by the veil of drowsiness and darkness, resulted in a hollow experience of sound. Daniel also describes the crow sound as a 'sound of non-communication and purposelessness',[53] labels which could apply to all music. Daniel, in *listening* the crows' cries *out* of the sound of the world worlding, is listening to the world musically (at least, 'musically' in the sense of non-fictional experimental music listening).

The overlap between sounds which can be interpreted as ambiguous, obscure, veiled and/or queer leads us back to *yūgen*, the primary aesthetic feature of nō. *Yūgen*, according to Zenchiku in his *Yūgen Sanrin* (幽玄三輪, Yūgen and the Three Upper Circles) treatise, is buddha nature.[54] As all phenomena in the heavens and earth, and in all realms, enact buddha nature inherently as they are (though not all phenomena realize their inherent buddha nature – per Dōgen, one needs to practice to manifest one's buddha nature), all phenomena (including sounds) also have *yūgen*.[55] But *yūgen* is a different kind of quality than buddha nature. A paradoxical and ineffable quality, *yūgen* is omnipresent but difficult to realize (for Zenchiku it is the supreme achievement of long practice; Zeami, in a treatise addressed to Zenchiku, says it is 'the most difficult' performance style[56]). Zenchiku, in the *Shidōyōshō*: 'The

[52] Daniel, 'All Sound'.

[53] Ibid.

[54] *Zeami Zenchiku*, 377.

[55] *Cf.* Matsuoka, who reads Zenchiku's 'pan-yūgen-ism' (*han'yūgenron* 汎幽玄論) as a last gasp of a centuries-long tradition that heralded the end of yūgen as a generative concept in the arts. Matsuoka, 'Yūgen ga enjaku suru toki', 40.

[56] *Zeami Zenchiku*, 194.

purity of gold is also yūgen. An untarnished mirror is also *yūgen*. The power of a sword is also *yūgen*. Stones and rocks are also *yūgen*. All the daemons and spirits are *yūgen*'.[57] It is the unaffected beauty of a young man, and also flowers blooming on an old tree. It is both something you perceive in the other (something nonhuman; something fictionally, surreally hollow; a supreme actor's performance), but also something you need to cultivate in yourself through practice. It defies linguistic description,[58] but also you – anyone – should know it when you see it.

Nishitani's description of the 'luminous scenery of Okunōtō' shows how the hollow can shine through in a landscape. It is a landscape that many people would describe as beautiful, but the practiced perception of Nishitani sensed a deeper hollowness through and beyond and within it. The 'soundscape' offers an infinite variety of potentially *yūgen* sounds, but practice in attentive listening is needed to perceive them. Our ears are always open, and sounds are penetrating our bodies every instant of our lives. But it's up to us to give them attention, to notice the *inter*penetration. All sounds are queer; all sounds are alive; all sounds enact buddha nature; all sounds afford being perceived as *yūgen*.

5.4.1 Jo Kondo's *Summer Days*

Summer Days (1970)[59] for clarinet and field recording is a one-off piece in Kondo's catalogue, a true experiment written in his third year of university, aged twenty-two. It stands out as one of the very first pieces written for unmanipulated field recording (as opposed to *musique concrète*) and instruments, written only one year after Schafer, Westerkamp, Barry Truax (b. 1947), and others inaugurated the World Soundscape Project in Vancouver.

[57] Ibid., 419.

[58] Zeami in *Kyūi* writes of the supreme level of acting, which he calls 'the style of the wondrous flower', that it 'obstructs the way of language, and extinguishes the operations of the mind'. *Zeami Zenchiku*, 174.

[59] Jo Kondo, *Mr.Bloomfield, His Spacing* (Tokyo: ALM Records, ALCD-13), track 3.

The story of its creation is very simple: having just purchased a tape recorder for the first time, he was testing it out by recording through the window of his childhood home in Kamakura. As Kondo relates it:

> listening to those sounds I recorded, the sound itself was somehow very musical, so, I thought, why not just present the sounds recorded as they were, which itself can already be a very musical experience. And I edited – not modulated or manipulated – but somehow edited the sounds I recorded, and I wrote *Summer Days* and presented it as my own work. And, a few years after I made this piece, I encountered Luc Ferrari's *presque rien* (1970) which came from the same year! I was very surprised, but at the same time very glad, because somehow I got the feeling that what I was doing was not totally wrong. Someone else was doing the same thing. It was a very good feeling.[60]

This is obviously not a soundwalk. However, as a listener using technology to mediate (to other, to queer) the experience of listening to the familiar, the experience Kondo describes that led up to the composition of *Summer Days* is quite like a fast-tracked version of the practice – the repetitive ritual – of soundwalking leading to a revelatory sonic experience. Like a soundwalker stravaiging a well-worn path, Kondo was in an environment he knew intimately. The act of field recording functioned as a trigger to listening attentively to the sounds that the brain unconsciously filters from our conscious perception (see Section 4.2.1), but the practice of attentive listening can train anyone's ears to hear more openly. As Kondo listened back to the recording, he heard it as music: he *listened* music *out* of the environmental sounds. Furthermore, he also listened out a hollow place in the sounds in which a clarinet part might manifest.

The piece remains incredibly fresh and vibrant, while at the same time being a non-fictional document of a 1970 sonic environment which no longer exists. Listening to it in 2025, it feels simultaneously present (as it is – the sound waves emanating from the speakers exist

[60] Jamieson, 'Varje ljud'.

in the same place as my ears, and my body) and old, from a time before I was born. All field recording – especially perhaps when a live instrument is playing with the pre-recorded sound – can exhibit heterochronicity, audibly inhabiting two different temporal places at once, the time of the recording being listened to now (past-in-the-present: the *shite*'s temporality) and the time of the listener/performer being interpenetrating with the recording (present-in-the-past: the *waki*'s temporality). The temporal complexity is increased in *Summer Days* since the tape of the field recording has been lost. Because it currently cannot be performed live, there are two distinct pasts simultaneously playing out into the present, both of which are irretrievable. A sense of nostalgia – and of the impermanence of things – pervades the listening experience of the piece today, though in essence it remains a document of the experimental listening practice of an incredibly inventive young composer whose explorations took him down a different (almost entirely concert music) path.

5.5 Listening out

Experimental listening is listening with attention rather than intention – acting as a good host for sounds, inviting sounds in rather than accosting and forcing them into your *basho* – and thence *listening out* those sounds which present themselves to you as guests rather than as captive, manipulable material. In a pure experience of experimental listening – where both the listener and the listened-to dissolve into a unity of sounding and listening – both the listener and listened-to share the roles of host and guest, each acting with grace towards the other.

As a practice, experimental listening is applicable to all situations: soundwalking, experimental music, meditation – but also listening to the quieter, ignored voices of those oppressed in socio-political situations in which you are also enmeshed, and to the nonhuman, nonsentient voices calling out with alarm using signs, symbols and hollow language that humans are somewhere between poor at and incapable of understanding. One of the great innovations of the Mahāyāna schools of Buddhism is the idea that the endless cycle of life and death (Sk. *saṃsāra*) is non-dually identical with nirvāṇa (*shōji-soku-nehan* 生死即涅槃). Awakening is not a ticket out of the cycle of life and death; it is a deeper understanding of this reality, as well as the ability and the responsibility to both improve this reality and help others achieve awakening. To the extent that experimental, non-fictional listening practice – wherever it is practiced – is a kind of listening meditation, those who have a profound awakening experience likewise have a responsibility to help others (because there are no true others, because the self is merely a hollow simulacrum, a sum total of all the phenomena in the universe reflected through your subjectivity) achieve a similar understanding, and allow each of the myriad phenomena to sound out from their own subject position while not masking the sounds of other phenomena.

6

Zenchiku and the promise of non-anthropocentric art

生きとし生けるもの、いづれか歌を詠まざりける
iki toshi ikeru mono, izureka uta wo yomazari keru
Every living thing, without exception, composes poetry.[1]

—Ki no Tsurayuki (紀貫之; *c.* 872–*c.* 945),
kana preface to the *Kokin wakashū*

Konparu Zenchiku's words and ideas have permeated this text, as his thought has permeated and altered mine for more than a decade. Though there are many aspects of Zenchiku's philosophical and artistic practice which are worth bringing into discussion with contemporary thinkers and artists, one which has been especially liberating for me has been the freedom with which he treats his source materials. Whether citing Chinese classics, the earliest mythological and historical texts in Japanese – the *Kojiki* (古事記, 712) and *Nihonshoki* (日本書紀, 720) – Buddhist texts, or the writings of his mentor and father-in-law Zeami, Zenchiku is not shy about repurposing previous authors' ideas and phrases to align with what he wants to say. Through Kegon Buddhist ideas of interpenetration and dependent origination, or allegoresis (the idea that homophonous words, or written Chinese characters sharing the same elements, implies identity or

[1] Klein, *Dancing the Dharma*, 69.

relationship[2]), Zenchiku discovered a web of interrelations which is fascinatingly complex and esoteric, if not always matching Modern academic standards of exegesis or citation. Noel Pinnington calls this 'creative misreading'.[3] Given the negative connotation of 'misreading' in Pinnington's formulation, I prefer (perhaps in a similarly oblique borrowing) Donald Landes' term for the phenomenologist Maurice Merleau-Ponty's reading practice: 'reading as expression'.[4] In alignment with Jo Kondo's practice of listening as 'listening out', we might also use 'reading out' to describe a Zenchiku-like practice of reading in the knowledge that each reader will subjectively take into themselves different aspects or meanings of any given text (Landes also uses the term '*exscribe*' for Merleau-Ponty's method,[5] of which 'read out' might itself be an exscription[6]).

This entire book has been a reading out of the tens, if not hundreds or thousands, of philosophers and artists whose work has left some trace in my brain and/or in my notebooks over my life. But that is especially true of this chapter, which will focus first on Zenchiku's theories and treatises, thence his nō. Towards the end, I will use some of my interpretations of Zenchiku's ideas to interpret artworks in very different temporal and geographical and generic worlds than Zenchiku's own.

2 According to Klein, '[i]t is evident from *Meishukushū* that Zenchiku believed in the signifying power of signs, that is, that the linguistic/symbolic relation of signifier and signified is not arbitrary, but motivated, and that homonyms and graphs can therefore be analysed to reveal hidden identities' and that he 'assumed that such associative identifications, when properly understood, conveyed something important about the true nature of reality: specifically, that associative identifications were a legitimate basis for the efficacy of rituals performed in connection with sarugaku noh'. Ibid., 90, 82.

3 Pinnington, *Traces in the Way*, 99*ff*.

4 Donald Landes, *Merleau-Ponty and the Paradoxes of Expression* (London: Bloomsbury, 2013), 37*ff*.

5 Ibid., 40.

6 Another post-Modern Western way of framing this kind of expressive reading out is 'queering', which I have explored in relation to Zenchiku's play *Mekari*: Daryl Jamieson, 'Zenchiku's Mekari: Staging Ambiguous and Hollow Worlds', *Humanities* 14 (2025): 113.

6.1 Zenchiku's treatises

It is inevitable that a few thousand-word summary of a creative artist and aesthetic theoretician's lifelong body of intellectual work will result in elisions and simplifications. My aim here is to flesh out some of the theories and ideas that have been alluded to in the first five chapters, and especially those which I have found generative in thinking about experimental music – and the place of 'difficult' art in society. I want to immediately flag at the start the somewhat surprisingly large body of work related to Zenchiku specifically in English for those who are intrigued and want to dive deeper: Arthur H. Thornhill's *Six Circles, One Dewdrop: The Religio-Aesthetic World of Konparu Zenchiku* focusses on the spiritual and syncretic religious influences on Zenchiku's earliest treatises; Mark Nearman's translation and interpretation of most (though not all) of Zenchiku's treatises over a series of four articles in *Monumenta Nipponica* under the title 'The Visions of a Creative Artist'; Paul Atkin's *Revealed Identity: The Noh Plays of Komparu Zenchiku* focusses on the plays first and foremost, but with copious reference to Zenchiku's thought; Noel Pinnington's *Traces in the Way: Michi and the Writings of Komparu Zenchiku* offers a more materialist analysis of the social context into which Zenchiku emerged and practiced; and Susan Blakeley Klein's *Dancing the Dharma: Religious and Political Allegory in Japanese Noh Theater* looks at allegory and allegoresis in Japanese mediaeval poetic and theatrical practice in general, with several chapters devoted to analysing both Zenchiku's theory and practice.[7]

Zenchiku's most developed conceptual framework for nō aesthetics is his *Six Circles One Dewdrop*. Like the Ten Ox Pictures (see Section 2.5) which had likely influenced it, *Rokurin ichiro* is a

[7] Principal Japanese sources for this section include the original texts by Zenchiku edited by Omote Akira and Katō Shūichi (*Zeami Zenchiku*, 323–424), and two books about Zenchiku: Takahashi Yūsuke, *Zenchiku Nōgakuron no sekai* (Tokyo: Keio University Press, 2014); and Nakazawa Shin'ichi, *Seirei no ō* (2003; repr. Tokyo: Kodansha, 2018).

series of drawings – six in Zenchiku's case – enclosed in circles (see Figures 6.1 and 6.2). In the earliest treatises, the textural explanations appended to each drawing are quite short, but these progressively get longer and more elaborated in subsequent developments of the framework. The vision of the six circles and one dewdrop was bestowed on Zenchiku by Sumiyoshi Daimyōjin, a *kami* associated with poetry.[8] The vision consists of:

1. *jurin* (寿輪) The circle of life (an empty circle)
2. *shurin* (竪輪) The circle of arising (a single vertical line bisecting the circle)
3. *jūrin* (住輪) The circle of abiding (a short vertical line)
4. *zōrin* (像輪) The circle of phenomenal forms (mountains, rivers, birds in constant flux – nature naturing, the world worlding)
5. *harin* (破輪) The circle of breaking (four straight lines extending beyond the edges of the circle dividing the circle into eight even wedges)
6. *kūrin* (空輪) The circle of emptiness (an empty circle)
   ichiro (一露) The one dewdrop (a sacred sword)[9]

The original vision was written down and shared with three scholars of three different traditions, presumably in order to help interpret the ambiguous oracle. These scholars were the Kegon abbot Nittō Shamon Shigyoku (入唐沙門志玉; 1383–1463), the Confucian scholar Ichijō

[8] *Zeami Zenchiku*, 412. See also Klein, *Dancing*, 87. Zenchiku claims to have received the vision on the thirteenth day of the ninth month, but he does not specify a year. Nearman postulates that the vision occurred after the death of Zeami in 1443 and before the spring of 1444. Nearman, 'Visions', Part 1, 235. If we accept both Zenchiku's and Nearman's accounts, that would date the vision to the thirteenth day of the ninth lunar month (19 October in the solar calendar) of 1443.

[9] *Ichiro* is decidedly not the 'seventh' in a series, but is an image of the interpenetration of all six circles. In the spirit of allegoretic readings of homonyms, Atkins references Buddhism scholar Tokiwa Gishin's (常盤義伸) insight that the *ro* (露) of *Rokurin ichiro* can be read not just as 'dewdrop' but also as 'exposure' or 'disclosure': Atkins, *Revealed Identity*, 22. This reading means that the function of the dewdrop/sword is to cut through all dualisms and disclose the truth that the hollow grounds everything. In Buddhist terms, 'all phenomena are Truth, just as they are' (*shohō jissō* 諸法実相), a phrase Zenchiku uses in his play *Bashō* (芭蕉).

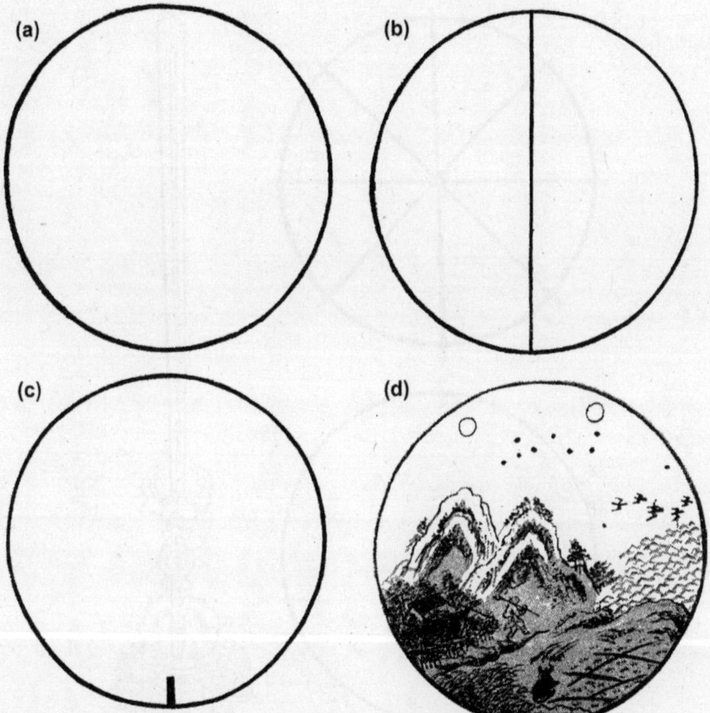

Figure 6.1 A *jurin* (The circle of life), b *shurin* (The circle of arising), c *jūrin* (The circle of abiding), d *zōrin* (The circle of phenomenal forms).

Kaneyoshi (一条兼良; 1402–81) and the Zen monk and poet Nankō Sōgen (南江宗沅; 1387–1463). Their comments and interpretations were woven into the initial versions of the treatise, though Zenchiku thereafter continued to develop and refine his own interpretations over a period of around two decades.

At the level of nō performance, the first three circles relate to the rhythmic structure *jo-ha-kyū* (序破急), which Zeami borrowed (*read out*) from *gagaku* (雅楽; orchestral music of the imperial court). The *jurin* is the preparation (mental envisioning), the *shurin* is breathing in (building anticipation and preparing the body for movement or vocal production), the *jūrin* is the action (decisive action: the note sung, the

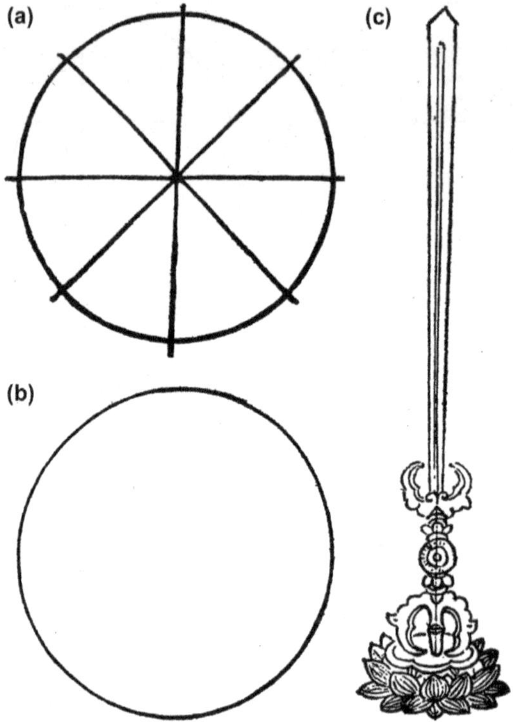

Figure 6.2 A *harin* (The circle of breaking), b *kūrin* (The circle of emptiness), c *ichiro* (One dewdrop).Images by Konparu Zenchiku, from *Rokurin Ichiro no Hichū* (Bunshō manuscript). In *Zeami Zenchiku*, 383–94.

body moved). The second set of three circles are more abstract qualities of performance: The *zōrin* is *monomane* (物真似; mimesis), the imitation of forms which is the basis of nō acting; the *harin* is the master actor whose training has become second nature and retreated into the unconscious (forgetting the self, in Dōgen's terms) which allows a new freedom in expression; the *kūrin* is the ultimate expression of *yūgen*, the return to youthful expression in an older, experienced master (new flowers budding on an ancient tree). Zenchiku uses the phrase *kōko kyakurai* for this 'return', a coinage of Zeami's which derives from the Buddhist term *kyakurai*, meaning to return to the conventional world after having achieved awakening (as in the final three cyclical circles of the Ten Ox Pictures).

To read these six circles in the context of twenty-first-century experimental listening practice, the first three would relate to the transition between passive hearing and conscious listening. The *jurin* is the ground of the hollow expanse, sounds sounding purposelessly and continuously whether we notice them or not. The *shurin* is turning your attention to the sounds. The *jūrin* is the meditative state of listening. The second trio of circles would be about what happens once the listener is abiding in the *jūrin* zone. The *zōrin* is listening to the sounds themselves without interpretation, imposition or manipulation. The *harin* is the pure experience of forgetting the self, dissolving the subject and object into an interpenetrative state of sounding and listening just as they are. The *kūrin* is the hollow expanse itself: identical in its emptiness to the *jurin*, but now we are conscious of the hollow expanse grounding both ourselves as listeners and the sounds as sounds. *Ichiro* serves as a non-dual frame around the entire process, reminding us that whether we are listening – or engaged in any other daily or artistic activity – or not, the hollow expanse grounds everything in conventional reality, and that every thing and every action is a phenomenon reflecting and interpenetrating every other phenomenon in the universe.

It is also worthwhile to interpret Zenchiku's circles as the life cycle of a sound, whether that is specifically a sound produced by a nō performer or any sound anywhere. From hollow silence (*jurin*), a sound arises into life (*shurin*). The sound is held, or sustained for a certain period of time, expressing its existence as a sound (*jūrin*). As all phenomena are alive and continuously in flux, some aspect of what we – from our human perspective – perceive as 'a' sound is constantly manifesting in new and subtly different forms (*zōrin*), whether this is changing amplitude or timbral quality, or simply the repeating wave forms that we perceive as pitch (e.g. 884 reiterations per second for an A_5). Sound – among the most ephemeral of phenomena – will soon die away (*harin*), either by modulating into a different sound or by returning to silence (*kūrin*). It is also notable that this understanding of the life cycle of a single sound, as exemplified by the second to fifth circles mirror one of the most common ways that the programmers of electronic synthesizers analysed and construed the development of each note. This method is generally known by its abbreviation AHDSR, which stands for Attack (akin to *shurin*); Hold (*jūrin*); Decay (*zōrin*); Sustain; Release (*harin*). The Sustain section of AHDSR does not have a correlative in Zenchiku's theory because while sustaining (without changing) a single sound is theoretically (artificially) possible with electronics, it is not realizable by human musicians or by any 'natural' sound. This correlation between how musical tones can be synthesized and Zenchiku's understanding of how sounds are produced shows that while Zenchiku's writings might be mystical in inspiration and esoteric in expression, he nonetheless has a deep, practical understanding of sound, and the *Rokurin ichiro* framework can also be interpreted as a practical framework for musicians and actors.[10]

In the earliest of Zenchiku's treatises (*Rokurin ichiro no ki* 六輪一露之記), he refers to the *jurin* as both the 'wellspring of *yūgen* in song and dance [i.e. nō performance] and a vessel in which the audience's feelings develop'.[11] That the hollow expanse of Buddhist emptiness is the source of *yūgen* – both an ideal of ephemeral, youthful beauty, but also complex, paradoxical, ambiguous obscurity – is perhaps unsurprising. The hollow encompasses all phenomena, even those which are impossible or inconceivable in the conventional world. The idea of the vessel is more generative, and more resonant with Ueda's idea of the 'hollow' as a new conception of emptiness. The empty (hollow) vessel as a metaphor for human potential has a venerable history in East Asia, stretching back to Kŏngzĭ's (孔子; Jp. Kōshi; also known as Confucius) *Analects* (*Lúnyǔ* 論語; Jp. *Rongo*). Zeami, in his *Yūgaku shudō fūken*, quotes this passage of the *Analects*. He writes that

[10] Or, as Klein might rejoin, a 'striking feature of the *Rokurin ichiro* texts is how abstract they are, and how resistant to interpretation—or rather how easy it is to project a variety of quite different interpretations onto them'. Klein, *Dancing*, 89.

[11] '歌舞幽玄之根源、見風聞曲而成㆑感之器也。' *Zeami Zenchiku*, 324.

a 'vessel' in this sense is Buddhist emptiness, and equates a masterful nō performer to a 'vessel'.[12] Zeami says that the master – a vessel of emptiness – has an intention[13] to manifest phenomena first in his mind and thence can manifest through his body on stage. The master actor as a hollow vessel can conjure up phenomena out of that emptiness. Zenchiku, however, puts his image of emptiness as vessel first in the series – not at a place of mastery, but as an attribute of all. Prior to being aware of our creative ability – our buddha nature – and prior to being able to effectively use it, it is still latently present in us. We are all a hollow vessel through which the hollow expanse can manifest phenomena; we all have the potential to express *yūgen*.

Meishukushū, Zenchiku's last treatise, is surely his most esoteric, perhaps the most esoteric and difficult to interpret of all nō texts.[14] In this text, Zenchiku attempts to allegorically identify Okina (翁), the old man of nō and the central figure in the proto-nō ritual piece *Okina*, with Sumiyoshi Daimyōjin, Kasuga Daimyōjin (春日大明神), the *kami* of Miwa (三輪) and Ise (伊勢) and the *kami* of the sun (and imperial progenitor) Amaterasu-ōmikami (天照大御神), as well as human figures such as the *waka* poet Narihira, and the semi-mythical Hata no Kawakatsu (秦河勝), purportedly the founder of the Konparu lineage (and thus a direct link to Zenchiku himself and his own artistic inheritance). There are many more figures from myth and history which Zenchiku claims to be non-dually identified with Okina, so much so that Nakazawa Shin'ichi (中沢新一) calls this an 'Okina monism'.[15] Pinnington sees this attempt to root the Konparu school in a mythical past and a present principally concerned with performing at religious institutions in Nara as a reactionary legitimizing strategy on the part of Zenchiku, in

12 Ibid., 166–7.

13 Here, Zeami is referring to the same quotation from Wèi Qìngzhī's *Shīrén yùxiè* – 'images in the intent' – that Zenchiku would also later use (see Section 5.2).

14 One reason for its relative impenetrability might be because the version we have is a draft, either because it was never completed (it was written at or near the end of Zenchiku's life) or the completed version has been lost. Nakazawa, *Seirei*, 149.

15 Ibid., 196.

contradistinction to the 'avant-garde' of Zeami and his father Kan'ami who had reduced or eliminated performances of *Okina* and principally performed for secular patrons and public audiences in Kyoto.[16]

Meishukushū is undoubtedly more theoretical, more philosophical (Nakazawa calls it the first work of structuralism in the Japanese language[17]), and less practical for the practice of music or theatre than any other text by Zenchiku. However, if Kan'ami and Zeami represent the modernizing forces of art in the service of capital (the pre-Modern equivalent of the market-driven classical composition identified by Marianna Ritchey[18]), perhaps Zenchiku's spiritual monist approach, rooted in tradition and a deep understanding of practice leading to freedom, is its experimental, non-fictional foil. If this slightly overstates the substantive differences between the two – Zeami and Zenchiku are more alike than different, Zenchiku treated Zeami as a mentor in most aspects of nō, and Zeami eventually backtracked on his abandonment of the traditional spiritual duties of the *sarugaku* nō troupes[19] – there is something to this small but real difference. After all, seen from outside the world of contemporary music, it's not as if there is a huge difference between experimental music and avant-garde music either.

6.2 Zenchiku's hollow worlds

My continually renewing interest in Zenchiku and his body of work is based on many factors, but two are of principal importance with regard to experimental listening and creation. One is his dramatization of humans in and as part of 'nature' in the sense it was understood in his time. In this, his work is in harmony with Zeami's. The other is his

16 Pinnington, *Traces*, 215.

17 Nakazawa, *Seirei*, 163.

18 Ritchey, *Composing Capital*.

19 Pinnington, *Traces*, 215.

resistance to Kan'ami and Zeami's secularization of nō, and what that means for the structure of his plays and the role of their performers.

In his treatises Zenchiku 'seems to regard the actor as a mere part of the vast universe, a conduit through which cosmic energies flow'.[20] The focus on ritual and appeasement of the *kami* appears to take precedence over the appeasement of the audience (though it is assumed that the audience will enjoy and hopefully receive spiritual benefit from viewing the performance). It is not a stretch to see a relationship between these characteristics and, say, Morton Feldman's approach ('I don't push the sounds around') or John Cage's ('The purpose of music is to sober and quiet the mind, thus making it susceptible to divine influences'[21]).

This focus on the spiritual and ritualistic aspect of performance – which is apparent not only in Zenchiku's theory but also in his practice – may come from some knowledge or speculation about the antecedents of nō. Zenchiku wrote about his putative ancestor, Hata no Kawakatsu, as the originator of the art of *sarugaku* nō in Japan, so he was clearly aware of and interested in this history. But how much he knew versus what he merely wanted to be true is a matter of speculation. For contemporary scholars, too, there is no agreement about what the principal artistic and dramatic forms and styles influenced the development of nō, and to what degree. But there are certainly explicit references to *kagura*, dance and music performances for *kami* which originated in shamanic possession rituals, in nō plays – including in Zenchiku's *Tatsuta* (龍田). And though there are no direct mentions in Zenchiku's treatises or plays, *jushi* (呪師) are thought to have been exorcists and public spiritual healers connected to Buddhist temples who did perform, according to historical records, with *sarugaku* performers.[22] Ortolani points out that

[20] Atkins, *Revealed Identity*, 47.

[21] John Cage, 'Autobiographical Statement' (John Cage Trust, 1990), johncage.org/autobiographical_statement.html.

[22] Benito Ortolani, 'Shamanism in the Origins of the Nō Theatre', *Asian Theatre Journal* 1, no. 2 (1984): 166–90. For a general discussion of the origins of nō, see Noel John Pinnington, *A New History of Medieval Japanese Theatre: Noh and Kyōgen from 1300 to 1600* (Cham: Palgrave Macmillan, 2019), Chapter 2.

> the *waki* role is often that of a monk because it derives from the role of the ascetic who, in many shamanistic rituals, induces the *miko*'s [巫女][23] divine possession. Honda [Yasuji (本田安次)] notes also that the *waki* was originally a flute player, the flute being the instrument used to bring about the descent of the god (*kamioroshi* [神下ろし]). The two parts of the classical ghost [*mugen* nō] plays are modeled on the incantation/conjuration and the actual possession of a medium resulting from the incantation—corresponding to the first act—and the apparition of the god, ghost, or demon in true form in the second act . . . .
>
> *Nō* music and *kakegoe* ([掛け声] the strange, guttural sound of the drummers' voices) have been traced to shamanistic rituals. The drums are traditional Japanese trance-inducing instruments; the flute, as mentioned before, is an instrument for conjuring the descent of the spirits; and the *kakegoe* are part of the invitation to the gods to manifest themselves.[24]

Thus we see that, for some scholars at least, there is a strong – if ultimately unprovable – link between nō and *kagura*, and thus shamanism and spirit possession of some kind. Whatever we might want to read out of Zenchiku's indisputable interest in spirituality and the history of nō (specifically the history of his own, the oldest, troupe), his resistance to the secularization of nō – if not necessarily in nō's on-stage themes, but in the focus on patronage and the human audience in what had only recently become a cash-based society[25] – was surely rooted in a sense that something valuable was being stripped away from the art.

One aspect of how Zenchiku's nō plays express his spiritual values is that they tend to avoid development and catharsis, dramatically or musically. The *shite* – unlike most of Zeami and others' *mugen* nō spirits

[23] *Miko* were originally female shamans. Their role gradually evolved into Shintō shrine maidens who perform music and dance.

[24] Ortolani, *Japanese Theatre*, 91–2.

[25] Pinnington, *New History*, 12–15.

who are attached to this world and achieve release at the end of the play – often are in the same state of limbo at the end as they are at the beginning: Both *Nonomiya* (野宮) and *Teika* (定家) end with the *shite* retreating back into their grave, unable to free themselves from attachment to this world. In terms of rhythm, Zenchiku's plays tend not to end with the relatively fast-paced rhythms of a climactic dance which are very common in nō and is implied in the basic *jo-ha-kyū* structure of the genre, but after the fastest-paced dance returns to the slowest type of congruent song (*ōnori*) to end the performance with a similarly broad rhythm as was at the start.[26] These returns to the start are aesthetic expressions of *kōko kyakurai*, and mirror the first and sixth circles in his *Six Circles One Dewdrop*. They show that the idea of 'progress' is an illusion (we can anachronistically read out of this a critique of Modernity's 'myth of progress'), illustrating instead the prevalent mediaeval Japanese Buddhist idea that opposites are non-dual reflections of each other.

Nakazawa offers another example of the non-dual logic transcended by Zenchiku: a subject is non-dual with its environmental surroundings (*shutai-soku-kankyō* 主体即環境).[27] Zenchiku's nō is not unique in his interest in the universality of buddha nature – or Okina – but he is notable for the frequency with which this topic appears in his work. In *Meishukushū* §16, Zenchiku claims, with reference to the Lotus Sutra, that everything is Okina's marvellous essence (*myōtai* 妙体): all the buddhas, the heavens and earth and all nature.[28] Zenchiku's description of 'nature' is expansive, including mountains-rivers-great-earth (*sengadaiji* 山河大地), the interwoven forest web of the myriad phenomena (as previously discussed in Section 5.2), and grasses-trees-bricks-stones (*sōmoku gaseki* 草木瓦石) (it is worth noting that human artefacts are included in this last metonym). All of these are aspects of

[26] Atkins, *Revealed Identity*, 223.

[27] Nakazawa, *Seirei*, 126.

[28] *Zeami Zenchiku*, 413. See also Takahashi, *Zenchiku Nōgakuron*, 190–2.

Okina and thus are also possessed of buddha nature. Though Zenchiku's staging of 'nature' is limited to plants, it is clear from his writings that, for him, all things have a sacredness.[29]

In two of Zenchiku's plays, *Bashō* (芭蕉, Plantain Tree) and *Kakitsubata*, the *shite* is the spirit of the titular plant. In *Kakitsubata*, the iris spirit is portrayed as vain and proud – she considers herself to be the most beautiful of all flowers because the poet Narihira (identified in the play as a bodhisattva and in *Meishukushū* as a manifestation of Okina) had so praised her. In the final moments, she awakens to her inherent buddha nature and her purple colour fades to white (casting off an attachment to worldly beauty and embracing the radical spiritual equality of all things). In *Bashō*, the spirit of the plantain tree is drawn to the abode of a monk who chants the Lotus Sutra, which is the sutra on which the idea of *sōmoku jōbustu* (the buddhahood of non-sentient beings) is based. The entire scenario is built on a hollow paradox, that of a plantain tree in snow,[30] and the entire play is thus manifesting the hollow expanse from the beginning to the end. It is one of the most text-heavy plays in the repertoire, with almost no action: the *waki* monk and the *shite* plantain tree discuss the Lotus Sutra and the buddhahood of plants and women, and then the plantain tree spirit dances. The final image intoned by the chorus is of the plantain spirit being blown away by the icy wind, leaving only a torn leaf as a sign she had been there. Of note is that – per Zenchiku's teacher Shōtetsu, and in Shunzei and Teika's poetic lineage – what is visible on stage (the purple robe, the figure of the *shite* playing the plantain tree's spirit) is of less importance than the words which tell us that the purple robe has turned white, that the plantain spirit has been blown away. Words – in this case, poetic, hollow words – manifest reality more than do our eyes.

[29] Though Zenchiku only staged the spirits of plants, his grandson Konparu Zenpō (金春禅鳳, 1454–1532) wrote *Hatsuyuki* 初雪, in which the *shite* is the spirit of a beloved chicken.

[30] This is not a strict meteorological impossibility, but plantains can only grow in temperate regions when they are specially protected through the winter by human farmers.

Other plays by Zenchiku also feature spirits of plants, or *kami* associated with plants. *Tatsuta* – in which the *shite* is a *kami* associated with autumn and the maple leaf – will be looked at in greater detail below. In *Teika*, the title character does not appear in human form at all, but the spirit of his lover Princess Shokushi (the main character) is trapped by their mutual attachment. Teika and his love for Shokushi is symbolized in the play by vines which wrap around her tomb. His spirit is in the vines and, despite not appearing as a character, the Teika vines are undoubtedly central to the plot.

Another play with nonhuman characters is *Mekari* (和布刈, *Seaweed Gathering*). *Mekari* is an enactment of a new year's dawn ritual, without any typically dramatic action. The play is an exploration of the non-duality of opposites and liminal spaces, set on the strait which divides the islands of Kyushu and Honshu. At the darkest part of the night before dawn of the new year, the ritual seaweed cutting ceremony (which still takes place at Mekari Shrine in Kita-Kyushu) is enacted in the liminal intertidal zone, between the low- and high-tide marks. The *shite* – called an Okina in the script – is an old fisherman who is actually a manifestation of a sea dragon king (i.e. is a manifestation of the sea), and the *tsure* (supporting lead) is a female diver who is actually a heavenly maiden (i.e. a manifestation of the sky). The *ai kyōgen* role in the interval between the first and second half of the play is a manifestation of the seaweed itself.[31]

6.2.1 Konparu Zenchiku's *Tatsuta*

What we know of the world is already always a construction through language – in conventional reality, the phenomena we lend our attention to are perceivable to us because we can name them.[32] And so, too, in the audience's perception of the nō stage, almost everything

[31] For a thorough analysis of *Mekari* see Jamieson, 'Zenchiku's *Mekari*'.

[32] This section's analysis is adapted from: Daryl Jamieson, 'The Buddhahood of Plants and Trees in Zenchiku's Nō: The case of *Tatsuta*', (forthcoming).

is constructed in the first instance through language. That said, there are other perceptual stimuli at play as well. Starting from the state of hollow emptiness and anticipation described by Ueda, the first signal of the start of *Tatsuta* – as with all nō plays – is not linguistic but sonic. Before any words or visual images, musical sound arises from out of the hollow expanse. This is the *oshirabe* (お調べ), where from behind the curtain, the four musicians – one *nōkan* (能管) flute player and three drummers, *kotsuzumi* (小鼓), *ōtsuzumi* (大鼓) and *taiko* (太鼓) – tune and adjust their instruments. Then the musicians and chorus (*jiutai* 地謡) enter, followed by the stagehands (*kōken* 後見) who bring on the sole prop – a small shrine which is placed at the centre of the stage.

The monks (the *waki* and his companions, who are carrying copies of the Lotus Sutra) then enter, beginning the play proper. Even before they arrive at Tatsuta Shrine they refer to the poet Saigyō (西行; 1118–90) in describing their journey.[33] They are already using poetry to shape their perception of their conventional world, and also of course constructing the audience's understanding of the twofold virtual world of the stage and the play through their words. When they are admonished by the shrine maiden (the *shite*, who is a manifestation of the Tatsuta *kami*[34]) not to ford the river lest they destroy the scenery, it is the monk whose mind leaps to a famous anonymous poem from the *Kokinshū* about not disturbing the brocade of leaves. But are there any leaves – or has the monk manifested their image out of season to rationalize to himself the shrine maiden's prohibition on fording? The shrine maiden actually has a different poem in mind, specifically about not breaking the ice. Going into the shrine proper, all the trees are bare but one, which still has a crimson raiment. Both of these images being painted with words alone – that of a newly-frozen river which still has autumn leaves on its surface, and that of a single tree keeping all its leaves when the other trees have lost all theirs – manifest events that, while not impossible,

33 Itō Masayoshi, ed., *Yōkyokushū*, vol. 2 (Tokyo: Shinchōsha, 1986), 309.

34 Tatsuta is a *utamakura* associated with the maple leaf and the season of autumn (Section 3.2).

are unusual. Furthermore, in Japanese poetic practice, crimson leaves (*momiji* もみぢ) are poetically associated with autumn, as ice (*kōri* 氷) and bare branches (*fuyugare* 冬枯れ) are with winter. The juxtaposition of these images is incongruous, if not conventionally impossible, and are thus preparing the audience for a potential awakening to the uncanniness of the twofoldedness of the world; in other words, they afford being interpreted as hollow.

In the second half, three poems are quoted. The first of these, by Ki no Tsurayuki, underlines the association with Tatsuta and autumn.[35] The second, by Kujō Motoie (九条基家; 1203–80), describes Mount Tatsuta's cherry trees:[36] Even these symbols of spring have turned crimson in accordance with the Tatsuta goddess' preference for that autumnal colour. The third poem, by Takamuko no Kusaharu (高向草春), likens the effect the thin layer of ice on the surface of the river has on the transparency of the water to the similar clouded effect rock sediment stirred up by a landslide on nearby Mount Mimuro (三室山) might have.[37] The imagery manifested by these poems – Tsurayuki's suggestion that autumn moors at the port of Tatsuta, Motoie's crimson cherry blossoms, Kusaharu's poetic allegory of the distortion of light caused by clouds of rock sediment and that caused by freezing over – affords being heard as hollow in and of itself. They also collectively create an uncanny world, with no clear temporal referent. As the poems quoted in the first half evoke both autumn and winter, the poems of the second half evoke not only autumn, winter,

[35] 年ごとにもみぢ葉流る龍田川湊や秋の泊りなるらん (Ibid., 315).
Toshi goto ni momijiba nagaru Tatutagawa minato ya aki no tomarinaru ran
Every year, crimson leaves float down the Tatsuta River, as autumn moors at this port.

[36] 今朝よりは龍田の桜色ぞ濃き夕日や花の時雨なるらん (Ibid.).
Kesa yori wa Tatsuta no sakura iro zo koki iuhi ya hana no shigure naruran
Since this morning, the colour of Tatsuta's cherry blossoms has deepened in the twilight, like the autumn rains [which colours the leaves].

[37] 神南備の三室の岸や崩るらん龍田の川の水の濁れる (Ibid.).
Kami nami no Mimuro no kishi ya kuzururan Tatsuta no kawa no mizu no nigoreru
Has there been a landslide at the sacred Mount Mimuro? The waters of Tatsuta's river have become clouded.

but also spring. The virtual world being constructed through the poetic language of the play becomes more and more hollow as it progresses.

The final scene plays out as the dream of the *waki* who has stayed up praying all night for the Tatsuta goddess to appear. Increasingly uncanny perceptual phenomena manifest on stage: As the *shite* goddess dances a *kagura* dance – the kind of dance which *miko* would once have danced to entertain the *kami* that had possessed them in early *kamioroshi* rituals – the *waki* monk interprets the sound of falling rain as if it were the voice of the ritual *suzu* bells (鈴) accompanying her. The wind whips up white caps on the surface of the water (though, how is this possible if the river has frozen over – right to the end the temporality of the play remains ambiguous), and these are allegorically, synaesthetically interpreted as white artificial flowers made as offerings to the *kami*.

When, near the end of the first scene, the *shite*'s multiple twofoldedness has been revealed by the chorus: they are both shrine maiden and goddess, human and tree, human and autumn itself, not to mention male (usually older) actor and maiden girl, and – for the most accomplished actors – human actor and divine goddess. These dualisms – which are dissolved and transcended in the hollow vessel which is the *shite* – are constructed through language, yes, but also the voice (the masculine voice singing in a feminine-coded style), the costumes and the mask. The mask is itself a holy being – made of wood – and the *shite* bows in front of the mask before putting it on. The mask is called an *omote* (面 true face), not a *kamen* (仮面 literally false face, the word commonly used for a mask which hides the wearer's face). As Ueda says, 'the shite must, through his acting, melt the omote and the visible part of his face into a physical unity . . . . He must unify himself physically with the concrete purity of the omote'.[38] As with the conventionally real sounds of rain and the image of the shrine maiden penetrating the hollow expanse (dream world) as, respectively, the

[38] Ueda, 'The Place of Man', 82.

sound of *kagura* and the vision of a dancing goddess, the audience, linguistically and perceptually aware of these dualisms and perhaps also the transcendence of them through the performance of the play, could be awakened to the interpenetration of the conventional and hollow worlds not just in the play but in conventional reality itself.

In *Tatsuta*, which is about those tinted leaves and the constellation of associations that have grown up around both the place and the leaves, we see enacted on stage an illustration of Shunzei's statement that, 'whether we seek out the cherry blossoms of spring or view the tinted leaves of autumn, if we did not have what we call poetry, no one would know the colour or the scent' (Section 3.1). As the monk cycles through the poems associated with the place he is in, these poetic layers occlude what is in front of him. As he falls into an early-morning dream at the end of the *ai kyōgen* interlude, the Tatsuta *kami* appears to him in the hollow expanse – which is also the hollow expanse of the stage, the hollow expanse which grounds our twofold being-in-the-world – dancing to the sound of *kagura* which is, in conventional reality, simply the rhythm of the rain. On a stage in which the hollow expanse is visible in its emptiness, trees and their spirits metamorphose into human form, dissolving the barrier separating different forms of being. Both trees and humans can be buddhas, as can all beings – sentient and non-sentient. It is also a world in which the *kami* – of Tatsuta as a place, but also of the maple leaves, of autumn, of nature itself – speaks out to prevent the despoiling of natural beauty by careless humans – and the humans listen to her.

6.3 Non-anthropocentric listening practice

Given the likely connection between shamanism and nō, and Zenchiku's interest in preserving the spiritual dimension of nō, we can infer that, at least in the ideal case of a supremely accomplished actor, in Zenchiku's practice the actor either becomes a vessel for possession by the divine or at least stages that shamanic possession for the audience. If, paraphrasing Cage, the purpose of nō is to prepare the mind to receive 'divine influences', Zenchiku's stand against secularization – and the subsequent abandonment (or minimization) of this concept in nō practice – is something we can learn from in the twenty-first century.

For listeners to sound (inclusive of interpreters, performers and composers) in any genre or format, I would not advocate spirit possession as *the* way to a better practice (it would seem, firstly, that a particular inbuilt talent as a medium – not to mention decades of training and practice – would be necessary for that to be the case). Zenchiku doesn't specifically advocate for this either, although there undoubtedly is a quality of spiritual ecstasy and the submission of the so-called 'self' in his fifth circle, the *harin*, as the borders of the circular world depicted by the first four circles are pierced through from every direction. In the most mature, Kanshō version of *Rokurin ichiro no hichū*, Zenchiku writes that the *harin* represents the nonduality of having complete mastery of the repertoire, but also should transcend it, to 'play in the undifferentiated expanse of the Dharma'[39] (i.e. reality). He also writes that the sound produced at this level will be a unique sound (*dokuon* 独音). It seems clear that, though practice and training are necessary, once mastery of the art has been achieved, it is submission to a mysterious, outside force that produces artists of true creativity and uniqueness.

'Playing in the undifferentiated expanse of the Dharma' is, essentially, Ueda's 'playing in the hollow expanse', where 'undifferentiated' points to a kind of Nishidian pure experience of non-discrimination between phenomena or a Kegon Buddhist non-obstructive interpenetration of phenomena and phenomena. Especially in the *harin*, which emphasizes interpenetration, playing in the hollow expanse is non-dual with the hollow expanse playing in you. It is from this submission to interpenetration by the forest web of myriad phenomena that unique

[39] '広大無偏ノ法界ニ遊ブ位ナルベシ' *Zeami Zenchiku*, 391.

sounds can be disclosed. Playing in conventional reality – things which already are known to exist – can only produce remixes and new combinations of previously known sounds. Attachment to a search for newness – like any attachment – precludes the extinction of the 'self' necessary for submission to interpenetration by myriad phenomena, so only by abandoning an intentional quest for novelty can the truly new become manifest.

'Undifferentiated' means the abandonment of all categorization of phenomena, and in the case of listening, this would include sound sources. Whether a sound is from an instrument, an insect, a mammal, a rock, an echo or waves crashing into the ocean (the ocean crashing into waves), what matters is the sound itself, in that moment of pure listening and pure sounding. However, as both Dōgen and Ueda insist, we cannot live in the hollow expanse – we should play in the hollow and live in (conventional) reality. *Harin* is both absolute control of the repertoire (i.e. the highest level of achievement in whatever skill you practice) and letting go of the conscious use of that skill. Then you will become a vessel for true creativity, and expression of the hollow expanse through whatever skill you practice.

A poem by Zen monk Shidō Bunan (至道無難; 1603–76, also pronounced Munan) explains the general case of this well:

> 生きながら死人となりてなりはてて思ふがままにするわざぞよき[40]
> *iki nagara shibito tonarite nari hatete omou ga mama ni suru wazazo yoki*
> Become a dead man, remaining alive; become thoroughly dead. Then do what you like, according to your own mind; all your deeds are then good.[41]

To paraphrase: if your 'self' dies while your body remains alive, you will be an open vessel to the hollow expanse of reality, and whatever sounds you listen out of reality will be good.

40 Suzuki Daitetsu, *Suzuki Daitetsu Zenshū*, vol. 20 (Tokyo: Iwanami Shoten, 1968), 233.

41 Bret Davis, *Zen Pathways: An Introduction to the Philosophy and Practice of Zen Buddhism* (Oxford: Oxford University Press, 2022), 169.

6.3.1 Hector Berlioz' *Les Troyens* Act 4: 'Chasse Royal et Orage'

I cannot claim to be a master in the practice of *listening out* through Zenchiku's *Six Circles One Dewdrop* framework to the extent that I can illustrate its full virtues. Zenchiku's conception of a master is someone with almost four decades of concentrated practice behind them, with artistic training in multiple tributary disciplines and spiritual training besides. While having been trained in comparable disciplines, I do not have the decades of practical experience that Zenchiku – and Zeami – clearly believe are essential. So, these case studies and examples are written in the spirit of someone on the path (which is not to imply that the path is something that can be exhausted of course, merely to recognize that I consider myself a relative beginner on it). This subsection's title also gives away that the two practical reflections on listening explored in this section are not, unlike those in previous chapters, from the experimental music subgenre. Non-fictional listening applies to all sounds, not just experimental non-fictional music, so I will be applying my ears to listenings out of sounds that the composers did not intend to be listened to in the open manner that Cage or Kondo expressly do.

That said, Hector Berlioz has certain traits that make him an ideal nineteenth-century composer to think about in the terms we have been discussing so far. One of these is his incredible ear, which allowed him to listen decidedly new timbres out of the orchestra. This was an ear developed as a conductor and orchestrator – that is, through practice – rather than orchestrating a short score which had been written at a piano, or notes which were composed without thinking about the sound quality of the instruments which would play them. Berlioz was a composer who – if not uniquely then unusually for his time – listened to sounds as whole beings, not solely as pitch and rhythm. To this end, he brought standard orchestral instruments together in combinations that had never been heard before and also used recently invented instruments in order to have as diverse a palette as possible.[42]

But Berlioz is also looking back, to Shakespeare in many works, and most importantly to the pre-Christian world of Rome through Vergil's (70–19 B. C. E.) *Aeneid*, the textual source of his grandest opera *Les Troyens* (1858). Act IV opens with a pantomime called the 'Chasse Royal et Orage' (En. Royal Hunt and Storm).[43] Berlioz' scenario for this pantomime scene (which lasts about nine minutes) is set in an 'African forest' (near Carthage, presumably, where the rest of the second half of the opera is set). Naïads, who, in Roman mythology, are minor female spirits of wells and springs (fresh water, but not river, deities) visually present the water element while the orchestra (dominated by woodwinds at the beginning) use tone painting techniques and conventional musical semiosis (e.g. using musical invariants symbolic of birdsong such as high woodwind instruments trilling and playing repeated tones) to indicate a pastoral 'nature' scene. This is somewhat undercut by the ominous tremolos and the descending chromatic line (which can symbolize death or mourning) that moves from the violins to the basses over the first minute (Rehearsal marks A–C). This falling motif brings a note of anxiety and instability into the scene, even when it is purely depicting 'nature'. The flux of nature is further underlined when the second violins and violas begin to use pizzicato, first as background accompaniment (D), and then as a counter figure (E), prefiguring the approach of rain (the titular storm).

From (E) solo saxhorns begin to play, then echo, a motif as if heard from a distance. This motif references a traditional hunting motif, but it is unusual rhythmically (it is five measures long, with a two-measure held note at the end; phrases of odd-number lengths are unusual in Western European art music), melodically (it is slightly

[42] In the 'Chasse Royal et Orage' of *Les Troyens*, for example, he uses four tenor saxhorns and an ophicleide.

[43] Hector Berlioz, *Les Troyens*, in *New Edition of the Complete Works*, vol. 2b, ed. Hugh Macdonald (Kassel: Bärenreiter, BA 5442/II, 1969).

chromatically inflected in a manner not possible on hunting horns – but can suggest the natural distortion of pitch that can occur when it is heard from afar) and timbrally (the hunting motif is typically heard on horns, not the then-newly-invented saxhorns). This motif is heard six times before the hunt begins to take off (H) in the full orchestra in 6/8 compound time, building rhythmic tension in (J) with hemiolas and slight syncopations, before being stopped suddenly by three unison trombones in a suddenly changed 2/2 simple metre heralding the start of the storm. It seems clear that 'nature' is being portrayed in regular, even phrases of simple metre, and the human hunters are portrayed in compound time, often syncopated, playing phrases of five or seven measures. When their worlds collide (Q–R, T, V–X), though they share a pulse, they are sounding in different wavelengths – the hunters (the titular Trojans) are thus rhythmically separated from nature.

At (W), the opera's main characters Aeneas and Dido enter the pantomime, embracing in the obscurity of a grotto. Nymphs, silvani and fauns – respectively female nature deities, male tree deities and male forest spirits, all performed by the chorus – enter to try to bridge the human-nature gap. Symbolizing nature, they sing in simple time in a mix of wordless vowels along with the single word 'Italie' (repeated five times). Lightning strikes a tree, and satyrs (ribald masculine spirits of remote natural locations) and the other male spirits dance and play with the burning branches. Then the storm gradually abates and, having delivered their message, the spirits disappear. As the hunters also retreat, a horn plays the hunting motif one last time, somewhat longer, more relaxed and more rhythmically regular than the previous versions.

The group of nature deities presented onstage as chorus members and dancers is meant to be understood by us human audience members as speaking via the wind in an attempt to push Aeneas away from Africa and towards his 'destiny' of founding Rome. However, we could read this instead as Aeneas listening the word 'Italie' out of the howling wind passing over the caves. In this case, the vowels howled by nymphs, silvani and fauns of the chorus in the course of nature naturing – the storm storming – become inflected with the consonants 't' and 'l' by the mind of Aeneas, who knows he must travel onward and is apt to read any setback (like a hunt ruined by a thunderstorm, flooding and fire) as a divine rebuke of his dallying in Carthage with Dido. Like the *waki* monk in *Tatsuta*, who experiences a goddess dancing to *kagura* music out of the sound of the rain, Aeneas too listens something that isn't there (in conventional reality) out of the sounds of the storm. In the *Zhōuyì*, the answer given by the oracle is merely an echo of the question asked (Section 4.1), and similarly, the question troubling Aeneas' mind is answered by the spirits as an echo of the question: 'Italie'. The sounds and echoes of 'nature' are a sutra that Aeneas is not properly (purely, attentively) listening to, and so his interpretation of those sounds is driving himself back into his own mind.

As audience members, we can be aware of the imperialist ideology which undoubtedly affects both Vergil's and Berlioz' artistic works,[44] and also aware of the 'speaking composition' nature of Berlioz' practice, and we can still listen out something other than what was put into it. There are affinities – and also, certainly, differences – between the classical Greco-Roman conception of nature and nature deities and the Japanese ones.[45] We can enjoy Berlioz' extraordinary orchestration for the sound of the sounds themselves, and also palimpsestically consider both Roman and Japanese (or other cultures') conceptions of nature spirits and how they communicate with humans (or, how humans listen oracular messages out of natural phenomena) in our own interpretation of 'Chasse Royal et Orage'.

[44] Peter Bloom, *Berlioz in Time: From Early Recognition to Lasting Renown* (Rochester: University of Rochester Press, 2022), 188*ff*.

[45] However, Nakazawa makes an interesting series of observations about the remarkable similarities between prehistoric Japanese gods and pre-Roman Celtic gods. Nakazawa, *Seirei*, 83*ff*.

6.3.2 Apichatpong Weerasethakul's *Sud Pralad*

Sud pralad (สัตว์ประหลาด, En. Tropical Malady) is a 2004 film by Thai director Apichatpong Weerasethakul. It is hard for me to think of a twenty-first-century work that has more in common with the aesthetics of Zenchiku's nō than this film, both in its dramatic form and its use of meaningful silence and restraint. In particular, the soundscape composition by Akritchalerm Kalayanamitr is notable for its strong presence in the second half of the film.

On a superficial level, the film, like *mugen* nō, has a two-part structure. The first part takes place in present-day conventional reality – a simple love story, told in gestures, glances and smiles – between Keng, a soldier stationed in a small town in rural north-eastern Thailand, and a local man, Tong. Keng takes the *waki* role, a visitor to this place, through whom we as the audience experience the narrative. In standard dramatic terms very little happens in the first hour other than scenes of everyday life in which Keng and Tong gradually and unaffectedly become closer to each other. As in a *mugen* nō, the *shite* – Tong in *Sud pralad* – departs from the *waki*'s (and audience's) view, dropping hints that there is something more to them than meets the eye. Tong wanders off into the forest – this development is somewhat reminiscent of Zenchiku's *Matsumushi* (松虫), in which one of two young male lovers disappears into the wild, never to be seen again. Keng overhears from local villagers that something mysterious and monstrous is killing the local cattle, and inter-titles tell a tale of a therianthropic Khmer shaman who can become a tiger.[46] This short section functions similarly to the *ai kyōgen*, explaining in plain language what has been happening and setting the stage for the more dreamlike (*mugen*) second half.

[46] In *Sud Pralad*'s shapeshifting storyline there is also some relation to the 1942 story '*Sangetsuki*' (山月記; En. 'Tiger Poet', also known as 'The Moon over the Mountain') by Nakajima Atsushi (中島敦; 1909–1942). This short story is about a poet who is so obsessed with poetry that he is driven insane and becomes a tiger, and it is quoted in an inter-title at the beginning of the film. Nakajima Atsushi, *The Moon over the Mountain*, trans. Paul McCarthy and Nobuko Ochner (Iowa City: Autumn Hill Books, 2011).

It is this second half which is of greatest interest, where Apichatpong's manifest interest in sound is given full reign: in the approximately forty minutes after the inter-title story there are only two lines of spoken dialogue, and these are spoken by Keng into an unresponsive walkie-talkie.[47] Tong, like the Khmer shaman, has become a tiger (or always had been a tiger) and during these forty minutes in which the soundscape of the jungle is the only audible sound Keng and Tong essentially hunt each other in an elaborate and compelling dance. Keng, fully human, tries to approach Tong-Tiger (who, when he appears in human form, is dressed only in tattoos) by becoming more and more animal-like: after losing his walkie-talkie, gun and other equipment, he covers himself with mud to mask his human scent. In other words, the technological, urban, Modernist items and concepts which conventionally – falsely – separate humans from 'nature' are being stripped from him.

At first, animal sounds (as opposed to the nearly-incessant insect sounds) – such as the deep lowing heard at 1:05:30 – are completely unidentified and sound mysteriously in the soundscape with no visual indication of their sources. Their ambiguity is a source of tension and fear for the audience, and, presumably, Keng. At 1:15:30, while Keng is asleep, the walkie-talkie erupts into life with short bursts of static noise interrupting the soundscape. This is a mirror of the former ambiguity, since we know the source, but Tong-Tiger, watching from a distance, does not. He is fascinated by it. By 1:27:55, having had the walkie-talkie – the last electronic sound-making/communication device – taken from him and destroyed by Tong-Tiger, Keng hears the sound of a monkey and he – and the audience, through subtitles – can understand the monkey's words. He tries unsuccessfully (1:31:55) to speak to a monkey by hooting, but the lack of subtitles shows us he is not yet able to talk back to nature – he is still only a listener. Tong-Tiger calls out with

[47] Apichatpong's interest in non-linguistic sound appears in several other films. There is, similarly, a lengthy section of *Blissfully Yours* (2002) without any speech, and his 2021 film *Memoria* is about a woman who hears a mysterious sound and enlists the help of a sound engineer to try to recapture it – a film about the very essence and materiality of sound.

guttural cries, similarly trying and failing to imitate human language. In lieu, perhaps, of the walkie-talkie, Keng (1:33:30) then sounds a kind of wooden bell – perhaps a cowbell – seemingly in an attempt to lure Tong-Tiger with its steady, un'natural' rhythm.

Any lingering sense of being in conventional reality or temporality is dashed (1:36:00) when walkie-talkie noise returns to the soundtrack (despite the machine having been broken beyond repair) and, visually, a dead cow's spirit is seen to rise out of its body and walk away. From this point, and especially after 1:40:50, the soundscape begins to drift into clearly fictional/hollow territory, circling back (*kōko kyakurai*) to sounds from earlier in this second half of the film: the steady rhythm of the wooden percussion returns (but Keng is not playing it), and the dead cow lows. Perhaps Keng and the cow both have experienced a kind of shamanic initiation, a death of their (conventional) selves and a rebirth into the (hollow) interpenetrative self, transcending the linear (Modernist) flow of time into a cyclical one.

In a movie where the silence of the jungle is very prominently and loudly present, it is notable that, in Keng's final confrontation with Tong-Tiger as a tiger, both shrouded in obscuring, *yūgen* darkness, the tiger does not move (aside from the slightly visible expansion and contraction of his breathing body), roar or make any identifiable diegetic sound at all. He speaks – of seeing himself in Keng as if he were a mirror, of devouring him, of birth, and of missing him – while a clearly terrified Keng, clutching only a tiny knife and a flashlight, stares back, his teeth audibly clattering. Tong-Tiger's words are spoken as a voiceover in clear human speech, as if Keng were hearing them in his head – markedly different from the monkey sounds earlier. And his speech mixes past, present and future tense: for Tong-Tiger – as in esoteric Buddhism – there is only the present; the past and future are both mere shadows and traces of the now. Keng submits to opening himself to a union of flesh and spirit, memory and blood with Tong-Tiger and, symbolically, with all of 'nature' – which is to say, with himself in the broadest possible interpenetrative understanding of 'self'.

After the cut to black, the jungle soundscape continues for almost five minutes while the credits play.

Sud pralad's structure and non-anthropocentric mode of storytelling – its transcendence of the boundaries between human and nonhuman – are very congruent with Zenchiku's visions of a spiritual narrative and dramatic art form (with, of course, differences in many details). In its use of both the noisy silence of purposeless sound and the silent silence of purposely not making sound, *Sud pralad* is also an exemplary use of hollow sound composition in a fictional narrative context. It employs a transition between seemingly non-fictional to seemingly fictional in order to underline the narrative shift from a story taking place in the conventional world to one exploring the radical implications of the hollow expanse.

7

Vessels of present silences

Centre Piece

Imagine a life.

Live it.

2003

Torna Haellestad, Sweden

—Ken Friedman[1]

7.1 *jurin*

Sounds sounding.
Worlds worlding.
All life sounds.
All sound is life.
All sound is alive.
All sounding things are alive.
All sound is vibration.
All hearing is being touched involuntarily.[2]
All listening is attending to the outside in ourselves.

1 Ken Friedman, *12 Structures: Scores by Ken Friedman* (London: The Centre of Attention, 2004).

2 For this reason, Mishima Yukio averred that music is the 'only masochistic art' because it envelops you, caresses you, and you can't control it or block it out. Okada Akeo, *Ongaku no kikikata* (Tokyo: Chūō kōron shinsha, 2009), 5–6.

All silent things are not silent, but merely seem so to our imperfect ears.

All sounding things are also listeners.

All things are listeners.

All sounds are listening.

In 'The Questions of the Kinnara King Druma', the titular king of the *kinnara* (semi-divine, semi-human skilled musicians in Brahmanical and Buddhist mythology) says of music that sounds are empty and 'abide in emptiness'.[3]

'All dharmas are like sound', meaning all phenomena are like sound.

All phenomena are waves on the sea of ultimate reality.

All sounds are waves on the sea of ultimate reality.

All sounds have 'the nature of emptiness'.

All phenomena have the nature of emptiness.

All words are sounds.

All words are nothing but sounds.

All words abide in emptiness.

All sounds are empty of inherent meaning.

All words are empty of inherent meaning.

All meaning the reader reads out of words are echoes of the reader's psyche.

All meaning or emotion a listener listens out of music or sound are echoes of the reader's psyche.

'Speaking' composition is fictional.

There is no 'speaking' music.

All music is 'listening' music.

John Berger, writing about Cy Twombly (1928–2011) and the quality of *écriture* in Twombly's art, says:

> A writer . . . [sees language] as a terrain full of illegibilities, hidden paths, impasses, surprises, and obscurities. Its map is not a dictionary but the whole of literature and perhaps everything ever said. Its obscurities, its

[3] Rambelli, 'Gagaku', 59. See Section 3.2.

> lost senses, its self-effacements come about for many reasons – because of the way words modify each other, write themselves over each other, cancel one another out, because the unsaid always counts for as much, or more, as the said, and because language can never cover what it signifies. Language is always an abbreviation.[4]

In the same way, every sound ever sounded in the past which subjectively meant something to someone (but can never mean anything inherently) is brought to bear on every sound sounded and heard in the present. How can any meaning emerge from this emptiness? If language – an instance of music, which is sound sounded by a human being with intentionality, which is an instance of sound as a whole, which is an instance of phenomena, which is a node on Indra's Net – is 'always an abbreviation' it is because the implicit 'unsaid', that which has been 'abbreviated', is the entirety of the hollow expanse (the emptiness, the nothingness) which grounds all reality. The blank page – a symbolic metonym of Zenchiku's *jurin*, the eternally empty sea which awaits the spark of moonlight on its waves to manifest living, sentient, creative phenomena – is not awaiting certainty nor is it a *space* awaiting domination, but it is a terrain (a *place*, a *basho*) of *yūgen*, of 'surprises, and obscurities', of *enchantment*.

All the sounds are always already sounding. You and I may not hear them all – we have physiological limitations that prevent us from hearing what dogs hear, what crickets hear, what moons hear. We cannot listen to them all either – there are simply too many sounds, even in our immediate vicinities and within our physiological capabilities, to attend to them all.

At the same time, we might notice when they stop sounding – will we listen to Sibelius' Seventh Symphony differently if a previously unremarked-upon second clarinet part is cut out? Will we listen differently to the nighttime soundscape if an insect we neither noticed nor heard is killed off by pesticides and thence the differently-hearing bats for whom they afforded being prey move on, or are killed off themselves?

4 John Berger, *Portraits*, ed. Tom Overton (2015; repr. London: Verso, 2017), 426.

7.2 *shurin*

Zenchiku, in his treatise *Rokurin ichiro hichū* (六輪一露秘注; Secret Notes on the Six Circles One Dewdrop), writes that 'supremely superior effects are created from the interval',[5] which he defines as the time between two actions. This means that the silence between the notes, the gap between events – the hollow emptiness – is where the magic of a performance lies. Nonetheless, that hollow emptiness can only be manifested by the sounds or actions on either side of it. Zeami names this empty interval *senu-hima* (せぬ隙),[6] and tells us in *Kakyō* (花鏡; A Mirror to the Flower) that if the performer intends to create this magical effect it cannot be achieved. That is because rather than being empty, it would be full of intent.[7] Thus, *shurin* – where the intention to create a frame, a vessel (and only the frame or vessel), for the ultimately more affecting, enchanted, unintentional and uncontrollable silence (interval) originates – is of vital importance for the listener (a category inclusive, as always, of performers and composers).

Poet, novelist, essayist and co-founder of the Dark Mountain Project, Paul Kingsnorth, suggests that human culture requires four elements:

1. A sacred source. A religious tradition, which speaks the name of God in its particular form.
2. Place. Nature itself, in its localized manifestation.
3. Culture from below. ('Folk culture')
4. Culture from above. ('High culture')

5 '無上々果しわざ、程より作'. *Zeami Zenchiku*, 396. Nearman, 'Visions', Part 4, 32.

6 Zeami's *senu hima* continues to be generative today, *e.g.* Ryoko Akama's 2015 album of that name on melange edition (Akama 2015, *senu hima*, https://melangeedition.bandcamp.com/album/senu-hima [accessed 18 August 2025]).

7 *Zeami Zenchiku*, 100. In Hare's translation: 'However, should it be apparent to others that you have adopted this frame of mind, that is no good. If it becomes apparent, then it is likely to turn into a dramatic technique in itself. Then it is no longer "doing nothing." At the rank of no-mind, one bridges the gaps between what comes before and after with such a stratagem, so that one's intent is even hidden from oneself.' Zeami, *Performance Notes*, 115.

These elements are deliberately ordered; they cascade downwards from the top.[8]

The creation of the particular cultural form of nō across Kan'ami, Zeami and Zenchiku's generations provides an example which is congruent with Kingsnorth's theory of culture. The sacred source, in this case, is the hollow ground of emptiness provided by Buddhism, along with the tutelary gods of nō such as Okina and those Indian, Chinese and Japanese deities that Zenchiku identifies with Okina. As is evidenced by the prominence of *utamakura*, rootedness in place is of supreme importance in *waka* poetics and nō theory and practice. Nō's roots lie in the folk songs of the field and the town, shamanic magic and Chinese acrobatics (see Section 6.2) – Kingsnorth's 'culture from below' – but its sophistication lies in combining those rustic forms with gagaku rhythmic and formal structures, *waka* poetics and spiritual-philosophical reflection across Buddhist, *onmyōdō* and Confucian traditions – 'culture from above'.

The flourishing of any culture, subculture or generic tradition is dependent on maintaining the four elements Kingsnorth identifies. If Kan'ami and Zeami were in danger of losing sight of the importance of nō's 'sacred source', one of Zenchiku's aims was to return it to its place of primacy in nō theory and practice. Musical modernism in its purest form forgot all but the fourth of Kingsnorth's elements – abandoning its sacred source at the dawn of historical Modernism, abandoning place in a historically understandable and excusable post-1945 reaction to the devastation left by competing nationalisms, and abandoning culture from below as a reaction against the instrumentalization of mass culture by capitalism (to take a generous view of the situation). Perhaps musicians now need to bring back the other three. Regarding element 3 ('culture from below'), I would not advocate for fusion with commercial popular music (which would only exacerbate the power

[8] Paul Kingsnorth, 'Exodus: A Theory of Culture', in *The Abbey of Misrule* (Substack, 2021), https://paulkingsnorth.substack.com/p/exodus.

and reach of the neoliberal global culture industry), but rather – in relation with element 2 ('place') – a kind of ethnographic approach to the roots of music and sound in one's place and in the musical tradition(s) one practices. A prime example of this would be the Icelandic composer Guðmundur Steinn Gunnarsson's (b. 1982) study of Icelandic folk *rímur* melodies, which led him to become 'aware of how deeply cognitive and cultural conditioning shape[s] the way we hear things'.9

In *At Work in the Ruins*, Dougald Hine, essayist and Kingsnorth's Dark Mountain co-founder, details how Modernism (i.e. Enlightenment and scientistic ways of thinking) has blinkered all of us into forgetting that there are other ways of knowing and other ways of listening. Identifying our current age as an age of revelation (meaning 'apocalypse' – note that Zenchiku's nō was classified by Atkins as a 'Theatre of Revelation'[10]), Hine identifies four things that can be done in such a time as ours – a time which reveals the hidden fractures in our conception of conventional reality, the Lacanian Real of Mark Fisher's Capitalist Realism. Those four things are:

1. Salvaging the good from Modernity;[11]
2. Mourn the good which cannot be salvaged;
3. Notice that things in Modernity were never quite as good as we were promised, that the cracks were always there;
4. Realize that, as Modernity was beginning, other ways of life, other ways of understanding the world, were being destroyed, and that picking up those threads – praxis and knowledge which

[9] Guðmundur Steinn Gunnarsson, 'A Circle With Four Corners: Guðmundur Steinn Gunnarsson's Rough Thoughts on Composition', in *The Foam We Removed From The Office* (blog, 2024), https://www.thefoamweremovedfromtheoffice.com/2024/06/14/a-circle-with-four-corners-gudmundur-steinn-gunnarssons-rough-thoughts-on-composition/.

[10] Atkins, *Revealed Identity*, 10.

[11] See also Vanessa Machado de Oliveira, *Hospicing Modernity: Facing Humanity's Wrongs and the Implications for Social Activism* (Berkeley: North Atlantic Books, 2021).

> Modernity found obsolete and worthless – which might be useful after Modernity has come to its end.[12]

This book has been a project of the fourth kind, an attempt to recover pre-Modern ways of listening to the world and being in the world which are less anthropocentric, ways of knowing the world and interacting with other, human and nonhuman, sentient and non-sentient beings – those other waves on the ocean of the Real – which are less destructive than the anthropocentric epistemologies of Modernity.

It is crucial – as with Boym's distinction between restorative and reflective nostalgias (Section 4.3) – that this gathering of discarded (i.e. repressed or oppressed) threads is done without attempting to return to the past wholesale. It is about re-learning ancient wisdom for the present; recovering a palimpsest's faded underwriting without erasing all of the overwriting. As Kirk Varnedoe wrote of Cy Twombly's use of ancient textual and visual elements in his paintings, it is an 'act of translation, of reconceiving the past in contemporary terms and by this traduction insisting on its presentness'.[13] Zenchiku, and the wider tradition of *mugen* nō can be, I insist, of the present.

7.3 *jūrin*

The *jūrin* is the circle of abiding, the circle of sounds (phenomena), having already been conceived of (*jurin*) and framed as music (*shurin*), being actually realized as music by a listener. Two such experimental works of sound abiding as sound will be discussed in this section.

12 Dougald Hine, *At Work in the Ruins: Finding Our Place in the Time of Science, Climate Change* (White River Junction: Chelsea Green Publishing, 2023), 198*ff*.

13 Kirk Varnedoe, *Cy Twombly: A Retrospective* (New York: The Museum of Modern Art, 1994), 46.

7.3.1 Frank Denyer's *Screens*

Screens (2018) by Frank Denyer, a composer who studied Japanese music and did ethnomusicological fieldwork with the Marakwet of Kenya, is a piece of music theatre[14] which knowingly plays with hiddenness and revelation, creating a contemporary kind of ritual music-theatrical experience of *yūgen*.[15] It resonates with Japanese aesthetics without being obviously derived from Japanese forms. The piece is for eight performers – female voice, muted violin, muted viola, bass flute, three percussionists (playing *jal tarang*,[16] Indian *santūr*,[17] a heavy wooden staff, two bass drums, crotales, among various other instruments) and a speaker – arrayed on and off a stage set with four folding dressing screens draped with heavy cloth. These screens completely prevent the audience from seeing those behind them, and also mute (reduce the volume and change the timbre of) the sounds played or sung behind them.

At the start of the piece, two percussionists are in the centre of the stage, visible, but with their backs to the audience, with the third percussionist offstage throughout the piece. The speaker sits in darkness at the side of the stage. The remaining four musicians are behind the titular folding screens (hidden from the audience behind the screen, each of

[14] 'Music theatre' is a subgenre of concert music in which the bodies of musicians are choreographed to a certain extent, and/or the musicians are placed on a stage with non-sonic elements being part of the performance instructions. It is not to be confused with 'musical theatre', a commercial genre of theatre of the type commonly found on Broadway in New York and the West End of London.

[15] *Screens* was released commercially on Another Timbre. Frank Denyer, *Screens*, performed by Octandre Ensemble (Another Timbre, at 220, 2023), track 3. A video excerpt can be seen as part of Suhail Merchant's documentary about Frank Denyer; *Some Sounds are Gates*, 57:14–1:05:32. Suhail Merchant, *Some Sounds are Gates* (YouTube, 2020), https://youtu.be/1XT0y5oMAvc.

[16] *Jal tarang* is a set of porcelain bowls filled with varying amounts of water to produce different pitches. It is of uncertain origin, though the name *jal tarang* itself is Hindi. Dutta and Chakraborty 2024: Sumita Dutta and Dipankar Chakraborty, 'The Untold History of Jal Tarang: A Critical Exploration of its Origin, Evolution and Preservation Initiatives', *Sangeet Galaxy e-Journal* 13, no. 2 (2024): 4–16.

[17] *Santūr* is a type of hammer dulcimer.

these four musicians also has a selection of percussion instruments – crotales, rattles and an item which is not a purpose-made percussion instrument, such as a tabletop – to play). Over the course of the piece, each of these four performers play from behind their screen, step out from behind the screen, play and step back behind it again. The combination of visible and invisible performers is constantly changing, which has not only visual but also acoustic effects, in that the (already very soft, and – in the case of the string instruments – already muted) music becomes more muted (obscured, ruined) when played from behind the screen.

As in nō theatre, Denyer employs the disorienting effect of a rhythm which never settles into a pattern which can be easily grasped – the percussive sounds, for example, though precisely notated, are consistently unpredictable in their rhythmic placement ('oddly intermittent', as Denyer puts it at the end of the text the speaker recites). Their timbre is also unpredictable, since, according to the score, '[n]o two knocks should sound the same'.[18] This instruction is an instance of Denyer inviting the performers-as-listeners (i.e. interpreters) to exercise freedom and their own expressivity in a score which otherwise tightly controls many musical parameters.[19] The wooden knocks are, from the audience's perspective, also unpredictable in their spatialization – the place (*basho*) from which they arise – since all the performers (not just the percussionists) perform knocks. When those knocks come from behind the screens there is no visual clue that a sound is forthcoming, and so the amplitude of each individual knock is its own surprise. Mason notes that the 'insistence on the uniqueness of each and every sound is the essence of Denyer's compositional voice',[20] the uniqueness of each

[18] Frank Denyer, *Screens* (2018; rev. 2021), preliminary notes.

[19] In this, *Screens* is unlike nō in that the performers in nō have much more freedom of rhythm: Even the *nōbayashi* (能囃子) ensemble leader alternates every half phrase between the two *tsuzumi* drummers.

[20] Christian Mason, liner notes to *Screens*, comp. Frank Denyer (Another Timbre, at 220, 2023), https://www.anothertimbre.com/pages/booklet-for-frank-denyers-screens.

sound's timbral quality, rhythmic place and sounding place emphasizes the unique *life* of each sound. Like all of Denyer's compositions, *Screens* is a complex and difficult score to perform, but this very difficulty is what necessitates the attention of the performers-*cum*-listeners to the life of the sounds themselves.[21] Denyer's score allows each sound to sound in a place where it can be heard as itself, and in non-hierarchical relation to all the other sounds. As Dōgen might say, each sound 'abides in its dharma position' (*jūhōi* 住法位). And, as Dōgen reminds us in '*Keisei sanshoku*', it was the unexpected sound of a pebble knocking against bamboo that afforded awakening for Xiāngyán.

The speaker unexpectedly comes forward from their obscuring darkness into the musicians' well-lit ritual space midway through the piece. They speak in plain, clearly articulated language about the piece.[22] This appearance of the speaker is akin to the *ai kyōgen* section of *mugen* nō in both its directness of expression and its rhythmic location at the midpoint of the piece. Their speech emphasizes the interrelatedness of sounds, and that any meaning that is to be found is not in the sounds but between them. The text of the speech reads, in part:

> 'between' these musicians . . .
> are – – sounds
> some sounds – – are – – words
> [. . .]
> occasionally – – perhaps – – some – sounds – are – gates
> gates – open or shut – [23]

The sounds, then, exist 'between' the musicians, as the musicians also exist between the sounds (much as, for Zenchiku, 'supremely superior effects are created from the interval', that is, the 'in-between'). As a

[21] Recall Section 1.4.1, where Greg Stuart is quoted as saying that extremely complex music is 'an invitation to make something, together'. Ritchey and Stuart, 'Accessibility and Instrumentality'.

[22] In both the recording on Another Timbre and in the documentary *Some Sounds are Gates* the speaker part is performed by the composer himself.

[23] Denyer, *In the Margins*, 82–3.

person is a phenomenon that emerges in the relations between two beings (Section 5.1), so a sound – not in its physical sense but in terms of its social meaning – is a phenomena emergent between two sounds, or between sounds and listeners (performers or audience). 'Some sounds', Denyer's text says, 'are words' – which can be read as signs and symbols, words in general being sounds which communicate (however imperfectly) meaning between humans – but 'some sounds are gates'. Gates to what, Denyer doesn't say, though – like words themselves – we might infer that some sounds are gates in the way that some sounds are hollow. Whether these gates are 'open or shut' is largely down to the relationship between the listener and those hollow sounds.

7.3.2 Eva-Maria Houben's *on the periphery*

One piece which is specifically about listening at a threshold – a gate – is *on the periphery* (2021), a text score by the German composer, organist and musicologist Eva-Maria Houben (b. 1955).[24] A piece which can be performed by any group of musicians of any size (it is scored for 'ensemble', with no other qualifications), it enacts a passage between the inner and outer, the conventional and the hollow – '*across borders, beyond frontiers and limits*'.[25]

The ambiguity of place is evident in the title: it is between two places, at a borderland that is neither in nor out of either, and is also transcendent of the idea of the border itself. The piece is in two sections – like *mugen* nō, like *Screens*, like many of the films of Apichatpong Weerasethakul, like Ueda's ontology of our twofold world. Part I's instructions direct the performers towards '*contemplating* sounds' (including gestures and actions sounding and not sounding, playing or not playing) 'that carry us away into irrelevancies'. The word 'irrelevancies' emphasizes the purposelessness, the non-teleological nature of the listener-

[24] Houben, like Pisaro-Liu, is a member of the Wandelweiser group of composers.

[25] Eva-Maria Houben, *On the Periphery* (edition wandelweiser, 2021).

performer's actions (one cannot achieve awakening when one is consciously attached to the goal of becoming awakened). But the first word – italicized by the composer to emphasize its importance – is '*contemplating*'. Contemplating – the Latin root of which is *templum*, a sacred place of meditation, also the root of the word temple (*OED*) – sound is listening with attention, observing the sacred life of sonic beings with the ear. It also recalls the Shunzei's appeal to Zhìyǐ's *Larger Treatise on Cessation and Contemplation* (Section 3.1). Though this is an instruction to ultimately create sounds, this act of creation is in the first place a listening. Any sound sounded is therefore listened out through contemplation.

And yet, contemplation is not a pure experience of sound; it is a mental mediation – an interpretation – of sound. Though the contemplation of sound is a practice which can lead to the opening of a gate to the hollow expanse, it is of the conventional world. In part II, the performers are enjoined to offer up the sonic gestures that emerged in part I. The text puts it as '*losing (and thereby transforming)* these poor and irrelevant expressions', ultimately 'entrusting them to silence'. What is crucial in this instruction is that the act of giving away these 'irrelevant' sounds to silence is not ending them, or even 'silencing' them, but setting them free. It transforms them from something created by musicians with meanings imposed by musicians, transforming them to sounds sounding of themselves in their own dharma position. Like all phenomena, they are then empty of meaning, neither irrelevant nor relevant, transcending this and all other dualities. To our ears, they become 'silent', but that does not mean that from the perspective of the sonic beings themselves they are no longer sounding; they have merely 'transformed'.

The transition – 'sliding gently across the hidden threshold between part I and part II' – can happen at any time; each performer can choose the time that, through their contemplation of the web of sounding beings in that time and in that place, seems right for the sounds they have listened out. The 'silence' that those listened-out sounds are being 'entrusted' to is not a lack of sounds but the lack of sounds made with intention – the lack of sounds made with any sense of purpose or teleology.

I have previously analysed this piece as a sacrificial ritual.[26] While I stand by that interpretation, it is important to realize that the sacrifice is not the sonic beings which are 'surrendered' into a nihilistic nothingness. It is music itself on the sacrificial altar – not sound, but the anthropocentric idea that music means something, that it is a universal language of feelings. It is not – and never has been – those things; sounds are 'irrelevancies' (per Houben), 'purposeless' (per Kondo). As Denyer contends, '[m]usic is a truly worthless occupation – that is its glory'.[27] And so, *on the periphery* is a sacrifice of even the idea of contemplatively making sound in favour of simply listening. It is, in the end, about the pure relationality of being to being – human beings, nonhuman beings, non-sentient beings. It is a communion with each other, with any and all listeners. And, as with Denyer's music, it is an invitation to enter – or at least peer through – a sonic 'gate' to the hollow expanse.

7.4 *zōrin*

Having sacrificed the Romantic, anthropocentric idea of music to the freedom of ateleological sonic beings, in the *zōrin* we are – per the ninth Ox Picture ('Return to the Origin') – radically unified with – interpenetrated by – all phenomena. Cage's poem on the ninth Ox Picture reads 'nothing's changed yet   something immense   asking';[28] Kuòān's circle shows a tree blossoming; Zenchiku's *zōrin* shows nature naturing. In the twenty-first century – indeed, throughout Modernity –

26 In a paper at the European Network of Japanese Philosophy's Eighth Annual Conference, *The Past in the Present*, held at Tallinn University in September 2024.

27 Denyer, *In the Margins*, 101.

28 Sugimoto, *Honkadori*, 183.

the sound of nature naturing has been increasingly masked by the noise of anthropocentric humanity aggressively doing anything but listening. Though self-improvement (refining one's listening practice) certainly has benefits for the 'self' (however we define that), and improving the self is an important aspect in any politically revolutionary movement,[29] are there any ethical, ecological or political dimensions or implications of a listening practice that treats sounds as beings?

As Federico Campagna writes: 'Although the task of reshaping the framework of reality – through which a particular world emerges to our experience – might appear at first to be far removed from active social engagement, its long-lasting consequences are more dramatic than any superficial revolution at the level of the immediate political system.'[30] Reconceiving our relations with other phenomena as one of infinite interpenetration, and embodying that in all aspects of our lives, can similarly radically change the ethical stance we take towards other beings, inclusive of radical changes in our social and political activities. Philosopher Takemura Makio (竹村牧男; b. 1948) writes that 'environmental problems are directly related to the issue of one's relationship to others',[31] and that a true universal awareness of the Kegon axiom of 'unimpeded interpenetration of phenomena and phenomena' would necessarily lead to the end of competition with our fellow beings and bring about universal compassion (and implicitly an end to the destruction of nonhuman beings and environments). He also notes that the Sanskrit word which is usually translated as 'compassion'[32] – *karuṇā* (Jp. *jihi* 慈悲) – in fact literally

[29] However well-intentioned, a revolution led by those who are mentally scarred by the system they wish to replace can only replicate it in more or less warped forms.

[30] Federico Campagna, *Technic and Magic* (London: Bloomsbury, 2018), 191–2.

[31] Takemura Makio, 'One Step Towards Buddhism as Philosophy', trans. Suhara Eiji, in *The Dao Companion to Japanese Buddhist Philosophy*, ed. Gereon Kopf (2009. Trans. Springer Nature, 2019), 78.

[32] Graham Priest suggests 'care' as a better translation than 'compassion' for the standard usage of *karuṇā*. Graham Priest, *Capitalism – its Nature and its Replacement: Buddhist and Marxist Insights* (London: Routledge, 2022), 20.

means 'sympathetic oscillation'. The term 'sympathetic oscillation' is also used in music, meaning two sounds whose waves are congruent in particular ways.[33]

The idea of sounds as living beings as presented in this book, though entirely rooted in East Asian philosophical traditions, may strike some as similar to theories of New Materialism, which ascribes something called 'agency' to nonhuman and non-sentient entities.[34] Andreas Malm, in his book *The Progress of This Storm: Nature and Society in a Warming World*, effectively argues that the advocates of New Materialism confuse agency with causation,[35] and agency only with intended consequences.[36] The cause of a particular effect does not imply the agential intention of the causer. Likewise, a particular intended action resulting in an unintended effect does not absolve the actor of causing that effect. The Buddhist idea of ascribing buddha nature to all things – to sounds, to moons, to dust, to humans, to fences, to shit, to light, to daemons, to dragons, to buddhas, *et cetera* – is crucially different from the ideas of the New Materialists in this idea of intention. Intention requires desire, which results in goal-oriented action. Conversely, buddha nature is definitionally without intention; the founding idea of Buddhism is Siddhārtha Gautama's Four Noble Truths, the second of which is that the cause of suffering (Sk. *dukkha*; Jp. *ku* 苦) is desire, craving or

[33] This refers to sound waves whose speed of oscillation (measured in Hertz) is related in simple whole-number ratios. There is an entire genre of experimental music based on explorations of these just intonation intervals which is tangentially related to the New York School of Cage and his companions and disciples, especially James Tenney. See Mark Sabat, *Plainsound Music Edition* (n.d.), https://www.plainsound.org.

[34] Indeed, much of so-called postmodern (or non-modern) philosophies often seem to be lifting ideas from Buddhism without actually understanding them. Or, more charitably, they often read like they are rediscovering ideas that they don't realize have existed, have been debated and refined, for thousands of years within the Indian and East Asian intellectual traditions. Needless to say, the quality of their arguments suffers for being unaware of the vast history of human thought which has already explored what they present as virgin territory.

[35] Andreas Malm, *The Progress of This Storm: Nature and Society in a Warming World* (2018; repr. London: Verso, 2020), 92.

[36] Ibid., 94*ff*.

attachment (Sk. *tṛṣṇā*; Jp. *ai* 愛). Beings who are resonating with and enacting their innate buddha nature do not have desires, or, at least, do not have desires that manifest intentional action. In other words, sounds – like all non-sentient beings – are alive, they enact buddha nature, but they do not have agency (they are, after all, *non-sentient*).

New Materialism is a profoundly anti-ethical ontology in that it absolves human beings from any responsibility to other beings, or any culpability for unintended consequences of actions we take. Graham Parkes points out that the realization in Mahāyāna Buddhist thought that this very world is *nirvāṇa* shifts the focus of 'our attention on this present existence as the only one, and on affirming and working to improve it'.[37]

Parkes additionally takes on several arguments presented against the merits, with regard to the current environmental crises, of the Kegon and Zen ideas this book has been exploring. One of these is Ian Harris' argument against

> those who aim to use the Hua-Yen [Kegon] doctrine of the mutual interpenetration of all things. . . . However, the category of 'all things' includes insecticides, totalitarian regimes and nuclear weapons and the argument therefore possesses some rather obvious problems. In short, it suffers from a certain vacuity from the moral perspective.[38]

A second is 'Critical Buddhist' Matsumoto Shirō's argument against the idea of *sōmoku jōbutsu* as a useful tool in reconceptualizing the human relationship with the natural world. Matsumoto writes, 'It is simply not logically possible to derive environmental ethics from an Eastern naturalism expressed in such phrases as "mountains, rivers, plants, and

[37] Graham Parkes, 'Kūkai and Dōgen as Exemplars of Ecological Engagement', in *Japanese Environmental Philosophy*, ed. J. Baird Callicott and James McRae (Oxford: Oxford University Press, 2017), 66.

[38] Ian Harris, 'Getting to Grips With Buddhist Environmentalism: A Provisional Typology', *Journal Of Buddhist Ethics* 2 (1995): 176.

trees are all enlightened." Such "naturalism" leads nowhere but to the "natural state of doing nothing . . . "'.[39]

Parkes responds to these arguments by pointing out that, for Dōgen, it is not any particular phenomenon and its buddha nature or its impermanence which is important,

> it's rather the organized totality of their dynamic interactions (which he calls *shitsu-u* 悉有, or 'whole-being') that's important. As with Kūkai, human activities and artifacts participate too; but since what's crucial is *zenki*, the dynamic functioning of all phenomena together, there would be every reason to eliminate, rather than celebrate, something as toxic as plutonium waste. Indeed, Dōgen would want to ask the deeper question concerning the desires that drive us to consume so much energy that we think such contrivances as nuclear power plants, with all the dangers and problems that they involve, are a worthwhile component in the whole. . . .
>
> The way of life, then, that Kūkai and Dōgen advocate involves energetic participation in the dynamic functioning of the whole world. Their discourses on natural phenomena encourage a respectful and reciprocal engagement with artifacts and things of nature and an attitude open to the wisdom expressed in their words and letters. And their ideas give every warrant for promoting (though it was unnecessary in their times) an overcoming of the hubris of our anthropocentrism in order to preserve and enhance the workings of Buddha-nature all over this green and blue planet.[40]

The practice of attentive, experimental listening explored in this book is only a small aspect of what Dōgen's or Kūkai's (空海; 774–835) conception of practice would have entailed. However, as the small is reflected in the large and *vice versa*, it is expected that, as Parkes suggests, the practice of attention to and attunement with the world

[39] Matsumoto Shirō, 'The Lotus Sūtra and Japanese Culture', in *Pruning the Bodhi Tree: The Storm Over Critical Buddhism*, ed. Jamie Hubbard and Paul L. Swanson (Honolulu: University of Hawai'i Press, 1997), 403

[40] Parkes, 'Kūkai and Dōgen', 83–4.

as a dynamic whole, with each being playing their part in that whole – each abiding in their Dharma position, neither dominating others nor shirking from their life-practice – will lead naturally to a resonant care for the environment inclusive of other human beings, as well as nonhuman beings, and non-sentient beings. Notably, though this attitude of attention, attunement and care describes the ideal of any phenomena within *shitsuu* (any node on Indra's net, any wave on the sea of existence), it also describes an ideal attitude towards playing music in an ensemble, especially the responsibilities involved in improvising with others, whether it occurs in the genres of jazz, free jazz or free improvisation.

7.5 *harin*

Cage's poem for the tenth Ox Picture ('Entering the Marketplace with Full Hands') reads 'not withheld from any form of life'.[41] It is an image of *kyakurai*, returning to the conventional world and helping others. This action of returning and helping is embodied by the figure of the bodhisattva (Jp. *bosatsu* 菩薩), an awakened one who devotes themselves to the salvation of other beings. Jay Garfield describes the motivation of the bodhisattva as a 'realization that not to experience the suffering of others as one's own, and not to take the welfare of others as one's own, is to suffer even more deeply from profound existential alienation born of a failure to appreciate one's own situation as a member of an inter-dependent community'.[42] If you embody an understanding of the interpenetration of the self with all other phenomena, radical empathy is inevitable, since any suffering is your suffering.

One of the most important and popular of the bodhisattvas is Kanzeon Bosatsu (観世音菩薩; Sk. Avalokiteśvara bodhisattva; Ch.

[41] Sugimoto, *Honkadori*, 184.

[42] Jay Garfield, *Engaging Buddhism: Why It Matters to Philosophy* (Oxford: Oxford University Press, 2015), 296.

Guānshìyīn púsà), also known as Kannon. The Chinese characters literally mean '[s/he] who hears the sufferings of the world'.[43] Through listening, Kannon perceives the suffering of all beings.[44] However painful listening to the suffering of all beings in the world is, not to do so would be to isolate oneself in a fictional, hollow world divorced from conventional reality. The ideal state of being is to comprehend reality through playing in the hollow expanse while abiding in reality, not to alienate oneself in unreality. When Cage writes that for this circle – for him, the tenth Ox Picture, which can be equated to Zenchiku's *harin*, the breaking free of the necessary strictures of training – the skills and insights of the self are 'not withheld   from any form of life', we can read out an injunction: through [listening] practice, extend (do not withhold) care, compassion, sympathetic resonance (*karuṇā*) to all beings, human, nonhuman, and non-sentient.

This injunction is to listen political freedom – the freedom *of* each being to exist in its own Dharma position, the freedom *from* each being's Dharma position being occluded by any other – out of an experimental, emancipated[45] listening practice. However, this is not a call for 'committed art'. Art which attempts to communicate a clear message, which committed art necessarily must do, cannot (if it is successful in its intention) be experimental because it does not grant the audience freedom of interpretation. This kind of art reproduces the hierarchy of a teacher—student or master—disciple relationship, as opposed to a community of equal interpreters (*sharing*, per Kondo's

[43] The veneration of Kannon is widespread across Asia, and they are depicted both in female and androgynous male forms.

[44] In Tang China (618–907) a set of thirty-three visual manifestations of Kannon was codified, including the Water-Moon Kannon (Jp. *Suigetsu Kannon* 水月観音), which depicts Kannon meditating in or near water on which moonlight is reflecting. Kim Hyein, *Sensōji shozō 'suigetsu kannon zō' no fukugen kenkyū: gekkō no hyōgen ni tsuite* (Doctoral Dissertation, Tokyo University of the Arts, 2018), 7*ff*.

[45] Jacques Rancière writes that 'Emancipation begins when we challenge the opposition between viewing and acting', which can just as easily be applied to the false dichotomy of listening and performing (or composing). Jacques Rancière, *The Emancipated Spectator*, trans. Gregory Elliott (2008; trans. London: Verso, 2009), 13.

formulation, 'an object of listening'). Furthermore, as Jacques Rancière says of committed art, for it to be effective, the viewer 'must already feel guilty about viewing the image that is to create the feeling of guilt';[46] in other words, committed art – though it certainly has a political function in strengthening the conviction of one's comrades – does not change minds.

Kondo's 'purposeless' music, Cage's 'means of writing music as strict with respect to my ego as sitting cross-legged'[47] – perhaps we could call this composing-zen (*sakkyoku-zen* 作曲禅) – are not denials of the beauty or emotion to be found in listening to music, but they are denials that the composer and their ego can communicate beauty or emotion through sound alone: 'sounds, when allowed to be themselves, do not require that those who hear them do so unfeelingly'.[48] They are also not denials of the political efficacy of listening, performing or composing practices. At one level, as Kondo writes, Modern capitalist societies impose purposefulness on all its citizens and try to ostracize those who are not sufficiently 'productive'. Therefore freedom 'is best cultivated through purposeless activity'.[49] Teleology, the myth of progress, and the myth that humans can exert control over the future are at the heart of capitalist Modernism, and a listening practice that seeks to subvert or protest this society cannot employ teleological progression (harmonic progression or rhythmic progression, to the extent these are considered different parameters), or exert manipulative control over the sonic beings that exist within the frame of the work, or attempt to control the human listeners who will hear the work. At another level, if a purposeless listening practice opens the self to the interdependence and interpenetration of all phenomena and an ethical-socio-political bodhisattva-like extension of practice, then who is to say that it is any less of a practice than just-sitting (*shikantaza* 只管打坐) zazen, the

46 Ibid., 85.

47 John Cage, 'Tokyo Lecture and Three Mesostics', *Perspectives of New Music* 26, no. 1 (1988): 7.

48 Cage, *Silence*, 10.

49 Kondo, *Homo audiens*, 80.

Buddhist way of poetry advocated by Shunzei, the way of nō, or any of the traditional arts.[50]

John Berger wrote that he judged the value of historical artwork 'according to whether or not it helped men in the modern world claim their social rights'.[51] We can expand that to judge any ideas of the past, to decide which dropped threads, in Hine's metaphor, to pick up and revivify. Graham Priest makes a convincingly argued book-length case for general Buddhist and Marxist concepts being complementarily crucial in overcoming the evils of capitalist Modernity in *Capitalism – its Nature and its Replacement: Buddhist and Marxist Insights*. I would similarly argue that the Buddhist cosmology remains liberatory in a way that scientistic Modernism is not.

One practical example of this is the Buddhist collective Jusatsu Kitō Sōdan (呪殺祈祷僧団) – literally curse-death-prayer-monk-group[52] – who were active in the early 1970s. This group – committed to what they termed 'the ultimate act of Buddhist terrorism'[53] – went to industrial sites across Japan and performed esoteric *abhichara* (阿毘遮迦) death curse rituals directed at the executives of companies whose factories were polluting rivers and causing great human and nonhuman suffering. Matsushita Takahiro (松下隆洪), one of the esoteric Shingon monks who was a member of the group, justified their dark magic activism, saying that

> rather than an anthropocentric western humanism, we need a Buddhist perspective which places humanity, and human beings themselves, in an equal position to all other living beings. Therefore, from this Buddhist perspective, polluting can only be understood as an act that seeks to destroy this cosmic environmental balance. . . . Interpreting

[50] Deep listening can also be employed for positive instrumental ends, such as the forensic audio analyses done by the NGO Earshot and the research lab Forensic Architecture, who investigate 'state and corporate violence' such as the Grenfell Tower Fire in London in 2017, or the ongoing genocide in Palestine.

[51] John Berger, *Why Look at Animals* (London: Penguin, 2009), 59.

[52] Osaka Koichiro, *Jusatsu Kito Sodan* (Hong Kong: Para Site, 2019), 39.

[53] Matsushita Takahiro, 'Kōgai kigyōnushi jusatsu to katakiuchi no fukken', *Gendai-no-me*, February 1971.

> the pollution problem as simply as the killing of living beings, the issue with regard to those who commit these murders becomes one of vengeance [and self-defence] . . . . We are not anti-pollutant *per se*. We are simply openly reviving the practice of vendettas on behalf of the dead and dying.[54]

When dismissed as irrational by their targets, Matsushita responded that 'We have no desire for our actions to be analysed by any "advanced science" that terrifies those involved and condones the killing of people with indifference.'[55] In addition to performing esoteric death mantras, the group also visited victims and prayed with and for them, practicing *karuṇā* as much as revenge. In this case, then, a thorough acceptance of Buddhist thought (and a practice steeped in playing in the hollow), applied to the conventional world of suffering that actually exists and we actually live in (and not a fictionalized hollow fantasy), leads not to fatalistic acceptance of the world, but a desire to change it for the improvement of all living things, sentient and non-sentient.

John Berger writes that 'Art is an organized response to what nature allows us to glimpse occasionally. Art sets out to transform the potential recognition into an unceasing one. . . . The transcendental face of art is always a form of prayer.'[56] David Graeber claimed something similar, that 'artistic avant gardes' (though I would argue that it is even more true of the experimentalists) are, like revolutionaries, and like politically-active Buddhists such as the Jusatsu Kitō Sōdan, aware that the conventional world is something collectively made by humans, and we could make it differently.[57] Everything conventional is empty of intrinsic identity and impermanent. We can, then, in a similar manner to that suggested by Ken Friedman (b. 1949), the experimental artist quoted as this chapter's epigraph, 'Imagine a world. / Make it.'[58]

[54] Ibid.

[55] Ibid.

[56] Berger, *Why*, 60.

[57] Graeber, *Revolutions*, 47.

[58] *c.f.* Goode, *The Forest*, 284–5.

7.6 *kūrin*

('Forgetting the Ox and the Person')

('time is provided   is possible   it follows   is transcended'

—Cage[59])

[59] Sugimoto, *Honkadori*, 183.

(月の万水に浮かび

花の匂ひの外に薫るが如くなり)[60]

('like the moon floating in myriad waters,

like the flower's scent permeating the atmosphere'

—Zenchiku)

[60] *Zeami Zenchiku*, 392.

7.∞ *ichiro*

The *Vimalakīrti sūtra* (Jp. 維摩経), with its dramatic structure, touches of humour, and a main character – Vimalakīrti – who was not a cosmic Buddha but a regular human (albeit a learned bodhisattva), was one of the most popular sutras in premodern and early modern Japan. It was also an important sutra in the development of Mahāyāna itself. Nāgārjuna studied it deeply when writing the foundational Mahāyāna text, the *Fundamental Wisdom of the Middle Way* (Sk. *Mūlamadhyamakakārikā*, Jp. *Chūron* 中論).

The framing device of the sutra is that, at the behest of the Buddha, the bodhisattva Mañjuśrī calls upon Vimalakīrti, who proceeds to debate and discuss the teachings of Buddha and the way of the bodhisattvas. In its eighth chapter, Vimalakīrti initiates a discussion of non-dualism. After the gathered Buddhist luminaries propound their ideas of conventional and ultimate realities, Mañjuśrī critiques them by saying that all explanations of non-dualism, by their very use of words, are necessarily dualistic. Finally, in the most famous episode of the sutra, Vimalakīrti is asked his opinion. He says nothing at all. To which Mañjuśrī replies: 'This is indeed the entrance into the nonduality of the bodhisattvas. Here there is no use for syllables, sounds, and ideas.'[61]

But this is not the outright valorization of silence that it seems on the surface. 'Silence' and 'sound' are also a dualism. The point is to hear the silence in sound, the sound in silence. Or, as Frey wrote, the silence 'present in the sounds' (see Section 1.2).[62] It is the embodied understanding of the equality – the non-differentiation – of silence and speech which is the gate to nonduality. Like the final three circles of the Ten Ox Pictures, cycling between hollow emptiness, absolute non-differentiation with all phenomena, and the *kyakurai* of the return to

[61] Dharmachakra Translation Committee, 'The Teaching of Vimalakīrti', in *84000: Translating the Words of the Buddha* (2017; rev. 2025), 8.34.

[62] Frey, 'The Architecture of Silence'.

the conventional reality; like the final three circles Zenchiku's *Rokurin ichiro*, the *zōrin*'s imitation of nature in its manner of operations,[63] the transcendence of the *harin*, the emptiness of the *kūrin*; speech, sound and silence interpenetrate each other, and all are equal – as are all things, in their dharma positions. The one dewdrop – 'Oneness disclosed' – contains all phenomena (*ji*), and all principle (*ri*). Zenchiku draws it, from the beginning, not as a dewdrop, but as a sword that cuts through dualities.

Like the Moon-Water Kannon, we practice listening to the world – its sufferings and its joys, its sins and its salvation, its sounds and silences – as one cosmic dewdrop, as a wave of moonlight on the ocean of reality.

[63] To paraphrase Cage's famous paraphrase of Thomas Aquinas' *ars imitatur naturam in sua operatione.*

Afterword

The hollow soundscape of Zushi Beach

Each morning, weather permitting, before composing or writing – or, when I used to teach just down the coast, going to work – I walk along Zushi Beach (逗子海岸). Every day the experience is different, which is what makes it a ritual practice, as well as a creative stimulus.

The beach itself is not particularly notable. If I didn't live a few minutes' walk away, I wouldn't make the effort to come. It's sandy, about 900m long, stretching in a crescent shape from the northwest to south. At the south end is a concrete seawall separating the beach from the mouth of the Tagoe River (田越川).[1] The beach, so far as I know, features in only a few commercially released experimental recordings. One of these is on Tsunoda's *Extract From Field Recording Archive* (CD 5 Track 2), titled 'Vibration through long and thick rope at seashore'. The titular seashore is identified as Zushi Beach in the liner notes.[2]

* * *

I am not a philosopher, at least not by training. I'm principally a composer and sound artist, who came to Japan to study in 2006 without any knowledge of its traditional music or religious thought. My purpose then was extractive and Modernist – I had come to study contemporary

[1] The Tagoe River is a minor *utamakura* place itself. Though it doesn't appear in many *utamakura* handbooks, it does appear in one of the most important scenes of the *Tale of the Heiki* (Heiki Monogatari 平家物語). It was on the banks of the Tagoe that Rokudai, the very last male member of the defeated Taira clan, was found and executed on the order of the victorious Minamoto Yoritomo. Takahashi Mutsuo, who lives nearby, includes the Tagoe River in his collection of original *utamakura* poems. Takahashi, *utamakura*, 45–7.

[2] Tsunoda, *Extract*, 25, 39.

composition under Jo Kondo, and also to learn just enough about nō to appropriate its unique rhythmic sensibility in my own music. This study of nō quickly overwhelmed me and my purposes, propelling me ever deeper in the study of mediaeval Japanese aesthetics, philosophy, religion, poetry, society, gender, sexuality and music. Almost twenty years later, I feel myself to still be a beginner in all these fields.

My compositions, after the first few months in Japan, began to change as I absorbed this knowledge. They continue to do so. My practice is not goal-directed, so who knows where it will go in future. All I can do is more fully sublimate my own ego in favour of just listening, and if what I listen out is sufficiently pleasing, record it in a way that I hope will allow other listeners to also listen something meaningful to them out of the resultant work.

* * *

I can't claim an identical approach to the soundwalk every time I do it. If I'm not in Zushi, of course the location varies. When I am in Zushi, there is still some variation, in that I enter right in the middle of the beach, and can either go north or south (I tend to alternate between the two). Some days I attempt to bracket my listening, attending to the layers of sounds as they are. I focus on the wash of the waves, the occasional cries of surfers, barking dogs, the hum of fishing boats leaving Abuzuri Harbour (鐙摺港) a few hundred metres away. In the summer months, lifeguards are warming up, practicing rescue techniques and CPR on dummies and the beach-side concession stands are prepping for a day of servicing the needs of swimmers and sunbathers. In all seasons, on the other side of my ear, the droning of traffic on the busy highway that borders the beach is omnipresent, but can, to an extent, be filtered out through focussed listening.

But some days I am not focussed, and other thoughts crowd my mind. If these are unrelated to the soundwalk I try to refocus. But sometimes they are intriguing complementary observations: the schools of tiny fish whose members grow every day, the crabs – some as small as a centimetre across, others as large as my fist – who move so slowly on the beach and so quickly in the water. One particularly unpleasant day there were dozens of rotting fish and bird carcasses strewn across the beach; on that day the olfactory observation masked any soundwalk I might have hoped to do.[3] Having lived and/or worked in Zushi for twelve years and counting, some days, inevitably, memory crowds in and establishes a sublayer to my perceptions – sometimes, stepping across the buoy rope, I hear Tsunoda's recording resonating in my head, or, coming to the line of concrete blocks which artificially delineate the border between the beach and the mouth of the Tagoe River, I think about its *utamakura* poetry too.

* * *

Having recognized the superficiality of appropriating only the *jo-ha-kyū* rhythmic structure of nō (which was in any case appropriated into nō by Zeami from *gagaku* music theory, itself rooted in Confucianism and Chinese aesthetics), my first attempts to grapple with the wider net (constellation, mesh, archipelago) of traditions that informed and thence grew out of Kan'ami, Zeami and Zenchiku's practices and theories of nō was poetry. Shunzei's idea of the Buddhist path of poetry and Ueda's idea of hollow words both pointed to art as being a complement to religion on the path to awakening. I set *waka* and other Japanese poems – *e.g. Dawn Prayers* (2011; Jp. 後朝の歌) for biwa, koto and viol, and *Spectral (for Kazuo Ohno)* (2012; Jp. スペクトル––––大野一雄氏に寄せて) for voice, biwa and shō – and used *waka* as found objects to construct pitch matrices to use as the basis of my compositions – for example *mountain/cherry/blossoms* (2012; Jp. 山桜花) for piano and *plaintive belling* (2013; Jp. 小雄鹿) for koto.

But I came to feel that this was still a superficial engagement with the cultural heritage of my adopted home.

* * *

[3] I did attempt to find out what had happened, but the beach was soon cleaned, and no newspaper or Twitter user commented on it, so I don't know the cause nor who cleaned it up.

As might be expected, and to the extent possible, sound is my focus on a soundwalk, and I walk and listen out for the subtly changing sonic phenomena which delight and surprise me. On high tide days, in the areas of the beach with an uncountable number of tiny fragments of shells, each wave breaks over this bed of calcium carbonate. The shells tumbling over each other create a rich and complex, high-pitched sonic event, beautiful and ineffable, different with every wave. These sounds are delightful as pure experiences of listening, and they also afford my listening out of them a metonym of the cosmic flux and sublimity of existence.

On summer days when the wind blows with uncommon strength, the slap of the powerful waves breaking echoes in hocket with the flapping of the canvas roofs atop some of the beach huts. On such a day the strength of the surf and wind masks the sounds of the highway. Walking the beach with ears open and eyes directed downwards or seawards, one can easily forget that one is in the centre of a bustling (if small) city, at the edge of a busy highway. In addition to the drone of the wind and the low-pitched percussive hocket of canvas and surf, there is also the continuous sound of taut rope being whipped by the wind against metallic flagpoles in a fast, semi-regular rhythm, the high-pitched, dull, bell-like sound audible for tens of metres even against the high surf and wind.

The flagpole itself is used to communicate warnings via large, coloured flags. Though there is no flag hoisted on most windy days, one will be when typhoons are approaching, or when there is a tsunami warning.

* * *

I began to delve more deeply into the syncretic religious aspects of mediaeval Japanese society which so clearly informed nō. At this time (around 2013) I was interested in comparing and contrasting it with early modern Western European Christianity. I wrote *Matsumushi* (2014; Jp. 松虫), an opera for mezzo-soprano and cor anglais (an onstage character) accompanied by violoncello and piano as a response to the idea of *mappō* (末法, the Buddhist age of the end of the dharma, the age in which the truth of Buddhism has passed out of history – which, by some theories, began in the sixth century, but by all measures will have started by now[4]), and as a response to, and companion piece for, Salvatore Sciarrino's music theatre still-life *Vanitas* (1981). *Matsumushi* is based on a nō by Zenchiku – this was also my first encounter with Zenchiku – and is centred around a homosexual love story, a longing for a youthful lover who has long ago died. From this piece the *Vanitas* trilogy grew, a series which also includes *fallings* (2016; Jp. フォーリングス), a music theatre piece for shō/u (笙・竽), viola and violoncello, and *Is nowhere free of bad tidings?* (2017; Jp. 憂きこと聞かぬところありや) for a quintet of traditional Japanese instruments to be performed in a garden.

At the same time, my interest in the soteriological potential of the poetry of place and landscape and interest in *utamakura* poetics both deepened. *Is nowhere free of bad tidings?* was my first site-specific piece, but I had also already begun the previous year to experiment with field recording as a way to sonically integrate the concept of 'place' into my concert music.

The *utamakura* series (2018–22), currently comprising six of a planned seven works, is the first major outgrowth of this aspect of my research. This series of pieces is for instruments and multimedia field recordings (sometimes audio only, some including video). Based on the example of Takahashi Mutsuo's *utamakura awase*, this series alternates between *utamakura* locations in the traditional Japanese canon and new ones outside of Japan – places with culturally resonant histories that, in their own traditions, have a similar function as *utamakura* places do in Japan (Takahashi's non-Japanese *utamakura*

[4] See Jackie Stone on the various theories in China and especially Japan about when the *mappō* Age began. Jackie Stone, 'Seeking Enlightenment in the Last Age: "Mappō" Thought in Kamakura Buddhism: PART I', *The Eastern Buddhist (New Series)* 18, no. 1 (1985): 30*ff*. On my personal engagement with *mappō* thought, see: Daryl Jamieson, 'An Artist's Response to the Climate Crisis Through Japanese *mappō* Thought', *Yin-Cheng Journal of Contemporary Buddhism* 1, no. 2 (2024): 215–28.

places are largely Greco-Roman; mine are in northern Europe). The pieces in the series are:

utamakura 1: *ponds of Nara* (2018) – for electric guitar and audio fixed media

utamakura 2: *Arnardalur* (2018) – for violin, piano and audiovisual fixed media

utamakura 3: *Saihōji* (2018) – for high voice, cor anglais, percussion and audio fixed media

utamakura 4: *St Dunstan-in-the-East* (2019) – for wind quintet and audio fixed media

utamakura 5: *Mount Kamakura* (2019) – for 17-string bass koto, Pierrot ensemble and audiovisual fixed media

utamakura 6: *Fårö* [not yet completed] – for viola d'amore, and audiovisual fixed media

utamakura 7: *Shiogama* (2022) – for 'cello, butoh dancer, audiovisual fixed media

In all these pieces of the *utamakura* series, the live instrumentalists are conceived of as *waki* – live, human interlocutors whose knowledge and skill serve as a medium to call forth the spirits (*kami*, if you will) of the places, represented by the sounds (and sometimes video) recorded at those places. Like Shunzei – who observed that if you visit an *utamakura* location you will notice that the conventional reality differs from the poetic (i.e. ultimate) reality, thus indicating the truth of transcendent ultimate reality above the flux of the world as we conventionally understand it – part of my intention in highlighting the differences of the soundscape as written about in the past and the soundscape I recorded in Modernity is to emphasize the destructive effects of industrialization and climate change on these oft-sung places.

* * *

One mid-August morning I arrive at Zushi beach just at low tide. Zushi beach is a tourist beach, so in summer, to make it prettier for out-of-towners to drink and get sunburnt on, the city regularly lays down tonnes of fresh, pristine sand. This is soon washed away and replaced, in a regularly occurring cycle that continues until the end of the season. The result of all this sand being washed away is that – especially in the late summer – the sea floor is very shallow for several metres away from the shore, and at low tide you can comfortably wade well beyond the inter-tidal zone.

Even in this artificially enhanced state, the shallow seafloor is texturally quite different from the inter-tidal zone it was so recently a part of. Here the sand undulates in imitation of the waves rolling over it, and small crabs and schools of baby fish abound, presumably safe in the knowledge that it is too shallow for larger predatory fish to swim there or for birds of prey to safely dive from above. The metres-long shallows mean that waves break well away from the shoreline and gently move along the shallows as an echo – the rhythm of the waves and these echoes, and their interpenetration at the shore as the stronger ones reflect back into the shallows is fascinating both visually and aurally. The rhythm is both regular and not regular;[5] in the longer pauses I fancy I can hear the tiny sounds of fishlings jumping and crabs scuttling. Is it my aural imagination, assigning the gurgles and clicks I hear in the general soundscape to the tiny creatures I can see with my eyes, or can I actually hear these small beings? Maybe it doesn't actually matter – sound is just touch, pitch is just rhythm and both are just ways human brains have evolved to make sense of an evolutionarily determined subset of signals. If I think I have heard these tiny sounds – and I have perceived *something* – that is enough. Who can tell me otherwise, and how could that affect my subjective experience?

* * *

[5] R. Murray Schafer's String Quartet 2: *Waves* (1976) is one concert work which takes its structure from the composer's deep listening to the rhythm of waves.

I increasingly began to feel that the sterility of the soundproofed concert hall and recording studio were places isolated from reality. In other words, these places are hollow vessels with their uses and potentials, but they are not conducive to the Uedan injunction to play in the hollow while abiding in reality. That is to say, while an artist might abide in reality and play in the hollow worlds of studios, the sounds themselves are confined in these 'soundproof' spaces, unable to themselves abide in reality.

I wanted to find a way to explore a truer experience of working with, playing with sounds and musicians in a dynamically unpredictable, living sonic environment. One aspect of this was working more with musicians improvisatorily responding to field recordings, an aspect of the collaborative compositional process the pianist Yasaka Kimihiro (八坂公洋) and I employed in developing the piano and audiovisual piece *Gotō (archipelago)* (2023; Jp. 五島(アーキペラゴ)).

This was also a driving force in the *Descants* series (2020–21; Jp. デスカント) – five pieces for solo instruments (shō/u, high voice, objects, viola and shakuhachi 尺八) in a 'natural' environment – as well as *Music to welcome moons into waves* (2025; Jp. 浪月楽) for ryūteki 龍笛, hichiriki/ōhichiriki 篳篥・大篳篥, shō/u and obbligato gakubiwa 楽琵琶 (all gagaku instruments) for performance outdoors. These pieces are conceived of as foregrounding the contingent sounds of the environment, with the composed instrumental part being a descant – in Western music practice, a contrapuntal counter-thematic melodic line that is sung or played above the principal music – sonically inscribed above the sound of nature naturing. In other words, the pre-composed music of these pieces (which can be flexibly adjusted in consideration of the beings already sounding in the listening-*cum*-performance place) is a palimpsestic, cultural layer modifying the listeners' perceptions of reality in the way that Shunzei described the effect of a remembered poem, or how the *waki* listens sacred *kagura* music out of the sound of the rain in Zenchiku's *Tatsuta*.

* * *

At low tide, the sand in the intertidal zone is saturated with seawater, which wants – like all water – to return to oneness with the sea. All along the beach, starting from the high-tide mark, tiny rivulets spring up, the smallest of rivers with the shortest of lifespans, destined to arise, flow with life and be extinguished within hours. And yet, they develop a visual form that looks, at least to my non-geographer's eye, like any aerial photograph of any undammed river system in the world. Though with a lifespan counted in hours as opposed to millennia, they are every bit as alive as the Amazon, as a mayfly is as alive as a great sequoia despite living vastly different lives, over vastly different lifespans. Can I hear the thundering flow of these metres-long rivers and centimetres-long tributaries? Do they cry out with suffering or with joy as the rising tide engulfs them?

* * *

I have not abandoned concert music, and my research into nō theory and Japanese aesthetics informs my concert works as much as my site-specific and field recording ones. Drawing on the structure of distributed leadership and flexibility of pulse in nō, after *Is nowhere free of bad tidings?*, my ensemble works have mostly eschewed scores in favour of parts with occasional aural cues for rough coordination. This is especially useful in theatre works, since it gives musicians the flexibility to follow the actors' play with the delivery of lines and enacting of gesture. One example of this is *The Seaweed Gatherers* (2022), a theatre piece I co-wrote with Scottish artists Graham Eatough and Miek Zwamborn adapting Zenchiku's *Mekari*, re-setting it on the Isle of Mull.

Even in solo concert pieces, like *Ro* (2021; Jp. 露) for piano, or *though frost settles* (2025; Jp. 霜は置くとも) for timpani and small percussion, I now prefer to use proportional notation and write each phrase on its own line, leaving plenty of white space which doesn't mean a pause – this style of notation gives the performer the same freedom as a theatrical actor has to decide how to pace themselves, and to respond to the hall and the listeners. As Chris Goode says about the silences in Harold Pinter's plays, 'a silence is communal, and that silence . . . must be sought collectively from the audience . . . *i.e.* waited for'.[6] Nō, a music drama with three to four instrumentalists, multiple actor/singers and usually eight chorus members, does not use scores either, and the actors and drummers in particular have a reasonably wide latitude to shape the rhythmic sense of their parts, and adjust depending on the situation.

* * *

On rare mornings, walking the beach under the rays of the morning sun, the moon still lingers in the sky. Though its light is too faint for me to make out its reflections, I nonetheless know they are there, glinting back from the myriad waves.

* * *

The final fluxion of nō practice, according to both Zeami and Zenchiku, is casting off any *conscious* sense of what you have embodied through decades of practice, and enacting nō through a beginner's mind. The performer abandons conscious thought of their training and simply becomes a conduit through which, to borrow Nishida's formulation, the world expresses itself.[7] Or a conduit through which buddha nature, or a *kami*, or a place expresses itself.

A soundwalking practice, and my intense listening practice of field recording, is the closest I have come to this, but I cannot report having 'accomplished' anything. Practice is simply practice, neither a means nor an end.

The pieces in which I exercise the least conscious control are my text scores, especially *from line (after Lee Ufan)* (2018; Jp. 線より:李禹煥の作品にちなんで), a piece for ensemble (any instruments) about the beauty of losing control of – ruining – delicate

6 Goode, *The Forest*, 74.

7 Nishida Kitarō, 'Seimei', in *Nishida Kitarō Zenshū*, vol. 11 (Tokyo: Iwanami Shoten, 1988), 289–370.

sounds, and *Descants* 3 (2021). Unlike the other four *Descants* pieces, *Descants* 3 requires the performer to construct a temporary ritual place, using *onmyōdō* geomantic principles (represented by appropriately coloured objects at the cardinal points and in the centre) to delineate the site of listening. The objects can be struck percussively, but they can also just 'be', sounding or not of their own volition. *Descants* 3 is kind of response to *4'33"* where it is not 'time' that frames the listening, but 'place'.

* * *

Every sound is a wave breaking against your ear. Does the moonlight reflect back from these waves too?

Bibliography

Akama, Ryoko. *senu hima*. Melange Edition, 2015. Compact Disc.

Akimoto, Kichiro, ed. *Fudoki*. Nihon Koten Bungaku Taikei, vol. 2. Tokyo: Iwanami Shoten, 1958.

Another, Timbre. 'Evan Johnson: Dust Book'. *Another Timbre* (2025). https://www.anothertimbre.com/products/evan-johnson-dust-book-marco-fusi-viola-damore (accessed 13 September 2025).

Aoki, Michiko Y. *Records of Wind and Earth: A Translation of Fudoki with Introduction and Commentaries*. Ann Arbor: Association for Asian Studies, 1997.

Atkins, Paul S. 'Depictions of the Kawara-no-in in Medieval Japanese Nō Drama'. *Asian Theatre Journal* 27, no. 1 (2010): 1–22.

Atkins, Paul S. *Revealed Identity: The Noh Plays of Komparu Zenchiku*. Ann Arbor: University of Michigan Center for Japanese Studies, 2006.

Atkins, Paul S. *Teika*. Honolulu: University of Hawai'i Press, 2017.

Barad, Karen. 'Nature's Queer Performativity'. *Kvinder, Køn & Forskning* 1–2 (2012): 25–53. https://doi.org/10.7146/kkf.v0i1-2.28067.

Barthes, Roland. *Image Music Text*. Translated by Stephen Heath. London: Fontana Press, 1977.

Berger, John. *Portraits*. Edited by Tom Overton. 2015. Reprint London: Verso, 2017.

Berger, John. *Why Look at Animals*. London: Penguin, 2009.

Berlioz, Hector. 'Les Troyens'. In *New Edition of the Complete Works* vol. 2b, edited by Hugh Macdonald. Kassel: Bärenreiter, BA 5442/II, 1969.

Beyer, Stephan V. *Singing to the Plants: A Guide to Mestizo Shamanism in the Upper Amazon*. Albuquerque: University of New Mexico Press, 2009.

Bialock, David T. 'From *Heike* to *Nomori no kagami*: *Onmyōdō* and the Soundscapes of Medieval Japan'. *Cahiers d'Extrême-Asie*, vol. 21, *The Way of Yin and Yang: Divinatory Techniques and Religious Practices* (2012): 165–99.

Bin, Kimura. 'Self and Nature—An Interpretation of Schizophrenia'. *Zen Buddhism Today* 6 (1988): 1–10.

Bloom, Peter. *Berlioz in Time: From Early Recognition to Lasting Renown*. Rochester: University of Rochester Press, 2022.

Bourriaud, Nicolas. *The Exform*. London: Verso, 2016.

Bowring, Richard. *Religious Traditions of Japan 500–1600*. Cambridge: Cambridge University Press, 2005.

Boym, Svetlana. *The Future of Nostalgia*. New York: Basic Books, 2001.

Bruce, Neil Spencer. 'Extending Soundwalking Practice: Soundsitting as an Inclusive and Complementary Method to Soundwalking'. *Acoustics* 5, no. 3 (2023): 788–97. https://doi.org/10.3390/acoustics5030046.

Cage, John. 'Autobiographical Statement'. *John Cage Trust*, 1990. johncage.org/autobiographical_statement.html (accessed 18 September 2025).

Cage, John. *The Selected Letters of John Cage*. Edited by Laura Kuhn. Middletown: Wesleyan University Press, 2016.

Cage, John. *Silence*. 1961. Reprint, Middletown: Wesleyan University Press, 2011.

Cage, John. 'Tokyo Lecture and Three Mesostics'. *Perspectives of New Music* 26, no. 1 (1988): 6–25.

Campagna, Federico. *Prophetic Culture: Recreation For Adolescents*. London: Bloomsbury, 2021.

Campagna, Federico. *Technic and Magic*. London: Bloomsbury, 2018.

Carta, Maria. *Nottes de incantu 1974-1992*. Recording Arts, 2005. Compact Disc.

Cheng Hsueh-Li. 'Confucianism and Zen (Ch'an): Philosophy of Education'. *Journal of Chinese Philosophy* 12 (1985): 197–215.

Chua, Daniel K. L. *Absolute Music and the Construction of Meaning*. Cambridge: Cambridge University Press, 1999.

Chua, Daniel K. L. and Alexander Rehding. *Alien Listening: Voyager's Golden Record and Music from Earth*. New York: Zone Books, 2021.

Cohen, Leonard. *The Future*. Columbia Records, 1992.

Daniel, Drew. 'All Sound is Queer'. *The Wire* 333 (2011): 42–7. www.academia.edu/15525147/ALL_SOUND_IS_QUEER (accessed 17 September 2025).

Davis, Bret W. 'Natural Freedom: Human/Nature Nondualism in Zen and Japanese Thought'. In *The Oxford Handbook of Japanese Philosophy*, edited by Bret W. Davis, 685–718. Oxford: Oxford University Press, 2018. https://doi.org/10.1093/oxfordhb/9780199945726.013.34.

Davis, Bret W. *Zen Pathways: An Introduction to the Philosophy and Practice of Zen Buddhism*. Oxford: Oxford University Press, 2022.

Denyer, Frank. *In The Margins of Composition*. London: Vision Edition, 2019.

Denyer, Frank. *Screens*. 2018; rev. 2021. Score.

Denyer, Frank. *Screens*. Performed by Octandre Ensemble. Another Timbre, at 220, 2023. Compact Disc.

DeWoskin, Kenneth J. *A Song for One or Two: Music and the Concept of Art in Early China*. Ann Arbor: Center for Chinese Studies at the University of Michigan, 1982.

Dharmachakra Translation Committee. 'The Questions of the Kinnara King Druma'. *84000: Translating the Words of the Buddha*, 2020. Revised 2025. https://84000.co/translation/toh157 (accessed 14 September 2025).

Dharmachakra Translation Committee. 'The Teaching of Vimalakīrti'. *84000: Translating the Words of the Buddha*, 2017. Revised 2025. https://84000.co/translation/toh176 (accessed 19 September 2025).

Dōgen. 'Dōgen Zenji Wakashū'. In *Dōgen Zenji Zenshū*, vol. 7, edited by Ōkubo Dōshū, 152–79. Tokyo: Shunshū sha, 1990.

Dōgen. *Shōbōgenzō*. Edited by Mizuno Yaoko. Tokyo: Iwanami, 1990.

Dōgen. *Treasury of the True Dharma Eye: Zen Master Dogen's Shobo Genzo*. Edited by Tanahashi Kazuaki. Boston: Shambala, 2010.

Dōgen. *The True Dharma-Eye Treasury*. Translated by Gudo Wafu Nishijima and Chodo Cross. 1994–99. Reprint, Berkeley: Numata Center for Buddhist Translation and Research, 2007.

Dōgen and Kōshō Uchiyama Rōshi. *How to Cook Your Life*. Translated by Thomas Wright. 1983. English edn. Boulder: Shambhala, 2005.

Duckworth, William. 'Anything I Say Will Be Misunderstood: An Interview with John Cage'. In *John Cage at Seventy-Five*, 15–33. Lewisburg: Bucknell University Press, 1989.

Dunscombe, Sam. *Two Forests / Oceanic*. Black Truffle, BT111, 2023. https://samdunscombe.bandcamp.com/album/two-forests (accessed 16 September 2025).

Dutta, Sumita and Dipankar Chakraborty. 'The Untold History of Jal Tarang: A Critical Exploration of its Origin, Evolution and Preservation Initiatives'. *Sangeet Galaxy e-Journal* 13, no. 2 (2024): 4–16.

Federici, Silvia. *Caliban and the Witch: Women, the Body and Primitive Accumulation*. New York: Autonomedia, 2004.

Feldman, Morton. *Give My Regards to Eighth Street: Collected Writings of Morton Feldman*. Edited by Bernard Harper Friedman. Cambridge: Exact Change, 2000.

Fisher, Mark. *Capitalist Realism: Is There No Alternative?* London: Zero Books, 2009.

Frey, Jürg. 'The Architecture of Silence'. *wandelweiser*, 1998. https://wandelweiser.de/_juerg-frey/texts-e.html#THE (accessed 13 September 2025).

Friedman, Ken. *12 Structures: Scores by Ken Friedman*. London: The Centre of Attention London, 2004. https://web.archive.org/web/20160328233307/http://www.thecentreofattention.org/exhibitions/Ken Friedman 12 Structures.pdf (accessed 19 September 2025).

Fujita Masakatsu. *Nishida Kitarō no shisaku sekai*. Tokyo: Iwanami, 2011.

Fujita Masakatsu. 'The Development of Nishida Kitarō's Philosophy: Pure Experience, Place, Action-Intuition'. In *The Oxford Handbook of Japanese Philosophy*, edited by Bret W. Davis, 389–416. Oxford: Oxford University Press, 2019. https://doi.org/10.1093/oxfordhb/9780199945726.013.21.

Fujiwara no Shunzei. 'Korai fūteishō'. In *Zokugun Shoruijū* vol. 16-b, 3rd edn, edited by Hanawa Hokiichi, revised by Ōta Tōshirō, 678–738. Tokyo: Zokugun Shoruijū Kanzeikai, 1989.

Furanku Berunāru [Bernard Frank]. *Fūryū to oni: Heian no hikari to yami*. Translated by Furanko Junko. Tokyo: Heibonsha, 1998.

Gagliano, Monica. *Thus Spoke the Plant*. Berkeley: North Atlantic Books, 2018.

Garfield, Jay. *Engaging Buddhism: Why It Matters to Philosophy*. Oxford: Oxford University Press, 2015.

Gibson, James. *The Ecological Approach to Visual Perception*. Boston: Houghton Mifflin, 1979.

Gilmore, Bob. 'Five Maps of the Experimental World'. In *Artistic Experimentation in Music: an Anthology*, edited by Darla Crispin and Bob Gilmore, 23–9. Leuven: Leuven University Press, 2014.

Ginsberg, Robert. *The Aesthetics of Ruins*. Rodopi: Amsterdam, 2004.

Goode, Chris. *The Forest and the Field: Changing Theatre in a Changing World*. London: Oberon Books, 2015.

Gottschalk, Jennie. *Experimental Music since 1970*. London: Bloomsbury, 2016.

Graeber, David. *Debt: The First 5000 Years*. Hoboken: Melville House, 2011.

Graeber, David. *Fragments of an Anarchist Anthropology*. Chicago: Prickly Paradigm Press, 2004.

Graeber, David. *Revolutions in Reverse: Essays on Politics, Violence, Art, and Imagination*. London: Minor Compositions, 2011.

Graeber, David. 'What's the Point If We Can't Have Fun?'. *The Baffler* 24 (2014). https://thebaffler.com/salvos/whats-the-point-if-we-cant-have-fun (accessed 16 September 2025).

Graeber, David and David Wengrow. *The Dawn of Everything: A New History of Humanity*. London: Allen Lane, 2021.

Griffiths, Paul. *Modern Music and After*, 3rd edn. Oxford: Oxford University Press, 2010.

Grisey, Gérard. *Écrits ou l'invention de la musique spectrale*. Edited by Guy Lelong and Anne-Marie Réby. Paris: Musica Falsa, 2008.

Gros, Frédéric. *A Philosophy of Walking*. Translated by John Howe. 2009; English edn. London: Verso, 2014.

Gunnarsson, Guðmundur Steinn. 'A Circle With Four Corners: Guðmundur Steinn Gunnarsson's Rough Thoughts on Composition'. In *The Foam We Removed From The Office* (Blog, 2024). https://www.thefoamweremovedfromtheoffice.com/2024/06/14/a-circle-with-four-corners-gudmundur-steinn-gunnarssons-rough-thoughts-on-composition/ (accessed 19 September 2025).

Harada Kaori. 'Hakuin zenji to nōgaku'. *Kokusai zen kenkyū* 3 (2019): 95–115. https://doi.org/10.34428/00011034.

Hare, Thomas Blenman. *Zeami's Style: The Noh Plays of Zeami Motokiyo*. Stanford: Stanford University Press, 1986.

Harris, Ian. 'Getting to Grips With Buddhist Environmentalism: A Provisional Typology'. *Journal Of Buddhist Ethics* 2 (1995): 173–90.

Hartley, L. P. *The Go-Between*. 1953. Reprint. London: Penguin, 1997.

Harvey, Jonathan. 'The Genesis of Quartet No. 4'. In *Identity and Difference: Essays on Music, Language and Time*, edited by Peter Dejans, 43–53. Leuven: Leuven University Press, 2004.

Harvey, Jonathan. 'Spiritual Music: "Positive" Negative Theology?'. In *Contemporary Music and Spirituality*, edited by Robert Sholl and Sander Van Maas, 311–25. London: Routledge, 2017.

Hayashi Ōki and Andō Chizuko, eds. *Kogorin*. Tokyo: Taishūkan, 1997.

Hesmondhalgh, David and Georgina Born, eds. *Western Music and Its Others: Difference, Representation, and Appropriation in Music*. Berkeley: University of California Press, 2000.

Hine, Dougald. *At Work in the Ruins: Finding Our Place in the Time of Climate Crises and Other Emergencies*. White River Junction: Chelsea Green Publishing, 2023.

Hirata, Catherine Costello. 'The Sounds of the Sounds Themselves: Analyzing the Early Music of Morton Feldman'. *Perspectives of New Music* 34, no. 1 (1996): 6–27.

Holt, Matthew. 'Capital as Fiction: The Communist Manifesto'. In *Literature and Politics: Pushing the World in Certain Directions*, edited by Peter Marks, 11–22. Newcastle upon Tyne: Cambridge Scholars Publishing, 2012.

Houben, Eva-Maria. *On the Periphery*. Edition wandelweiser, 2021.

Ingold, Tim. *Being Alive: Essays on Movement, Knowledge and Description*. 2011. Reprint. London: Routledge, 2022.

International Organization for Standardization. *Acoustics — Soundscape: Part 2: Data Collection and Reporting Requirements*. Geneva: International Organization for Standardization, 2018. https://www.iso.org/standard/75267.html (accessed 17 September 2025).

Ishihara Yuko. 'Dialogue as Human Existence: Ueda Shizuteru's Zen Buddhist Philosophy and a Care Ethics of Play'. In *Care Ethics and Beyond: Moral, Epistemological, and Cross-Cultural Perspectives*, edited by Seisuke Hayakawa and Michael Slote, 73–92. Cham: Palgrave Macmillan, 2026

Ishihara, Yuko and Katsunori Miyahara. 'Real harmony of the self: Enactivism and the Kyoto School'. In *Considering, Questioning and Re-Imagining Harmony: Multicultural, Multihistorical and Multidisciplinary Reflections*, edited by Karyn Lai, Rick Benitez, Chenyang Li, 169–88. London: Bloomsbury, 2025.

Itō Masayoshi, ed. *Yōkyokushū* vol. 2. Tokyo: Shinchōsha, 1986.

Izutsu Toyoko. 'Preliminary Essays'. In *The Theory of Beauty in the Classical Aesthetics of Japan*, by Izutsu Toshihiko and Izutsu Toyo. The Hague: Martinus Nijhoff Publishers, 1981.

Jamieson, Daryl. 'An Artist's Response to the Climate Crisis Through Japanese *mappō* Thought'. *Yin-Cheng Journal of Contemporary Buddhism* 1, no. 2 (2024): 215–28. https://doi.org/10.15239/ycjcb.01.02.10.

Jamieson, Daryl. 'The Buddhahood of Plants and Trees In Zenchiku's Nō: The case of *Tatsuta*'. Forthcoming.

Jamieson, Daryl. 'Does a Sound have Buddha-Nature? Kegon Thought and the Aesthetics of Sound'. *The Journal of East Asian Philosophy* (2024). https://doi.org/10.1007/s43493-024-00042-x.

Jamieson, Daryl. 'Field Recording and the Re-enchantment of the World: An Intercultural and Interdisciplinary Approach'. *The Journal of Aesthetics and Art Criticism* 79, no. 2 (2021): 213–26. https://doi.org/10.1093/jaac/kpab001.

Jamieson, Daryl. 'Hollow Sounds: Toward a Zen-Derived Aesthetics of Contemporary Music'. *The Journal of Aesthetics and Art Criticism* 76, no. 3 (2018): 331–40.

Jamieson, Daryl. 'Spirit of Place: Zeami's *Tōru* and the Poetic Manifestation of *Mugen*'. *Japanese Studies* 42, no. 2 (2022): 137–53. https://doi.org/10.1080/10371397.2022.2101991.

Jamieson, Daryl. 'Uncanny Movement Through Virtual Spaces: Michael Pisaro's Fields have Ears'. *MUSICultures* 45, no. 1–2 (2018): 238–54.

Jamieson, Daryl. 'Varje ljud har sitt eget liv'. *Nutida Musik* 291 (2023): 6–26.

Jamieson, Daryl. 'Zenchiku's *Mekari*: Staging Ambiguous and Hollow Worlds'. *Humanities* 14, no. 113 (2025). https://doi.org/10.3390/h14060113.

Janz, Tobias and Chien-Chang Yang, eds. *Decentering Musical Modernity: Perspectives on East Asian and European Music History*. Bielefeld: transcript, 2019.

Johnson, Evan. *Lists, Little Stars: Piano Music 2003–2020*. London: all that dust, 2021.

Jones, David. *The Anathemata*. 1952. Reprint. London: Faber & Faber, 2010.

Josephson-Storm, Jason Ā. *The Myth of Disenchantment: Magic, Modernity, and the Birth of the Human Sciences*. Chicago: University of Chicago Press, 2017.

Kakimoto Akihiro. 'Future Museum with Chocolate, Celery, and Grapefruit'. *So Good* 24 (2020). https://www.sogoodmagazine.com/pastry-recipes/future-museum-chocolate-celery-grapefruit-akihiro-kakimoto/ (accessed 13 September 2025).

Kakinuma Toshie. 'Oral History Interview with Shiomi Mieko', translated by Tomii Reiko. *Kyoto City University of Arts*, 2014. https://www.kcua.ac.jp/arc/ar/shiomi_eg_1/ (accessed 13 September 2025).

Kamei Shin. '*Kieyuku Tsuki:* Chiyo nōhime shichihenge monogatari *no shohon*'. *Bunken tankyū* 39 (2001): 68–76. https://doi.org/10.15017/10338.

Kamens, Edward. *Utamakura, Allusion, and Intertextuality in Traditional Japanese Poetry*. New Haven: Yale University Press, 1997.

Kamo no Chōmei. 'Mumyōshō'. In *Kabunshū Nōgakuronshū*, edited by Hisamatsu Sen'ichi, 35–98. 1961. Reprint. Tokyo: Iwanami Shoten, 1974.

Kasulis, Thomas P. *Engaging Japanese Philosophy: A Short History*. Honolulu: University of Hawai'i Press, 2019.

Katagiri Yōichi. *Utamakura Utakotoba Jiten Zōteiban*. 1999. Revised. Tokyo: Kasamashoin, 2001.

Katō, Hilda. 'The Mumyosho'. *Monumenta Nipponica* 23, no. 3–4 (1968): 351–430.

Kaye, Nick. *Site-specific Art: Performance, Place and Documentation*. London: Routledge, 2000.

Keene, Donald. *Travelers of a Hundred Ages*. New York: Henry Holt and Company, 1989.

Kim Hyein. *Sensōji shozō 'suigetsu kannon zō' no fukugen kenkyū: gekkō no hyōgen ni tsuite*. Doctoral Dissertation, Tokyo University of the Arts, 2018.

Kingsnorth, Paul. 'Exodus: A Theory of Culture'. In *The Abbey of Misrule*. Substack, 2021. https://paulkingsnorth.substack.com/p/exodus (accessed 19 September 2025).

Klein, Susan Blakeley. *Dancing the Dharma: Religious and Political Allegory in Japanese Noh Theater*. Cambridge, MA: Harvard University Press, 2021.

Klein, Susan Blakeley. 'Esotericism in Noh commentaries and plays Konparu Zenchiku's Meishukushū and Kakitsubata'. In *The Culture of Secrecy in Japanese Religion*, edited by Bernhard Scheid and Mark Teeuwen, 229–54. London: Routledge, 2015.

Kondo Jo. *Homo audiens*. Translated by Daryl Jamieson. Cologne: MusikTexte, 2022.

Kondō Jō. *Mimi no shikō*. Tokyo: Seidosha, 1985.

Kondo Jo. *Mr. Bloomfield, His Spacing*. Tokyo: ALM Records, ALCD-13. Compact Disc.

Kopf, Gereon. '"The Self That Is Not a Self": Ueda and Kuoan's Ten Ox Pictures'. In *Tetsugaku Companion to Ueda Shizuteru: Language, Experience, and Zen*, edited by Ralf Müller, Raquel Bouso, and Adam Loughnane, 317–36. Cham: Springer, 2022. https://doi.org/10.1007/978-3-030-92321-1_21.

Koyama Hiroshi, Satō Kikuo, and Satō Ken'ichirō, eds. *Yōkyokushū*, vol. 1. Tokyo: Shōgakukan, 1973.

Knowles, Alison. 'Proposition'. In *Fluxus Performance Workbook*, edited by Ken Friedman, Owen Smith, and Lauren Sawchyn, 69. London: Performance Research e-Publications, 2002.

Kuusela, Anttoni. 'Listening Without a Listener – Understanding the Self and the Activity of Listening to Music Through Nishitani Keiji's Philosophy'.

The Journal of East Asian Philosophy 4 (2025): 123–36. https://doi.org/10.1007/s43493-024-00046-7.

LaBelle, Brandon. 'Minor Acoustics: Sound Art, Relationality, and Poetic Listening'. In *The Oxford Handbook of Sound Art*, edited by Jane Grant, John Matthias, and David Prior, 453–70. Oxford: Oxford University Press, 2021. ps://doi.org/https://doi.org/https://doi.org/10.1093/oxfordhb/9780190274054.013.30.

Landes, Donald. *Merleau-Ponty and the Paradoxes of Expression*. London: Bloomsbury, 2013.

Larson, Kay. *Where the Heart Beats: John Cage, Zen Buddhism, and the Inner Life of Artists*. London: Penguin Press, 2012.

Leach, Elizabeth Eva. 'The composer Grimace'. *Musicology, Medieval to Modern*, 2010. https://eeleach.blog/2010/12/29/the-composer-grimace/ (accessed 13 September 2025).

Li, Lin. 'Teaching Beyond Words: "Silence" and its Pedagogical Implications Discoursed in the Early Classical Texts of Confucianism, Daoism and Zen Buddhism'. *Educational Philosophy and Theory* 52, no. 7 (2020): 759–68. https://doi.org/10.1080/00131857.2019.1684896.

Lorde, Audre. 'Poetry is Not a Luxury'. 1977. In *Teaching Black: The Craft of Teaching on Black Life and Literature*, edited by Ana-Maurine Lara and drea brown, 125–7. Pittsburgh: University of Pittsburgh Press, 2021.

Loughnane, Adam. 'Ueda and Heidegger: Playing in Hollowness, Abiding in Actuality and the Risk of Poetic Language'. In *Tetsugaku Companion to Ueda Shizuteru: Language, Experience, and Zen*, edited by Ralf Müller, Raquel Bouso, and Adam Loughnane, 247–62. Cham: Springer, 2022. https://doi.org/10.1007/978-3-030-92321-1_17.

Macfarlane, Robert. *Mountains of the Mind*. London: Granta, 2003.

Machado de Oliveira, Vanessa. *Hospicing Modernity: Facing Humanity's Wrongs and the Implications for Social Activism*. Berkeley: North Atlantic Books, 2021.

Malm, Andreas. *The Progress of This Storm: Nature and Society in a Warming World*. 2018. Reprint. London: Verso, 2020.

Mancini, Simona, Aurora Mascolo, Gabriella Graziuso, and Claudio Guarnaccia. 'Soundwalk, Questionnaires and Noise Measurements in a University Campus: A Soundscape Study'. *Sustainability* 13, no. 2 (2021): 841. https://doi.org/10.3390/su13020841.

Marra, Michael F. *Essays on Japan: Between Aesthetics and Literature*. Leiden: Brill, 2010.

Mason, Christian. Liner notes to *Screens*, composed by Frank Denyer. Another Timbre, at 220, 2023. https://www.anothertimbre.com/pages/booklet-for-frank-denyers-screens (accessed 19 September 2025).

Matsumoto Shirō. 'The Lotus Sūtra and Japanese Culture'. In *Pruning the Bodhi Tree: The Storm Over Critical Buddhism*, edited by Jamie Hubbard and Paul L. Swanson, 388–403. Honolulu: University of Hawai'i Press, 1997.

Matsuoka Shinpei. *Embodied Performance: Warriors, Dancers, and the Origins of Noh Theater*. Translated by Janet Goff. New York: Columbia University Press, 2024.

Matsuoka Shinpei. 'Managing the Poetic *topos*: The Aesthetics and Methods of *waka* and Zeami's noh Plays'. *Nō and Kyōgen* 12 (2014): 56–73.

Matsuoka Shinpei. 'Yūgen ga enjakusuru toki: Ikkyū Zenchiku no sekai'. *Bungaku* 7, no. 2 (1996): 32–40.

Matsushita Takahiro. 'Kōgai kigyōnushi jusatsu to katakiuchi no fukken'. *Gendai-no-me*, February 1971.

McLuhan, Marshall. *Understanding Media*. 1964. Reprint. London: Routledge, 2001.

Melia, Nicholas. 'Stille Musik—Wandelweiser and the Voices of Ontological Silence'. *Contemporary Music Review* 30, no. 6 (2011): 471–95. https://doi.org/10.1080/07494467.2011.676897.

Melia, Nicholas and James Saunders. 'Introduction: What is Wandelweiser?'. *Contemporary Music Review* 30, no. 6 (2011): 445–8. https://doi.org/10.1080/07494467.2011.676893.

Merchant, Suhail. *Some Sounds are Gates*. YouTube, 2020. Film. https://youtu.be/1XT0y5oMAvc (accessed 19 September 2025).

Mika, Carl, Vanessa Andreotti, Garrick Cooper, Cash Ahenakew, and Denise Silva. 'The Ontological Differences Between Wording and Worlding the World'. *Language, Discourse & Society* 8, no. 1(15) (2020): 17–32.

Miller, Cassandra. *Duet for Cello and Orchestra*. Composed 2015. Published. London: Faber Music, 2021.

Miller, Cassandra. 'Duet for Cello and Orchestra'. On *Faber Music* website. https://www.fabermusic.com/music/e3017d0d-f43e-4015-9b67-892fa1b210cf (accessed 14 September 2025).

Miller, Cassandra. *'O, Zomer!'*. Another Timbre, 2018, at126. Compact disc.

Montgomery, Will. 'Quiet storms: Toshiya Tsunoda'. *The Wire* (2011). https://www.thewire.co.uk/in-writing/essays/p=9937 (accessed 16 September 2025).

Morrison, Ryan. 'Study Guide: Tanizaki Jun'ichirō "In Praise of Shadows" (In'ei raisan; 1933)'. 『*Behold My Swarthy Face*。』(2014) http://www.beholdmyswarthyface.com

Muller, A. Charles, ed. *Digital Dictionary of Buddhism*. (2025). http://buddhism-dict.net/ddb (accessed 31 October 2025).

Nakajima Atsushi. *The Moon over the Mountain*. Translated by Paul McCarthy and Nobuko Ochner. Iowa City: Autumn Hill Books, 2011.

Nakazawa Shin'ichi. *Seirei no ō*. 2003. Reprint. Tokyo: Kodansha, 2018.

Nearman, Mark J. 'The Visions of a Creative Artist: Zenchiku's *Rokurin Ichiro* Treatises Part 1'. *Monumenta Nipponica* 50, no. 2 (1995): 235–61.

Nearman, Mark J. 'The Visions of a Creative Artist: Zenchiku's *Rokurin Ichiro* Treatises Part 2'. *Monumenta Nipponica* 50, no. 3 (1995): 281–303.

Nearman, Mark J. 'The Visions of a Creative Artist: Zenchiku's *Rokurin Ichiro* Treatises Part 3'. *Monumenta Nipponica* 50, no. 4 (1995): 485–521.

Nearman, Mark J. 'The Visions of a Creative Artist: Zenchiku's *Rokurin Ichiro* Treatises Part 4'. *Monumenta Nipponica* 51, no. 1 (1996): 17–52.

Nickel, Luke. 'Scores in Bloom: Some Recent Orally Transmitted Experimental Music'. *TEMPO* 74, no. 293 (2020): 54–69. https://doi.org/10.1017/S0040298220000261.

Nishida Kitarō. *An Inquiry into the Good*. Translated by Masao Abe and Christopher Ives. 1911. Translation. New Haven: Yale University Press, 1990.

Nishida Kitarō. 'Basho'. In *Place and Dialectic: Two Essays by Nishida Kitarō*, translated by John W. M. Krummel and Shigenori Nagatomo, 49–102. Oxford: Oxford University Press, 2012.

Nishida Kitarō. 'Seimei'. In *Nishida Kitarō Zenshū*, vol. 11, 289–370. Tokyo: Iwanami Shoten, 1988.

Nishitani Keiji. 'Ikebana'. In *Japanese Philosophy: A Sourcebook*, translated by Jeff Shore, edited by James Heisig, Thomas Kasulis, and John Maraldo, 1197–200. Honolulu: University of Hawai'i Press, 2011.

Nishiyama Mika. 'Keiaiji, Hōji'in Monzeki'. In *Amamonzeki, A Hidden Heritage: Treasures of the Japanese Imperial Convents*, edited by Patricia Fister and Monica Bethe, 54–61. Chicago: Paragon Book Gallery, 2009.

Ogawa, Tadashi. *Phenomenology of Wind and Atmosphere*, translated by Lorenzo Marinucci. Sesto San Giovanni: Mimesis International, 2021.

Okada Akeo. *Ongaku no kikikata*. Tokyo: Chūō kōron shinsha, 2009.

Oliveros, Pauline. *Sonic Meditations*. Sharon: Smith Publications, 1971.

Ono Yoko. *Grapefruit*. 1964. Reprint. New York: Simon & Schuster, 2000.

Ortolani, Benito. 'Shamanism in the Origins of the Nō Theatre'. *Asian Theatre Journal* 1, no. 2 (1984): 166–90.

Ortolani, Benito. *The Japanese Theatre: From Shamanistic Ritual to Contemporary Pluralism*. 1990. Revised. Princeton: Princeton University Press, 1995.

Osaka Koichiro. *Jusatsu Kito Sodan*. Hong Kong: Para Site, 2019.

Parkes, Graham. 'Kūkai and Dōgen as Exemplars of Ecological Engagement'. In *Japanese Environmental Philosophy*, edited by J. Baird Callicott and James McRae, 65–86. Oxford: Oxford University Press, 2017.

Pinnington, Noel John. *A New History of Medieval Japanese Theatre: Noh and Kyōgen from 1300 to 1600*. Cham: Palgrave Macmillan, 2019. https://doi.org/10.1007/978-3-030-06140-1.

Pinnington, Noel John. *Traces in the Way: Michi and the Writings of Komparu Zenchiku*. Ithaca: Cornell University Press, 2006.

Pisaro-Liu, Michael. *Fields Have Ears*. Another Timbre, 2012, at47. Compact disc.

Pisaro-Liu, Michael. *Fields Have Ears (1)*. Kyushu University Design YouTube, 2022. https://youtu.be/_4ZxdFXMj7w (accessed 15 September 2025).

Pisaro-Liu, Michael. 'Some Thoughts on the "Fields Have Ears" Series (and a Few Remarks on the Current Gravity Wave release)'. *Gravity Wave Blogspot*, 2012. http://michaelpisaro.blogspot.jp/2012/03/some-thoughts-on-fields-have-ears.html (accessed 15 September 2025).

Pisaro-Liu, Michael. 'Ten Framing Considerations of the Field'. In *The Experimental Music Yearbook*, edited by Sara Roberts (2010). https://www.experimentalmusicyearbook.com/ten-framing-considerations-of-the-field (accessed 16 September 2025).

Pisaro-Liu, Michael. 'Wandelweiser'. *wandelweiser*, 2009. https://wandelweiser.de/_texte/erstw-engl.html (accessed 13 September 2025).

Priest, Graham. *Capitalism – Its Nature and its Replacement: Buddhist and Marxist Insights*. London: Routledge, 2022.

Rambelli, Fabio. 'The Dharma of Music: Gagaku and Buddhist Salvation in Medieval Japan'. *Japanese Journal of Religious Studies* 48, no. 1 (2021): 45–71. https://doi.org/10.18874/jjrs.48.1.2021.45-71.

Rambelli, Fabio. *Vegetal Buddhas*. Kyoto: Italian School of East Asian Studies, 2001.

Rancière, Jacques. *The Emancipated Spectator*. Translated by Gregory Elliott. 2008. Translation. London: Verso, 2009.

Raud, Rein, et al. *Forgetting the Self*. Tallinn: Haus galeriis, 2024.

Riddoch, Malcolm. 'Imagining the Sounds Themselves'. In *The Oxford Handbook of Sound and Imagination* vol. 1, edited by Mark Grimshaw-Aagaard, Mads Walther-Hansen, and Martin Knakkergaard, 54–77. Oxford: Oxford University Press, 2019. https://doi.org/10.1093/oxfordhb/9780190460167.013.3.

Ritchey, Marianna. *Composing Capital: Classical Music in the Neoliberal Era*. Chicago: University of Chicago Press, 2019.

Ritchey, Marianna and Greg Stuart. 'Accessibility and Instrumentality: A Conversation'. *e-flux* 154 (2025). https://www.e-flux.com/journal/154/666348/accessibility-and-instrumentality-a-conversation (accessed 13 September 2025).

Rodd, Laurel Rasplica. *Shinkokinshū*. Leiden: Brill, 2015. https://doi.org/10.1163/9789004288294.

Rutherford-Johnson, Tim. Liner notes for *Bára Gísladóttir: Orchestral Works*. Copenhagen: Dacapo Records, 2024.

Rutherford-Johnson, Tim. *Music After the Fall: Modern Composition and Culture Since 1989*. Oakland: University of California Press, 2017.

Rutt, Richard. *Zhouyi: A New Translation with Commentary of the Book of Changes*. London: RoutledgeCurzon, 2002.

Sabat, Mark. *Plainsound Music Edition*. N.d. https://www.plainsound.org (accessed 19 September 2025).

Saunders, James. 'Testing the Consequences: Multipart Series in the Work of the Wandelweiser Composers'. *Contemporary Music Review* 30, no. 6 (2011): 497–524. https://doi.org/10.1080/07494467.2011.676898.

Schafer, R. Murray. *The Thinking Ear: Complete Writings on Music Education*. Toronto: Arcana Editions, 1985.

Scheid, Bernhard and Mark Teeuwen, eds. *The Culture of Secrecy in Japanese Religion*. London: Routledge, 2015.

Schmidt-Hori, Sachi. *Tales of Idolized Boys: Male-Male Love in Medieval Japanese Buddhist Narratives*. Honolulu: University of Hawai'i Press, 2021.

Sedgwick, Eve Kosofsky. *Tendencies*. Durham: Duke University Press, 1993.

Seel, Martin. *Aesthetics of Appearing*. Stanford: Stanford University Press, 2005.

Seymour, Richard. *The Disenchanted Earth: Reflections on Ecosocialism & Barbarism*. London: Indigo Press, 2022.

Shaw, Miranda. 'Nature in Dogen's Philosophy and Poetry'. *The Journal Of The International Association Of Buddhist Studies* 8, no. 2 (1985): 111–32.

Shikishi, Princess. *String of Beads: Complete Poems of Princess Shikishi*. Translated by Hiroaki Sato. Honolulu: University of Hawai'i Press, 1993.

Shirane, Haruo, edr. *Traditional Japanese Literature: An Anthology, Beginnings to 1600*. New York: Columbia University Press, 2007.

Shōtetsu. *Conversations with Shōtetsu*. Translated by Robert H. Brower. Ann Arbor: Center for Japanese Studies, 1992.

Sigurðsson, Geir. 'Making More Sense: A Confucian-Hermeneutic Path to Aesthetics'. *Journal East Asian Philosophy* (2024). https://doi.org/10.1007/s43493-024-00039-6.

Smith, Linda Catlin. 'On Listening: A Lecture'. *Linda Catlin Smith: Composer* (1992). http://www.catlinsmith.com/writings/on-listening-a-lecture (accessed 16 September 2025).

Smolicki, Jacek. 'Introduction'. In *Soundwalking: Through Time, Space, and Technologies*, edited by Jacek Smolicki, 1–17. London: Routledge, 2023.

Spence, Charles. 'Sound: The Forgotten Flavor Sense'. In *Multisensory Flavor Perception: From Fundamental Neuroscience Through to the Marketplace*, edited by Betina Piqueras-Fiszman and Charles Spence, 81–105. Amsterdam: Woodhead, 2016. https://doi.org/10.1016/B978-0-08-100350-3.00005-5.

Stone, Jackie [Jacqueline]. 'Seeking Enlightenment in the Last Age: "Mappō" Thought in Kamakura Buddhism: PART I'. *The Eastern Buddhist (New Series)* 18, no. 1 (1985): 28–56.

Stravinsky, Igor. *Chronicle of My Life*. London: Victor Gollancz, 1936.

Sugimoto Hiroshi. *Honkadori Azumakudari*. Yokohama: Kuma Publishing, 2023.

Sugimoto Taku. *Gakufu to kaisetsu*. Tokyo: Saboten Shobō, 2018.

Sugimoto Taku. *May*. Bandcamp, 2021. https://takusugimoto.bandcamp.com/album/may (accessed 15 September 2025).

Sugimoto Taku. *May (Tama)*. YouTube, 2021. https://youtu.be/R8V3uecqZBA (accessed 15 September 2025).

Suzuki Daitetsu. *Suzuki Daitetsu Zenshū*, vol. 20. Tokyo: Iwanami Shoten, 1968.

Svensson, Kristofer. 'A Buddhist Musical Poetics'. *Intimating Emptiness*. Blogspot, 2015. https://intimatingemptiness.blogspot.com/2014/10/a-buddhist-aesthetic-theory.html (accessed 13 September 2025).

Takahashi Mutsuo. *Shishin nisennen: Susanoo kara 3/11 e*. Tokyo: Iwanami Shoten, 2011.

Takahashi Mutsuo. *Utamakura Awase*. Tokyo: Shoshi Yamada, 2005.

Takahashi Yūsuke. *Zenchiku Nōgakuron no sekai*. Tokyo: Keio University Press, 2014.

Takei Jiro and Marc P. Keane. *Sakuteiki: Visions of the Japanese Garden*. Tokyo: Tuttle Publishing, 2001.

Takemitsu Tōru. *Confronting Silence*. Translated and edited by Yoshiko Kakudo and Glenn Glasow. Berkley: Fallen Leaf Press, 1995.

Takemura Makio. 'One Step Towards Buddhism as Philosophy', translated by Suhara Eiji. In *The Dao Companion to Japanese Buddhist Philosophy*, edited by Gereon Kopf, 71–81. 2009. Translation. Springer Nature, 2019. https://doi.org/10.1007/978-90-481-2924-9_3.

Tamagawa, Kiyoshi. *Echoes from the East: The Javanese Gamelan and Its Influence on the Music of Claude Debussy*. London: Bloomsbury, 2019.

Tellenbach, Hubertus and Kimura Bin. 'The Japanese Concept of "Nature"'. In *Nature in Asian Traditions of Thought: Essays in Environmental Philosophy*, edited by J. Baird Callicott and Roger T. Ames, 153–62. Albany: State University of New York Press, 1989.

Thornhill, Arthur H. III. *Six Circles, One Dewdrop: The Religio-Aesthetic World of Komparu Zenchiku*. Princeton: Princeton University Press, 1997.

Thornhill, Arthur H. III. '*Yūgen* after Zeami'. In *Nō and Kyōgen in the Contemporary World*, edited by James R. Brandon, 36–64. Honolulu: University of Hawai'i Press, 1997.

Tsunoda Toshiya. *Extract From Field Recording Archive*, liner notes translated by Yuko Zama. Erstwhile Records, ErstPast 001-5, 2019. Compact Disc. https://erstwhilerecords.bandcamp.com/album/extract-from-field-recording-archive (accessed 16 September 2025).

Tsunoda Toshiya. *Low Frequency Observed at Maguchi Bay*. hibari music, hibari-11, 2007. Compact Disc.

Tyler, Royall. *Joy, Despair, Illusion, Dreams: Twenty Plays from the Nō Tradition*. New York: Columbia University Press, 2024.

Ueda Shizuteru, *Jūgyūzu*, edited by Ueda Shizuteru and Yanagida Seizan. Tokyo: Chikuma Shobō, 1992.

Ueda Shizuteru. *Kotoba*. Tokyo: Iwanami shoten, 2008.

Ueda Shizuteru, 'Language in a Twofold World'. In *Japanese Philosophy: A Sourcebook*, edited by James Heisig, Thomas Kasulis, and John Maraldo, 766–84. Honolulu: University of Hawai'i Press, 2011.

Ueda Shizuteru. 'The Place of Man in the Noh Play'. *The Eastern Buddhist NEW SERIES* 25, no. 2 (1992): 59–88.

Utz, Christian. *Musical Composition in the Context of Globalization: New Perspectives on Music History of the 20th and 21st Century*. Bielefeld: transcript, 2021.

Van Goethem, Ellen. 'The Four Directional Animals in East Asia: A Comparative Analysis'. In *Feng Shui (Kan Yu) and Architecture*, edited by Florian Reiter, 201–16. Berlin: Humboldt-Universität zu Berlin, 2011.

Varnedoe, Kirk. *Cy Twombly: A Retrospective*. New York: The Museum of Modern Art, 1994.

Vickery, Lindsay, Michael Terren, Sam Gillies, and Josten Myburgh. 'Between the Real and the Imaginary: Ecostructural Approaches to Composing with Field Recordings and Acoustic Instruments'. *Proceedings of the 2016 Annual Conference of the Australasian Computer Music Association* (2016): 81–9.

Vovin, Alexander. *Man'yoshu: A New English Translation Containing the Original Text, kana Transliteration, Romanization, Glossing and Commentary*, vol. 14. Leiden: Brill, 2012.

Watson, Chris. *Chris Watson*. Bandcamp. https://chriswatsonreleases.bandcamp.com (accessed 16 September 2025).

Westerkamp, Hildegard. 'Soundwalking'. *Sound Heritage* 3, no. 4 (1974): 18–27. https://hildegardwesterkamp.ca/writings/writings-by/?post_id=13&title=soundwalking.

White, Gordon. *Ani.mystic: Encounters with a Living Cosmos*. London: Scarlet Imprint, 2022.

Wilde, Oscar. *The Critical Writings of Oscar Wilde: An Annotated Selection*. Edited by Nicholas Frankel. Cambridge, MA: Harvard University Press, 2022.

Wittgenstein, Ludwig. *Tractatus Logico-Philosophicus*. London: Kegan Paul, Trench, Trubner & Co., 1922.

Yamagami Shimpei. *Epiphany*. Tokyo: bookshop M, 2023.

Yamagami Shimpei. *helix*. Tokyo: minä perhonen, 2022.

Yamagami Shimpei. *Liminal (Eyes) YAMAGAMI*. Tokyo: bookshop M, 2022.

Yonezawa Kengo, Tani Hideaki, Nakajima Shin'ichirō, and Uchida Hiroyuki. 'Development of the Japanese version of the 30-item Mystical Experience Questionnaire'. *Neuropsychopharmacolgy Reports* 44 (2024): 280–4. https://doi.org/10.1002/npr2.12377.

Yusa Michiko. 'Japanese Buddhism and Women: The Lotus, Amida, and Awakening'. In *The Dao Companion to Japanese Buddhist Philosophy*, edited by Gereon Kopf, 83–133. Dordrecht: Springer, 2019. https://doi.org/10.1007/978-90-481-2924-9_4.

Zeami Motokiyo. *Performance Notes*. Translated by Tom Hare. New York: Columbia University Press, 2008.

Zeami Motokiyo and Konparu Zenchiku. *Zeami Zenchiku*. Edited by Omote Akira and Katō Shūichi. Tokyo: Iwanami Shoten, 1974.

Index